Brian & Debby Peterman

THE
ROADLESS
YAAK

"To build a road is so much simpler than to think of what the country really needs."
—Aldo Leopold, *A Sand County Almanac* (1949)

Books by Rick Bass

THE

Reflections and Observations

ROADLESS

About One of Our Last

YAAK

Great Wild Places

EDITED BY RICK BASS

Introduction by Mike Dombeck

THE LYONS PRESS
GUILFORD, CONNECTICUT
AN IMPRINT OF THE GLOBE PEQUOT PRESS

Permissions Acknowledgments

Rick Bass, "The Community of Glaciers" from *Audubon,* December 1999

Tom Franklin, "Pieces of Sky" from *Black Warrior Review* (Vol. 27.1, 34-38).

Debra Gwartney, "Traveling Close to Home" from *Open Spaces* (Vol. 2, Issue 4, 1999-2000).

Laurie John Lane-Zucker, "Ghost Print" from *Orion Afield* (premier issue).

Roy Parvin, "Solstice" from *Northern Lights* (Spring 1999).

Janisse Ray, "Up Against Openings" from the *Missoula Independent* (August 28– September 4, 1997).

Bob Shacochis, "Grouse, Grouse, Grouse" from *Domesticity* (Scribners, 1994).

Annick Smith, "The Best Last Place" from *Big Sky Journal* (Summer 2000).

Text Design: M.A. Dubé

Printed in the United States of America

10 9 8 7 6 5 4 3 2 1

Library of Congress Cataloging-in-Publication Data

The roadless Yaak : reflections and observations about one of our last great wilderness areas / edited by Rick Bass.
    p. cm.
 ISBN 1-58574-545-6 (hardcover : alk. paper)
 1. Natural history--Montana--Yaak Valley. 2. Nature conservation--Montana--Yaak Valley. I. Bass, Rick, 1958-
 QH105.M9 R625 2002
 508.786'81--dc21
                                        2002008908

Printed on recycled paper.

First Edition/First Printing

CONTENTS

PREFACE

"I DON'T KNOW EXACTLY WHAT A PRAYER IS," WRITES MARY Oliver in her poem *The Summer Day*. "I do know how to pay attention, how to fall down into the grass, how to kneel down in the grass, how to be idle and blessed, how to stroll through the fields, which is what I have been doing all day."

It is with this kind of gratitude, even reverence, that I thank the poets, scientists, and essayists who have contributed to this anthology. All generously agreed to take time away from their work and busy lives, and to visit the Yaak, and to testify afterward—if they were so moved—on behalf of the last remaining roadless areas in the Yaak. Implicit in their accepting that invitation, I think, is the understanding by these artists and scientists that each of these roadless areas is more beautiful and enduring than any one artist's book, or any one artist's oeuvre. The Yaak is honored by the gift of their generous spirits.

These last little roadless areas in the Yaak are public lands: lands owned by you, by me, by these writers and scientists, and by all Americans. Lands whose beauty provides inspiration, lands whose biological integrity provides refugia for an amazing assemblage of rare and sensitive and threatened and endangered species; lands that still, against the overwhelming odds of the last century, and standing even now before the juggernaut of the century oncoming, have managed to retain the grace of their initial creation; fifteen last gardens where all the various and intensely interconnected cycles of life, from the infinitesimal to the grand, are still free to play out at the original pace with which they were first designed by a Creator.

You can feel it immediately, entering such lands—such small remaining gardens. So great is the power and mystery—indeed, the health—that emanates from these last roadless cores that you can feel the difference, even standing at the edge of one of these last gardens.

The Yaak Valley lies in the extreme northwesternmost corner of Montana. It is a semi-permeable island, bounded to the north by the haze of Canada's corporate clear-cuts, to the west by the high stone cliffs of Idaho, to the south by the broad and rushing Kootenai River, and to the east by a giant hydroelectric project created in the 1970s, Lake Koocanusa.

Still, the island lives—is connected, even if only tenuously, to the rest of the wild pulse of the West—and in many ways can be thought of as the heart of the wild pulse of this portion of the West. Nothing has ever yet gone extinct in the Yaak, for example—not since the time of mastodons and mammoths—though many of the populations are down to a single- or double-digit tally, like a reverse kind of Noah's Ark: as if we are unable to heed any one story, nor any command, for too long, without trying to unravel it.

Five or six wolves; only a very few known breeding female grizzly bears, in the lowest elevation they can be found in the continental United States—interior rain forest grizzlies, rare even among the rare. One population of inland redband trout, a type of landlocked salmon; a scattered handful of enclaves of Coeur d'Alene salamanders, wood toads, water howellia, and bull and Westslope cutthroat trout. One occasional woodland caribou. Harlequin ducks, great gray owls, eagles and falcons, wolverines, and lynx.

In addition to being the heart of diversity, the Yaak is also a vital linchpin, the narrowest bottleneck in a chain of wildness that extends north from the Yellowstone country all the way up toward the Yukon. And in addition to being the wild heart of diversity and a linchpin, the Yaak is a crossroads, linking not just north with south, but east with west. Nearly one million acres lie due north of the Kootenai River, resting in a magical seam of diversity that conjoins uniquely the Pacific Northwest maritime weather systems, and their associated species, with the glaciated mountainscapes of the northern Rockies, and their species.

Mountain goats, bighorn sheep, moose, and elk can all be found north of the Kootenai. Indeed, much of the story of the Yaak is that it is a land of two things, with twice the abundance, and twice the diversity. Bald eagles and golden eagles; wolves and coyotes; mule deer and white-tailed deer; lynx and mountain lions. If it's wild, there's a good chance it lives in the Yaak.

Unlike the rest of the northern Rockies, no single tree species dominates the Yaak, though the larch trees perhaps best typify the place: unique, ancient citizens of the forest that are both coniferous and deciduous, occupying perfectly this northern seam where both strategies make sense, and where there is still the possibility, still opportunity, to live and prosper, both ways—the larch producing their seeds within the protection of cones and casting them down into the ashes left behind by wildfire, yet shedding their needles each season, only to then grow them anew in the next season. A land of fire, but a land of rot, also.

For an ecosystem of such dynamic extremism, the solutions of preservation—the opportunities for protecting these fifteen wild gardens—are astoundingly moderate: so easy that any politician could promote them without fear of being called bold or radical or, perhaps worst of all, visionary. Conservative, maybe, but never visionary.

Protect the last of the last. Establish corridors of connectivity that keep the wild archipelago of these fifteen gardens linked and interconnected, braided together, breathing and pulsing, so that they may continue to serve as reservoirs of wildness— reservoirs of diversity, and even magic. Continue to harvest the small-diameter trees that flourish along the infrastructure of existing roads—thousands of miles of taxpayer-built roads, here in the Yaak, and in all of our national forests. Move steadily away from the old industry of the subsidized high-grading liquidation of old growth, and toward a more sustainable economy of restoration.

The puzzle pieces for a solution are all still here, in the Yaak. Here, such a solution almost—not quite, but almost—assembles itself.

This book is not so much about solutions or opportunities, however, as it is about a celebration of beauty, and of a wildness that is fast diminishing under the weight of an ever-enlarging world, and in the absence of permanent protection.

When Mike Dombeck was chief of the U.S. Forest Service, he would regularly ask his employees, "How do we expect to be relevant as a public agency in the next fifty years?"

Wilderness was one of the many answers that came up regularly—protecting and providing that option into the future, rather than foreclosing on that possibility, that treasure, forever.

Something that will become evident, reading these essays, is that the Yaak is not a tourist destination. Far from it, as Roy Parvin and others point out. It is a biological wilderness, not a recreational wilderness, and as such can be thought of as a gold standard of ecological diversity, replete with low-elevation swamps and fens and bogs, mosquitoes and beetles and fungi whose complex life cycles, Doug Chadwick reminds us, we'll probably never understand fully, but which serve as the underpinning of all life and health within the ecosystem.

To provide permanent protection for these fifteen unprotected wilderness gardens in the Yaak—and in the other roadless areas in the national forest system—is a critical first step in developing a mature land ethic that looks not just at the recreational needs and desires of humans, but also at the less glamorous needs of the rare and threatened and endangered and sensitive species that reside still within the responsibility of our stewardship, or, as Terry Tempest Williams has called it, "our wild registry."

It is not too late. There is still time.

It's interesting, too, how many times the concept of healing appears in these essays. There is nothing in the Yaak if not the potential for restoration.

Just as I am grateful to these writers for giving voice to their support for such a notion, so too am I reminded that they are grateful to the Yaak, and other wild places, for the simple comfort provided by the knowledge, as Wallace Stegner wrote, that such places even still exist.

As a Montana resident, and as an American citizen, I'm extremely grateful to the efforts of nonprofit grassroots organizations such as the Montana Wilderness Association (PO Box 635, Helena, MT 59624) and, closer to home, the Yaak Valley Forest Council (YVFC, 155 Riverview, Troy, MT 59935), whose supporters are comprised exclusively of landowners and residents in the Yaak. All of the proceeds from the sale of this book will be donated to the YVFC, as well as to reimbursing the Round River Conservation Studies program, which helped support the making of this book. Please feel free to give generously. Your support of these vital organizations—particularly the place-based YVFC—is greatly encouraged. A copy of this book has been distributed to each member of Congress, to the president and vice president, and to the chief of the U.S. Forest Service. We desperately need for you to write a letter asking for protection for the Yaak's last roadless areas, and send a copy of it the the addresses listed at the back of the book. And my gratitude goes again to these thirty-six contributors who stepped forward—and to readers such as yourself who are taking the time to listen to their testimony, their experience.

— *Rick Bass*
June 2002

INTRODUCTION:

CONSERVATION FOR A NEW CENTURY

By Mike Dombeck

VISIONARY IS A MUCH OVERUSED WORD. A VISIONARY IS ABLE to look beyond life's urgent press of immediate business and focus on the truly long-term important things. Few single words, however, lend themselves with more ease to the life and work of Aldo Leopold. Whether the issue was his evolving understanding of the role of large predators such as wolves, the importance of education, the imperative of wilderness, or extending a land ethic to economic and social issues, Leopold charted a course and defined a legacy that our culture struggles to measure up to more than half a century later.

Mindful of Leopold's ability to separate the important from the urgent, when I was Forest Service chief I challenged my personnel and others to get beyond the controversy *du jour* and ask, "What is it society will need from—value most about—the national forests in fifty years?"

At root, this is a question of values. And discussions of values are difficult, particularly for large bureaucracies. Often, we cloak our discussions of the need for clean water, more wild places, old growth, and unfragmented landscapes, ecologically sustainable timber harvest, in thick environmental impact statements that read as though a biologist were mimicking a patent lawyer. Perhaps part of this analysis and documentation is a defense to maintain the status quo while social values and expectations continue to evolve. The leadership challenge is to keep up with changing times and values and look beyond the headlines.

If we have learned anything over the past decade, it's that difficult, value-laden issues don't become easier with neglect. They snowball out of control into courtrooms across the country. The Yaak, and other public lands like it around the country, are filled with important value-laden issues that I hope we can respond to with vision.

My introduction, like much of this book, has a focus on values and the passionate feelings people have for wild places. How would Aldo Leopold or Theodore Roosevelt or others whom we today view as visionaries treat the Yaak, and the other wild places that remain in our ever-developing landscape? I believe that living within the ecological limits of the land, and not allowing short-term economic gains to override the land legacy we bequeath to future generations, is among the strongest demonstrations of patriotism that I know.

All of us, as citizens of the United States, together own hundreds of millions of acres of land. This is our birthright, a gift from our forebears, many of whom died securing the land and the freedoms we enjoy. Our public lands—more than five hundred million acres—are uniquely American. Other cultures have their great Pyramids or works of art. England and Spain have their great sea captains, Rome and Athens their great temples, and the Far East its dynasties. We in the United States have our public lands, the remnants of our wild frontier. It was this frontier that shaped our character as a people and a nation. Our heroes are the likes of Davy Crockett, Tecumseh, Daniel Boone, Sacagawea, Lewis and Clark, and Chief Joseph. We admire them for their endurance and skill, tested by the vast wild places of the American frontier.

At one time we viewed our public land as a vast storehouse of inexhaustible resources. Whoever was capable of exploiting those resources for personal profit could do so, in the name of progress and civilization. Too often, the result was environmental disaster. It was the tragedy of the commons, a tragic part of our history. Overgrazing the western rangelands, and the cut-and-run timber era that ended a century ago, which eliminated all but a few acres of old-growth forests in my home state of Wisconsin and throughout much of the East and upper Midwest, are just a few examples. The fires, floods, and erosion that followed degraded our lands and waters, sometimes for generations to come.

Good land management requires that we take the long view and live within the limits of the land. It requires that we not use up the land or forests, leaving future generations to pay the price of poorer quality of life. Land conservation needs must be placed ahead of the two-, four-, or six-year election cycles and economic cycles. Good long-term land stewardship—loyalty to the land—is the ethical and patriotic thing to do.

Everyone should be well aware that timber harvest off national forests has declined by more than 75 percent—from twelve billion board feet in the late 1980s to about two billion board feet by 2000. Make no mistake, although we in the Forest Service did what was expected of us at the time, we were cutting too many trees for too long, and it resulted in public opposition and distrust that led to court injunctions and social and economic uncertainty. Wild places like the Yaak, the Bitterroot, and the Monongahela were clearly abused. In the late 1980s, as concerns over the spotted owl reached a boiling point, the timber industry likely could have settled for legislation that would have reduced harvest in the Pacific Northwest from five billion board feet to two or three. But no agreement could be reached. Currently we harvest less than one billion board feet in the Pacific Northwest.

This example speaks to the dilemma we find ourselves in today. The debate over forest management continues to be driven by outdated models from the bygone big-timber-harvest era. We should be talking about the condition we want on the land. We should be talking about what we leave rather than the board feet of timber we take. Applying yesterday's debate to a new era can have insidious effects. It can perpetuate distrust and division. It can stifle dialogue and consensus. It can compromise our ability to resolve difficult conservation issues. Land management decisions must be based on ecological sustainability and watershed function.

I envision a future where the seventy million acres of national forest that by the Forest Service's own analysis are at high or moderate risk of wildfire—in many cases due to past management practices and fire suppression—are managed to restore watershed function, ecosystem integrity, and forest health. Many of these acres are overstocked with off-site species that have replaced native species or, put simply, have too many of the wrong species of trees. These small-diameter trees could provide material to develop value-added products that may substitute for traditional lumber, help reduce our reliance on wood imports, and provide local jobs. We must conserve this nation's forests without exporting environmental problems to other countries.

It is unlikely we will ever again see the timber-harvest levels of the 1980s taken from our public forests. Nor should we. Yet we must be willing to slow our consumption rates of natural resources if our land ethic can extend over state lines and through private boundaries, and finally to other nations of the world.

Related to the issue of forest health is our own national commitment to conservation and restoration—what Aldo Leopold called the land ethic. No other nation has ever enjoyed the wealth and prosperity we take for granted today. Our challenge is to ensure that we make the necessary investments in maintaining and restoring our environmental capital so it will continue to pay dividends for generations to come. Unfortunately, federal spending on natural resources and the environment as a percent of total spending is half of what it was in 1962.

Helping as best as they can to fill this deplorable void are nonprofit grassroots community groups such as the Yaak Valley Forest Council and collaborative ventures such as their Headwaters Restoration Project, which unites conservation organizations such as Trout Unlimited and the Cutthroat Foundation with state, federal, and local agencies like the U.S. Forest Service, the U.S. Fish & Wildlife Service, and Montana Department of Fish, Wildlife and Parks, to help repair injured watersheds. Efforts like these, if successful across the rest of the 192 million acres of our national forests, will bear dividends whose value will be apparent when a citizen of Salt Lake City, Los Angeles, or Missoula turns on his tap and drinks clean water from a national forest; a parent in Vermont takes her daughter fishing in the Green Mountain National Forest; a small mill operator in Montana sends twice as much wood fiber to market from a single tree due to research and development; and a private landowner in Illinois bequeaths to his children twenty acres of healthy, diverse, and productive forestland through forest legacy conservation easements.

The term *multiple use* does not mean we should do everything on every acre simply because we can. We must protect the last best places, and restore the rest. Many areas are simply not appropriate for certain activities, such as hard rock mining. For many years Congress has been unable to reach consensus on updating the 1872 Mining Law, a vexing and outdated statute that is the product of an era when women and most minorities could not vote. The Mining Act's antiquated royalty provisions are well known and simple. None exist. It is a blatant giveaway of public resources. In addition, it allows privatization of public land for $2.50 to $5 per acre, sometimes to foreign or multinational mining companies. Every other natural resource use—timber, grazing, oil and gas, recreation—is subject to approval or rejection by field managers for environmental or safety reasons. Only hard rock mining is exempt.

Congressional inaction does not, however, diminish our responsibility to use the best science to protect the most scenic, most diverse, most special places. Two such very important places are the Rocky Mountain Front and the Cabinet Mountain Wilderness, at the southern end of the Cabinet-Yaak ecosystem. The Bush administration and even some within my own Forest Service support a huge copper and silver mine in the very same Cabinet Mountain Wilderness.

Stewart Udall, Secretary of the Interior in the Kennedy and Johnson administrations, left office in 1969 saying that this was an archaic law badly in need of change. The last failed attempt to change the 1872 Mining Law was in the early 1990s, early in the Clinton administration. It nearly succeeded, but Congress adjourned just before the job was complete. The Republican sweep of the House and Senate in 1994 sucked the momentum out of the reform of the 1872 Mining Law.

Updating the 1872 Mining Law should be at the top of the list of conservation priorities for congressional and administration action. Instead, the current Bush administration has chosen to relax the conservation provisions of the mining regulations developed by the Bureau of Land Management over the past couple of years.

Our public servants have a long and storied history of working to protect the incredible fish, wildlife, cultural, and scenic resources of these areas, from Bob Marshall's efforts to protect the wilderness now memorialized by his name to Gloria Flora's decision in 1998 to prohibit oil and gas leasing in the area. The Cabinet Mountain Wilderness, just to the south of the Yaak, was one of this nation's first ten "flagship" wilderness areas designated under the 1964 Wilderness Act.

Wild places and natural areas like those that still exist are of increasing importance to a society that can afford to protect them. The writer T. H. Watkins once said, "In natural regions, as in public libraries, we should not be allowed to do everything we can merely because we can do it."

The Forest Service's wilderness legacy is a crown jewel. When you consider the contributions of former employees such as Bob Marshall, Arthur Carhart, and Aldo Leopold, it would not be an overstatement to say that Forest Service employees practically invented the wilderness concept. In recent years I have become concerned that our national commitment to the Wilderness Act has diminished, and that the resources to protect and manage the wilderness have not kept pace with our needs. When he was Forest Service chief, my predecessor Jack Ward Thomas asked the question, "When I think of wilderness, I wonder who will be the next ones to step up, lead, and sacrifice for this precious resource? Who will see that the wilderness doesn't get inched away from us, one compromise at a time?" There is no end to the intangible, even spiritual benefits that wild places and roadless lands provide for us—in the Yaak, and all across this country.

Growing up, I was a fishing guide in northern Wisconsin's Chequamegon National Forest. My entire family shares a passion for hunting, particularly deer hunting in the deep woods of our wild, remote national forests. When my daughter Mary missed her first deer, she felt bad, like we all do. But in previous years she'd taken her first two deer with one shot each. I told her two out of three isn't bad. It certainly tops her dad's record.

It is this firsthand, personal experience that has served as the catalyst for me as we move ecologically sustainable land management into a new century. This direction, provided we stay the course, will have enormous payoffs for hunters, particularly those who cherish a variety of hunting experiences. The rich array of choices on public lands is the true gold standard by which all hunting and outdoor recreation pursuits are measured. When America's population doubles near the end of this new century, where will tomorrow's hunters go for choice and variety in the quest for a quality experience?

National forests may be the last best places where a variety and choice of hunting experiences will still be possible.

Why build more roads on our national forests? The national forests already contain more than 380,000 miles of roads, yet over the past decade they received funding to maintain less than 20 percent of these roads. In the 1.5-million-acre Chequamegon and Nicolet National Forests of my home state of Wisconsin, 79 percent of the land is within a quarter mile of a road. Why build more roads in the last remaining wild places when we cannot take care of the roads we already have?

During the public comment period on the roadless rule from 1998 to 2000, we learned that the future use of forest areas was of utmost concern to the public. In response to an overwhelming volume of support, President Clinton asked that we develop a policy for determining the future uses of roadless areas. It is time to stop kicking this issue to the next generation. It is time we made a decision. This task is a national challenge for us all—and let me define *us*.

Us means nonmotorized and motorized recreationists, hunters, anglers, hikers, outdoor enthusiasts, campers, artists and writers, seniors and young people, thrill and solitude seekers, rural and urban citizens, wealthy and poor. We need to come to terms as a nation about how we want these unspoiled lands used. What do we want to leave for future generations? Some claim the roadless initiative was a fleeting ploy by the Clinton administration for an environmental legacy in its waning years. The need for a roadless policy for the national forests has been festering for more than twenty-five years. The issues are not new; the science that supports limited road building to protect the ecosystems is not new. The very first roadless area inventory was conducted by the Forest Service in 1926.

One hundred years ago President Theodore Roosevelt felt that the public and their public lands were inseparable. Things have not changed as we embrace the next one hundred years. A favorite Roosevelt quote of mine is this: *"Public land, land that belongs to everyone and thus to no one, is one of the permanent homes of the American spirit."* And it is in the American wilderness that this spirit can be most profoundly felt.

The writer A. Q. Mowbray once said, "The measure of a modern industrialized nation can be taken by observing the quality of its works in the two extremes of its environment—cities and wilderness." In four centuries we have lost most of the original American wilderness. We have actually paved over more acreage in this country than we have designated as wilderness! The love of wilderness and the tragedy of its loss are common threads in early American literature. Both are driving themes in James Fenimore Cooper's famous *Leatherstocking Tales.* Henry David Thoreau is famous for his wildland walks through the Massachusetts countryside. The solitude he found was balsam for his soul. "In wildness is the preservation of the world," he proclaimed.

Despite early calls for wilderness conservation, the rate of wilderness loss accelerated with the expanding frontier. In 1909 Aldo Leopold could still rejoice in experiencing, as he put it, "wild country to be young in" out west, where "there were grizzlies in every major mountain mass." That's no longer true in the lower forty-eight states. Leopold well understood the threat to our remaining wilderness areas—the "blank spots on the map," as he called them. He worked tirelessly, and his efforts paid off—in 1924 the first wilderness was designated, the Gila Wilderness on the Gila National Forest in New Mexico.

Arthur Carhart—another Forest Service employee—was also working for wilderness protection. In 1926, partly thanks to his efforts, another area was designated for special protection. Today we know it as the Boundary Waters Canoe Area in Minnesota's Superior National Forest. That same year Forest Service Chief William Greeley initiated the first inventory of roadless areas. The inventory was limited to areas larger than 230,400 acres. The Forest Service identified seventy-four tracts, totaling fifty-five million acres.

By the 1930s the wilderness movement was off the ground. But Forest Service regulations for designating and managing wilderness areas remained weak until 1939. That's when Bob Marshall—yet another Forest Service employee—drafted much tougher regulations for protecting wilderness areas. Aldo Leopold and Bob Marshall, joined by a few others, founded the Wilderness Society in 1935. By 1964, with support from the society, the Forest Service had set aside nine million acres of wilderness. But there was something missing: a common standard of wilderness management.

Also, because wilderness designations received only administrative protections, any future administration could reverse them. Wilderness was far from secure.

In the 1940s and 1950s and beyond, roads were needed to penetrate old-growth forests for timber supply to support our troops during World War II and, later, to help realize the American postwar dream of owning a single-family home. Millions of acres of wilderness were lost. But people like Howard Zahniser led a movement to give wilderness permanent protection through an act of Congress. The wilderness movement laid the foundations for wilderness as we know it today. In 1964 the Wilderness Act created the National Wilderness Preservation System. As Congress so poetically proclaimed in the memorable words of Howard Zahniser, principal author of the Wilderness Act, a wilderness is "an area where the earth and its community of life are untrammeled by man, where man himself is a visitor who does not remain." Leopold, Marshall, Carhart, Zahniser—we are privileged to enjoy the benefits of their foresight.

Since 1964 the National Wilderness Preservation System has grown from 9 to 105 million acres. Today we have more than 650 wilderness areas in forty-six states, thanks to the visionaries who still inspire us. Without them, this vision would never have become a reality—without the many agencies, private citizens, and organizations whose contributions to wilderness protection have been so vital over the years.

Despite our many gains, I remain concerned about the future of wilderness. We live in a society dominated by high-tech gadgetry that makes our lives easier even as we grow farther removed from our wilderness heritage. In a world of technological innovations that know no bounds, who will speak for the wild places—for the natural landscapes that yearly give way to parking lots, urban sprawl, our insatiable consumption of natural resources, and other indicators of what too many view as "progress"?

Too often, from 1950 onward, we in the Forest Service allowed our commitment to multiple use to imply that we couldn't be "for" wilderness without being "against" multiple use. Many accused us of only arguing for the protection of "rock and ice" as wilderness, leaving the prairie, old growth, and other more "productive" ecosystems open to development. All ecosystems should be represented in our Wilderness

Preservation System, but are not yet. For example, tallgrass prairie and bottomland hardwood are missing and should be added.

Today the National Wilderness Preservation System accounts for about 5 percent of the land area of the United States. That might not sound like much, and in fact it's not nearly enough. The scarcity of wilderness makes it all the more precious. We need what wilderness can give us. Wilderness provides us with clean water and air. Wilderness provides habitats for plants and animals, including a refuge for endangered species; all too often, wilderness is their last, best hope for survival. Wilderness provides solitude, a refuge from the noise and traffic that plague us in our daily lives. Wilderness provides scenic beauty, a place for quiet reflection on what it means to be alive. And let's not forget—wilderness provides economic benefits to communities through tourism and recreation, and to society at large through clean water and clean air.

Our most respected conservationist president was Theodore Roosevelt. Yet his rise appalled many of the political leaders of his own Republican party. As governor of New York, Roosevelt had shown a troublesome tendency toward the protection of natural resources and the reining in of corporate power. Roosevelt's initiatives in New York flummoxed the high, mighty, and influential. They thought they had found a convenient solution to get this "bull out of their china shop" when they had drafted Roosevelt for the vice presidency. Little did they know that six months later, "that damned cowboy" would be President.

Roosevelt's White House tenure from 1901 to 1909 defined modern conservation. He understood and believed in science. Not since Jefferson had someone so well versed in the sciences occupied the White House. His conservation legacy is immense—more than 250 million acres of national forests, national monuments, national parks and refuges.

There are important lessons to be learned from the past, especially in land management, where we must always take the long view. Perhaps the most important lesson is: Don't use up the land for short-term gain, or for any reason. Humans may not be able to control climate change or desertification, but we do influence it. We need only to look to parts of the Middle East to see the stark result of overuse of the land by too many people for too long.

The Bush administration, and subsequent leaders, will do well to follow the example of what Teddy Roosevelt did one hundred years ago. We should provide a conservation vision for this new century—a vision that has as its premise "the greatest good for the greatest number, in the long run."

I invite communities of places such as the Yaak, as well as communities of interest, to begin a dialogue. The roadless issue, and others, will not get easier with neglect or endless gridlock. Our challenge as a nation of outdoors lovers is to find common ground, and solutions for the future, while the opportunity is still within our grasp.

I think about how one man, Aldo Leopold, shaped the past fifty years of conservation and wonder. Leopold live his life and raised his children as "plain and simple members of the land community." What an incredible understatement, and what incredible humility exists in such a thought.

I hope readers of this book, and all those who care about our last remaining public wildlands, can acknowledge the shared goal: that in the coming fifty years our children's children will celebrate those leaders who, in an era that demanded tough choices, chose integrity over expediency; long-term values over short-term profit; and always to err on the side of the land.

CHAPTER 1

TRAVELING CLOSE TO HOME

By Debra Gwartney

SOMETIMES MY THIRD CHILD, A TALL AND DETERMINED THIRTEEN-year-old who's taken on the family job of keeping track of the promises I've made to the children, asks me if we are still going to move to Wales and live there for a year. We're going to try hard to do that, I tell her. I say it because Wales is the land of our ancestors, and I suspect something—maybe a small thing, but there nonetheless—stays unsolved in each of us because we've not breathed its air or walked its trails. I've read my children Welsh novels one after the other until we can picture the green, rolling landscape, the craggy hillsides, the gray sheets of slate, and the mushy wetlands that have swallowed swords and small children whole. Grieving women painted blue, keening from the mountaintops.

A map of Wales (hugged, as it is, by England) hangs on the wall of our spare bedroom, smudged by our fingertip travels along the coastal highway. We stumble our tongues across the vowel-laden names of towns and villages, sailing already to this strange and mysterious place that tugs at whatever ancestral fiber remains in my bones.

We won't forget our plan, I tell Mary. And if it turns out Wales is impossible, we'll find another place that will feed a part of our history and our future. A good, long time far off from here where the five of us can make sense of what's different than what we know.

It's not that our everyday life in Oregon is bad—it's just that it feels like it's always about going our separate ways. At eight every morning, we split like dandelion dander blown into the air, caught up in the snarl of traffic and strangers on the way to school and work. We race to a piano lesson, get to some friend's birthday party, another trip to the grocery store, let an evening hike unravel because of a forgotten meeting, a camping trip fall away because of some pressing teenage social requirement.

I want these willowy daughters—girls who've never let fear yank them back from dark corners, but who plow headlong into curiosity—to know a remote landscape, to be fed by it. So getting to such a place sounds like a good idea, an idea to advance upon immediately. But then I think: We'll go as soon as Mary finishes that year of advanced band, as soon as the youngest competes in that gymnastics tournament; as soon as the older girls' unruly teenage scenes are no longer part of what I have to manage on a day-to-day basis, so I can turn my thoughts to piecing together a long trip and money, housing, clothing.

But years have passed in this way of thinking. My daughters, now almost adults, are moving away, one by one. And I've fallen into the oldest human story: In the waiting until the time is right, the time has passed. I'm feeling the edges of resignation. The desire, the determination, to get my children off into a wild and completely foreign place is dwindling, settling down to soft coals, barely glowing. Just a little smoke in the distance.

"Why don't we hike the Appalachian Trail together?" was my thin plea at dinner not long ago. "It'll take us about five months; we'll live on the trail, pick up extra supplies in towns we come across." My daughters smiled a little, shrugged at the suggestion that would pass like a breeze through the house, and then the youngest mentioned that she had to build a diorama of a scene from *Mrs. Frisby and the Rats of NIMH* and have it ready for school the next morning, and a shoe box was not to be found anywhere in the house. I got up from the table to help her look while the other girls went off to their own rooms to listen to music alone, or to the telephone to call a friend.

Watching my daughters grow up and away, I find myself left with this question: In the absence of immersing ourselves completely in a far-off place, have I given my children any sense of the richness of life outside the urban patterns that dictate our days? Do they know how to fight for the preservation of a place that's not their own? We go camping a few times every summer. We know how to stake a tent and cook pancakes and fat turkey sausages over a campfire. We hike, we startle our skin pink by jumping in cold rivers and lakes, we rent cross-country ski equipment and traipse around the snowy mountains an hour from our home. And once in a while, I scrape together enough money that we can drive to Portland, fly to Spokane, rent a car, drive another four or so hours toward the Canadian border through all of the northern Idaho towns I visited with my own family when I was a girl, to the remote Montana valley where our dearest friends live and work.

We've been in the Yaak in every season: smelled the sweet pungency of myriad blossoms in the spring; in the fall, watched moose, heads sagging from the weight of their mossy green web of antlers, pull drinks of water from a pond with their dipper mouths; picked tiny wild strawberries from green meadows, and reeled mica-shiny fat trout out of the streams in the summer. One daughter once rounded a corner to run into a black bear and her two cubs; another time two saw a mountain lion crouched in the distance, tail switching. And we've wound our way through the woods, led by our friend Rick, who often stops to show the girls the dull charcoal-colored pellets of elk scat, a delicate hawk feather, a tiny tent of porcupine quills, a tangle of moose skeleton, the strange whistle gullet from the throat of a grouse. At the tops of these mountain hikes, we've stood still in the preternatural quiet, just letting the world be.

It's been five years since the five of us have gone to Yaak, to the farthest-off place we've been together. That was the time we went to have Thanksgiving with Rick and Elizabeth and their daughter. The massive amount of snow the valley gets every winter was already down that year—foot after foot of it plowed into walls on the side of the roads. And it was cold. Our first night in Yaak, the temperatures dipped to twenty-six degrees below zero. While we had always before seen moose, elk, and deer weaving through the trees as we made our way down the last few miles of narrow road to the cabin, this time we saw only white. And ice. Just a few hours after we'd arrived at the small house, I'd dashed back to the car for something and found the cans of soda pop the girls had left in the backseat exploded. Jagged metal broken open on the floor; brown, sweet icicles hanging from the ceiling and mashed into the seats.

The cabin's water pipes were frozen, refusing to give up even one drop of liquid. Elizabeth and I started Thanksgiving morning by hauling in clean, fresh snow to melt on the wood-burning stove; Rick kept it up through the day. We'd use it to cook with and to clean the pan where onions and celery had sizzled, spiced with freshly rubbed sage for the stuffing, and to scrub off the potatoes that would boil until they could be mashed into clouds. In the living room, the girls, who were thirteen, eleven, eight, and six at the time, folded themselves in the cumbersome elk skins that Rick had covered us with the night before, layers of musky animal fur that had kept us pinned to piles of down sleeping bags. The five of us slept together on the living room floor that way. The cold woke me only once; I shoved a few logs onto the dying fire, my face warmed by the orange glow, squeaked the hot cast-iron door of the woodstove closed with a stick, and then touched the only exposed parts of my daughters: the chilly rounded tops of their heads. In the morning, the raw logs that made up the walls of the tiny house were coated with ice, inside as well as out. The girls got up to rub their hands over the cold glass-encased wood, which melted into puddles as the fire got roaring.

Elizabeth and I, in the course of making Thanksgiving dinner, went back and forth to the stove to warm our feet, which became fat with numbness while standing over the kitchen sink despite wool socks and thick slippers. But we kept a steady beat: kneading the dough for rolls, rolling the piecrusts, scooping out the ripe, yellow butternut squash for the casserole.

No TV, of course—there was no electricity. The girls stayed close to the fire and read, they played checkers and card games, they told stories to the baby, they bundled themselves up in thick natty sweaters and heavy coats to make a run for the outhouse a hundred feet from the house, stopping each time on the way back to yank four-foot icicles off the cabin's eaves, sticking their tongues to the dry surface of the ice, shrieking for help with guttural calls when the cold grabbed tender skin and refused to give it back, rescued with a splash of water. They kicked snow into a flurry; jumping into piles of it until they were buried, and then ran in the house, cheeks red and ears brimmed with fire, to unfold themselves like fans in front of the stove.

In the afternoon, we called the girls over to help us set the table—Elizabeth and I talked about how it would only make sense to use paper plates instead of asking Rick to haul more snow in for water. But Rick groaned and delighted the girls in proclaiming, with a booming voice, his love for packing buckets in and out of the house. So we got out the best wedding china, pale and fragile as a field of March crocus, the crystal goblets, the crisp linen cloth. The table loaded with steaming gold and brown heaps of food could have been set anywhere, in any city or village—but out the huge picture window behind our laden feast was a scene that could only be Yaak. Snow blew across the icy pond, whirling up twisted ghosts. Giant fir and pine trees trembled under their winter weight, their tops tipping toward each other in the dark forest, as if they were sleeping through the long season of cold.

My daughters had told me that they (as I had when I was young) fantasized of living in a hollowed-out tree; cooking simple, earthy roots and berries they'd gathered themselves over a small fire in the middle of the empty trunk and fashioning furniture—chairs and shelves and tables—from what they'd found in the forest around them. This rough-hewn cabin—a thin barrier from pure wilderness—was as close as they'd ever come to living that way, and I could see they reveled in it.

I grew up in Idaho and I'm raising my children in Oregon, so Montana hardly seems foreign, and a long weekend isn't time enough to have a full sense of a place, but the Yaak is where my children and I, together, have fallen headlong into the glory of the unfamiliar, into the last of the planet's wildness, the unpredictability of the natural landscape, the authentic hush possible only away from the clamor.

But is it enough? Have their less than a dozen short visits to Yaak carved out a wilderness in their hearts?

That Thanksgiving, after dinner, after fine china was wiped down and left in the sink to steam under hot, melted snow, we decided to get out in the last bit of daylight, which edged through the windows in thin, creamy patches. The thermometer hung above the creaky porch read minus fifteen degrees. Over our full bellies, we layered sweaters, coats, hats, gloves, more wool socks, boots, and stomped our way outside. Rick brought two wooden sleds out of the shed, and the four girls began a raucous race over the icy pond, metal runners scratching long notes through the crisp, still air. The two pulling fell often, sprawling on the ice like snow-angels; the two being pulled tipped over each time the sleds slung out in a curve—girls jackknifing across the glassy surface, then rolling like potato bugs as the long skid stopped. Elizabeth, holding her bundled baby, and I watched the children play, their laughter carried into the dark wood and the coming night. Just as we were getting ready to call them in, my daughters goaded me into getting on one of the sleds. I plopped down and held the wooden slatted sides with clenched mittened fingers and pushed my boots hard against the metal plate at the end, since I knew that my bones had long ago lost the amazing resiliency to hit hard and then pop up again.

Each girl took a portion of the rope in her hand and, together, they started to run, boots spraying up a wake of white, all four of them howling their pleasure into the sky. The last of the sun faded over us, my family, as we pounded, jolted, slid across the cold world—traveling as if nothing could hold us back.

CHAPTER 2

THE SLOW AND DIFFICULT TRICK

By Chris Wood

Many have gone and think me half a fool
To miss a day away in the cool country.
Maybe. But in a book read and cherish,
Going to Walden is not so easy a thing
As a green visit. It is the slow and difficult
Trick of living, and finding it where you are.

—Mary Oliver

A CONFESSION. I'VE NEVER BEEN TO THE YAAK OR, FOR THAT
matter, Thoreau's Walden Pond. Living in Washington, D.C., however, I do know
something about Mary Oliver's admonition to find Walden wherever you are. The
essays, poems, and stories within this book are a poignant reminder to those of us who
spend our time in the wilds of the nation's capital that roadless areas in countless Yaaks
across the national forest system are more than fodder for political arguments or small
isolated green patches on Forest Service maps.

And all of us who care about national forests have our own Yaak stories to tell.
One bleary evening, in the final days of completing the Roadless Area Conservation
Rule, a member of the roadless team told me how he left his job as a timber cruiser in
a particularly remote national forest after seeing the effects of his work the next hunting season.

"That moonscape made me leave, Chris. And now it's come full circle. We are
doing something important. Something lasting." Embarrassed, he stopped.

I mumbled something about how the team's work would stand the test of time. He looked up as if I hadn't spoken, and said, "Dammit. They care. People really care about these places."

Although I cannot capture the spirit of the Yaak, I can try to explain the rationale for—the spirit, if you will—of the Roadless Area Conservation Rule, a policy that would have prohibited new road construction and most commercial timber harvest on the Yaak's last few roadless lands and another fifty-eight million acres of roadless areas of national forests.

I believe the roadless rule, a bureaucratic endeavor, as all federal rule makings are, represented the best of democracy in action. A record-breaking six hundred local meetings and 2.2 million postcards, letters, e-mails, and faxes—an astonishing 95 percent supporting stronger protection of roadless areas—serve as testament. Instead of preparing canned and trite responses that neatly fitted a preordained conclusion, the Forest Service allowed public sentiment to shape the outcome and content of the rule—affirming the value of public involvement in management of public lands. Never before, and likely never again, will a federal proposal receive such widespread public support.

If implemented, the roadless rule would have quelled the controversy over how to manage our last wild and unfragmented public forests. It would have helped secure the conservation of lands providing habitat for nearly 25 percent of all animal species listed for protection under the Endangered Species Act. It would have reduced the amount of taxpayer money spent trying to build roads or offer timber sales in remote and hard-to-reach landscapes. Equally important, it would have allowed the Forest Service to live up to its brag, emblazoned on letterheads and coffee mugs, as the World's Foremost Conservation Organization. The cost? Less than two-tenths of one percent of the nation's timber supply.

Would have. Instead of defending the roadless rule from legal challenges by the timber industry and the state of Idaho, the new Bush administration chose to reopen and then weaken the most popular public land conservation initiative of the past century. Regardless of the White House's political machinations, the era of building roads and putting up commodity timber sales in roadless areas is, or very well should be, over. As my high school geometry teacher often said in response to my never-sharp mathematics, "How many times do we have to beat this dead horse to death?"

For decades, controversies over roadless areas plagued local forest managers. Environmentalists, the source of many of the comments calling for roadless protection, were driven largely because Forest-Service-inventoried roadless areas represent the reservoir of future wilderness areas. Although newspapers across the country hailed the roadless rule as the most important public lands conservation measure since the creation and expansion of the national forest system, the motivations of the Forest Service were as much practical as visionary.

Facing an $8.4 billion road maintenance backlog that kept growing exponentially through neglect, the agency received its wake-up call when a House of Representatives amendment to an appropriations bill in 1997 came within a single vote of eliminating 80 percent of forest roads funding—in large part to slow road construction into undeveloped roadless areas. From such mundane beginnings the roadless rule was born.

Critics—and there were many—dubbed the roadless rule as bold, liberal excess. In reality, protecting roadless areas was not a particularly bold action for the Forest Service so much as a way to minimize an $8.4 billion taxpayer liability. Similarly, not cutting the few remaining old-growth forests is not liberal—it is the essence of conservative when so few remain. Just as designating wilderness is not excessive, it is the single most conservative action the government can take regarding public lands.

Bold? Advocating development of an oil field in a protected wildlife refuge in Alaska for six months' worth of oil is bold. Cutting our last remaining old-growth forests: That's liberal. What could be more excessive, if not regressive, than an agenda based on rolling back protections for the few remaining wild and unfragmented public lands? That maintaining the status quo and retaining options for future generations can be cast as liberal demonstrates just how meaningless terms like *conservative* have become, with regard to conservation.

The ecological and economic arguments for protecting roadless areas are well established. The philosophic underpinnings of the roadless rule extend back to the westward expansion of the thirteen colonies.

The shortsighted may believe, or hope, that a single presidential election will spell the fate of roadless protection. But protecting our remaining wild places is more than a political debate dependent on the whims of four-year election cycles. It speaks to our willingness to recognize our heritage—to not forget from whence we came. Egypt has its Pyramids, Italy its splendid churches, and Africa its ancient cultures. We have our wild places. Landscapes that tested westward migrants in search of gold, land, plunder, freedom, and new opportunity. Protecting these last remaining wildlands affirms our national identity and recognizes that we will leave this knowledge to interpret, experience, and judge for our children and our children's children.

Our children's children. My wife, Betsy, is extraordinarily close to her grandmother. The first time I met this remarkable ninety-three-year-old woman, she beat me in a cutthroat game of croquet. What makes Betsy and her grandmother most remarkable is the rarity of their relationship. Our attitude toward wild places is not unlike the way the majority of us view our grandparents. They bake great cookies and have an older generation's aptitude for fixing broken appliances. Not until they are gone do we realize their importance to us—the firmament and grounding they provided, the wisdom they possessed. So it is with wild places.

Aldo Leopold, a former Forest Service employee, once wrote, "Wilderness is a resource that can shrink but not grow." The U.S. Forest Service has a long and paradoxical relationship with roadless areas and wilderness. Arthur Carhart fought to preserve the Boundary Waters wilderness in Minnesota. Leopold helped create the first wilderness on the Gila National Forest in New Mexico. Bob Marshall first called for the protection of large roadless areas. These Forest Service employees of seventy-five years ago are conservation legends celebrated today. Lesser known are the agency's contemporary rank-and-file wilderness heroes, and they are many.

It is only a slight overstatement to say that the U.S. Forest Service invented the wilderness ethic. But if environmentalists were polled, most would probably place the Forest Service somewhere between *disinterested observers* and *despoilers of wilderness.* Such sentiments may be born more of misperception than fact. The greatest resistance in 2000, however, to creating a new wilderness program in the Forest Service came from within the agency.

The Forest Service's uneasy relationship with wilderness and roadless area protection reflects our frontier heritage. Even today, five generations removed from Manifest Destiny and "taming" the wilderness, some view our remaining wild places as an "impediment" to productivity. The whole concept of limits—and roadless protection is about nothing if not limits—is anathema. It's almost anti-American.

In 1912 James Bryce, the British ambassador to the United States, predicted:

> *What Europe is now, is that toward which you in America are tending. Presently, steam cars stop some 12 miles away from the entrance of Yosemite. Surely development should come no closer. . . . If you were to realize what the result of the automobile will be in that wonderful, that incomparable valley, you would keep it out.*

Today Yosemite—"that wonderful, that incomparable valley"—suffers from daily traffic jams and has been described as at times resembling a downtown urban area. We need roadless areas if for no other reason than they are so improbable, so unlikely in our productive, connected, call-me-as-soon-as-you-get-this society. The Chilean poet Pablo Neruda once wrote:

> *For once on the face of the earth*
> *Let's not speak in any language.*
> *Let's stop for one second*
> *Moving our arms so much . . .*
> *If we were not so single-minded*
> *About keeping our lives moving*
> *And for once could do nothing,*
> *Perhaps a huge silence*
> *Might interrupt this sadness*
> *Of never understanding ourselves*
> *And of threatening ourselves with death.*

If you prefer more homegrown reason and advocacy, consider Wallace Stegner's oft-quoted words to the Forest Service in 1960, four years prior to passage of the Wilderness Act:

Without any remaining wilderness we are committed wholly, without
chance for even momentary reflection and rest, to a headlong drive into our
technological termite-life, the Brave New World of completely man-con-
trolled environment. We need wilderness preserved—as much of it as is still
left, and as many kinds—because it was the challenge against which our
character as a people was formed. The reminder and the reassurance that it
is still there is good for our spiritual health even if we never once in ten
years set foot in it.

Stegner's words speak to a national trend toward forgetfulness. Each new idea, fashion, or product becomes the standard against which we measure our experience and
progress. In the span of a single generation we have seen the majority of our populace
move from rural to urban areas. Today 80 percent of us live in urban areas and sub-
urbs. What are the effects on our national psyche—not to mention what Aldo Leopold
called a "land ethic"—from this collective belief that food comes from grocery stores,
and energy from power plants?

Smaller phones that fit in a breast pocket of a fishing vest; little machines that pay
bills, send and receive love letters, and buy gifts for friends and family. Whole communities carved from woodlands and old farms in the span of a few months. Products,
gadgets, and development that in the name of improving our quality of life, our ability
to stay connected, leave our communities ever more frayed, the human inhabitants ever
more stressed.

Most Thanksgivings, I get together with the friends I grew up with. Roadless areas
are the public lands' equivalent of seeing your old friends from home. Like windows
into our past, they ground us and keep us in check. They remind us where we came
from. Who we were before we became so busy doing Important Things. That is precisely why we need to protect all the roadless areas we have and as many more as
Congress will allow as wilderness. *Too much wilderness* is an oxymoron. It is like having
too many old friends from home.

Without roadless areas, our only connection, the only tributes to the tenacity of our
forebears, would be composed of plaster and paper, in parks and dusty books. Leopold
once told the planners of a monument to the extinct passenger pigeon:

24

There will always be pigeons in books and in museums, but these are effigies and images, dead to all hardships and to all delights. Book pigeons cannot dive out of a cloud to make the deer run for cover, nor flap their wings in thunderous applause of mast-laden woods. . . . They know no urge of seasons; they feel no kiss of sun, no lash of wind and weather. They live by not living at all.

Effigies and images cannot compare to the Real Thing. Do not misunderstand. I do not want an antitechnology society of Luddites. Innovation and development allowed our nation to become great. In the final analysis, however, it is respect for our lands and waters—the sort of humility that allows roadless areas to persist—that will sustain us, and allow us to endure.

CHAPTER 3

THE LOGGERS

By Bob Love

I'VE WORKED AS A LOGGER IN THE FORESTS OF NORTHWEST Montana for nearly twenty-five years. In the early part of my career I was a timber faller for a large company, cutting for their high-lead yarders on national forest timber sales. When that outfit folded in the mid-1980s, I hired on with an independent contractor who did the same type of work, but on smaller sales. As the flow of federal timber declined in the late 1980s, he decided to work exclusively for Plum Creek Timber on its land.

At that time Plum Creek was "liquidating its assets" (cutting the best and leaving the rest) in order to satisfy corporate debts and quarterly profit reports. As I grew increasingly dissatisfied with this so-called forestry, I publicly voiced my opposition to it. Even though many of my fellow loggers privately agreed with me, few of them were willing to bite the hand that fed them. As I became more estranged from the logging community and frustrated with my inability to affect the system, I decided to make some career changes.

While my livelihood depended on sustainable forest management, I was being paid to satisfy the insatiable appetites of sawmills. This obviously wasn't in the best interests of the land, my family, or my community. I decided to use my skills to benefit the land, or find another trade. I had to shift my priorities from forest removal to forest retention. Since this contradicted what was happening on industrial and public lands, the only option left to me was to become an independent contractor for private nonindustrial forest owners. I started down this road eight years ago, and have thoroughly enjoyed the journey.

At the same time I was openly challenging conventional forestry practices, I became familiar with some local environmentalists; we were attending many of the same hearings, workshops, and field tours. The underlying assumption of these affairs was that loggers and environmentalists disagreed on everything; consequently, all the players stuck to the script. The deeper the adversaries dug in their heels, the more convinced the Forest Service became that resolution was impossible.

I realized that if either side "won" we would all lose, and sensed that reasonable people could find some common ground if a few of us were willing to drop our defenses and step out of the trenches. Acting on this intuition, I called Steve Thompson of the Montana Wilderness Association. We organized some tours where loggers and MWA members looked at good and bad forestry, without Forest Service intervention.

We found plenty to argue about, but in the absence of the contrived contentiousness that normally framed our meetings, we got to know one another more intimately. As we shared rides, lunches, opinions, and stories, we began to see one another as neighbors rather than members of special-interest groups. For the first time, loggers and environmentalists approached the Forest Service with a unified front and offered a cohesive vision for the future. Essentially, we agreed that the timber frontier was closed, and that we had to learn to live within limits. The Forest Service didn't know what to make of this. Although some employees were supportive, we encountered institutional resistance, and the true believers in the environmental and logging communities regarded us as traitors.

This all happened more than a decade ago. Some of the relationships formed during that time deepened into friendships, while some friendships that existed prior to that period disintegrated. At any rate, our voluntary cease-fire encouraged more thoughtful, civil discussions about public forest issues, and led to the creation of the Flathead Forestry Project. FFP is an ad hoc group dedicated to restoring trust among the timber industry, conservationists, and the Forest Service by promoting small timber sales and stewardship projects in our national forests. The group has been meeting for eight years and has had some influence on Forest Service policy, despite bureaucratic inertia and the active resistance of some industrial trade groups and environmental organizations.

A key principle that emerged from those initial conversations, and still guides the FFP, is that we don't have to enter roadless areas to find logs. There's plenty of work to do in the roaded frontcountry, where we've consistently eaten dessert before cleaning our plate. I recall several Forest Service tours of proposed timber sales where we drove past forty miles of salvage, thinning, fuel-reduction, and restoration work, only to arrive at an alpine basin at the end of a road where nobody thought we should be working anyway. But instead of addressing the challenging and complex issues associated with previously managed forests, we have chosen to reckon damages, assign blame, and antagonize one another, to the detriment of the land and our communities. The failure of the Clinton-era debate about roadless area management was that it occurred in the absence of more urgent deliberations about the treatment of roaded areas.

In a global context, our nation is like a gated community. We may be the only people in the world who can afford to spend so much time and energy bickering with one another about the fate of wildlands. Our circumstance is both tragic and fortunate. Tragic, in that our ability to preserve backcountry while we neglect the stewardship of the frontcountry has been facilitated by unsustainable resource extraction from other places. Fortunate, in that the ecosystems of our national forests are resilient and relatively intact. I believe our thoughtful interaction with these landscapes is warranted and desirable, and the responsible thing to do.

I was at a party a few years ago when a woman approached me and said she'd heard I was "quite a conservationist." When I replied that I tried to be, she remarked, "That's good, because I'm not on the loggers' side at all." When I told her I worked in the woods, she seemed to be more perplexed than embarrassed, and bolted away without saying a word. Her reaction reflects a political climate that stifles independent thinking, provokes animosity between people who should be allies, and strengthens the corporate influence on public resource issues. Although it's widely assumed that most loggers aren't conservationists, I know many who are, and I believe we all should be.

As a logger, I support timber management in our national forests. As a hunter and backcountry wanderer, I advocate the preservation of wilderness and roadless areas. We can and should have both. To achieve this balance we need to pay attention, proceed cautiously, and learn to ask the land what it can provide, rather than make demands of it. Ideally, the forestry we practice in our national forests should honor the spirit—the wildness—of the land. It should work in concert with natural cycles and patterns, respectfully harvesting the forests' interest rather than plundering their capital, attuning local economies to the land's productive capacity. Finally, this forestry should be more labor- than capital-intensive, and more manual than mechanical, so that our national forests would provide opportunities for young people to learn the land and make a career of caring for it, and become sanctuaries for the skills and wisdom that are discounted in corporately managed forests.

But when I compare my utopian version with reality, I'm not very optimistic. The polarization in our communities is increasing. The Forest Service is still being whipsawed between environmental and industrial lobbyists who have no affinity with rural communities and landscapes. As loggers become more mechanized, foresters design timber sales to match the machinery, and the site-sensitive projects suited for small loggers and restoration specialists fall through the planning cracks. And I don't see many young people pursuing a career in the woods.

But I'm going to keep swimming against the current—I'm convinced there are some deep pools upstream. And, paraphrasing Robert Frost, I'd like you to come, too.

CHAPTER 4

PIECES OF SKY

By Tom Franklin

I WAS THERE, IN THE YAAK, NINE YEARS AGO, BEFORE I KNEW what trouble the valley was in, a time when I could barely see past my own troubles. My cousin Ken and I left Mobile, Alabama, and drove twenty-five straight hours to Rapid City, South Dakota, and slept in a Kentucky Fried Chicken parking lot, shivering under our coats, in a rented Chrysler. The next day Ken strummed his acoustic guitar as I drove from there into Wyoming, then Montana, higher and higher, and colder, even in July. I wore a pair of brand-new snakeskin cowboy boots, and we'd stopped at each state line and I'd taken pictures of the boots with my mother's camera. Every mile that clicked off the odometer was the farthest I'd been from home, so I hoped my life was being reshaped as we drove, heading into red swelling sunsets with snowcapped mountains shrugging across the horizon.

I'd left behind me the hospital morgue where I worked, where I pushed corpses around on gurneys and took amputated limbs wrapped in biohazard bags and miscarried fetuses in plastic buckets and stored them on shelves in the freezer until Tuesday, which was the day I carted them to the incinerator, where I fed them piece by piece into the fire like a trapper tossing in sticks of furniture with winter howling and knocking outside. I'd also left behind the old Toyota pickup truck my father had loaned me, a faded brown diesel with slow-leaking tires and holes where the radio had been. Left too a cheap, one-room apartment and the woman I was married to—or, really, she had left me.

I brought the twelve-dollar sleeping bag that was my bed in the empty apartment, and the cowboy boots, charged at Sears on the way out of town. A limp leather fishing cap because I thought you needed a cap in Montana. Several field guides from the library—mammals, birds, reptiles, and trees of the Northwest. I'd read about the Yaak and heard rumors of it, that it was wilderness, mythic, and I brought Ken because I didn't want to travel to such a place alone. He told me, as we neared Libby, that he'd never liked my ex-wife, had never thought she seemed to love me. He wasn't the first person to say that. In response, I told him how, in the morgue, I always looked at the faces of the dead as they came to my care. I would fold back the sheet and see a man with his dentures safety-pinned to his hospital gown, or a woman with ice packs over her eyes because she'd checked the organ donor box on her driver's license.

I told Ken one of the last things my ex-wife had said to me was, "I don't like the way you look, or smell, or feel." Told him she'd spent the last two days we lived together in our rented house assembling a giant puzzle: covered bridge, autumn leaves, clouds. I'd tried talking to her but knew she'd said all she wanted to say, our problems as enormous as the sky outside. I'd sat across from her at our dining table and watched her fit the last section of the puzzle with fingers that had chewed nails. Then I watched as she picked the puzzle apart, piece by piece. And then she shuffled the pieces and, after lighting a cigarette and calling the cat into her lap, started to work again, organizing by color, searching for the four corners. That, I told Ken, was what my marriage had been.

It was raining, the temperature dropping, when we headed north out of Troy, mountains all around but often obscured by trees. We drove, the wipers swishing, until we saw a small sign that said YAAK, and we turned onto a muddy dirt road, both of us worrying that the Chrysler might get stuck. "Should we go back?" Ken wondered aloud, but I was driving.

After half an hour of skidding and steering around mud holes, I pulled the car down a hill into a campground near the river. There were several sites, all vacant, no cars or people or dogs, just mosquitoes, empty trash cans, and barbecue grills full of water. The noise of the river and, above that, the rain.

"We'll never get a fire started," Ken sad, glancing at the gray sky.

We set up the cheap pup tent I'd brought, then silently unloaded our gear into it. We were both a little cranky from the trip, and wet. We'd driven over twenty-three hundred miles to camp in the rain? What place was worth that?

"Feel like a hike?" Ken asked, opening an umbrella.

No, I told him. I wanted a drink.

The "town" of Yaak was a few miles farther north. The mercantile had closed for the day, but the Dirty Shame was open for business. I parked the Chrysler beside a blue Nissan pickup, the only vehicle there. Inside the saloon, a man named Dick McGary was reading a Missoula newspaper. *Missoula,* I thought, sitting at the bar, remembering how far *south* that city was from here. Ken had uncased his guitar and was plucking it while I studied the dollar bills stapled to the walls, the names of people from everywhere. We were the only customers at the time and, as it turned out, the only customers that night.

McGary set Bud Lights in front of us. "Where you guys from?"

I told him.

He raised his eyebrows. "You *drove* here? From southern Alabama?"

We both nodded.

"Jesus. Why?"

Ken paused in his playing, and I tried to tell how I thought I needed someplace like a wild valley to give me back what I couldn't put into words. I didn't explain myself very clearly, I guess.

McGary grunted and said other tourists came up here, too—too damn many—that we weren't the first. "Nobody from as low as you, though," he said.

I got quiet then, feeling diminished, as McGary told us about the valley, its tiny population, the severe winters, what to do if we hiked and came across a grizzly, how to avert our eyes, slump our shoulders, and make ourselves nonthreatening. But it was the opposite, he said, for a mountain lion. For one of those, you wave your arms and charge it. Outside the rain was picking up, spattering the roof, the crack beneath the door flickering with lightning, low rumble of thunder rolling in from the mountains.

The night was cold, midforties maybe, and the rain kept falling. I peeled my wet socks off and laid them like strips of raw bacon on the floor of the tent and climbed into the twelve-dollar sleeping bag. Not nearly drunk enough, I hugged myself and shivered. Next to me, Ken snored and flounced and kicked the way he had in our childhood, talking in his sleep and somehow managing to get nearly crossways in the tiny tent. Between us lay his guitar, which he'd refused to leave in the car, and the walls jostled each time we moved, rain dripping through the ceiling. Half numb from cold, I remembered hearing that if you lie very still, you'll be warmer, so I tried that. It was strange, as sleep didn't come, to comprehend that I was in Montana, the Yaak Valley, nothing but a trail of boot-pictures to tell of the journey. More strange, though, wasn't my being here, but that I'd had the idea to make the trip, surely—and sadly—the most outrageous thing I'd ever done. And yet still I felt no magic, no myth. Lying in the dark, surrounded by wilderness, it occurred to me that all I felt was the old familiar loneliness, and that land like this was not for the lonely. Perhaps I'd traveled here because I was *after* the Yaak, as if this valley were a place you could mine for the opposite of loneliness, whatever that is. Maybe it was wrong to come here wanting to take something, rather than to give. Maybe that's true for every place.

At dawn—I'd barely slept—I pulled the cowboy boots over a dry pair of socks. The rain had stopped in the night. I shrugged into my coat and took the hat from my pocket. Moving Ken's guitar, I crawled out to a cold and quiet world, the kind of silence I've seldom heard, a silence that included the clucking of river and the drip of rain, yet absent of all the others like myself. Around me trees stood shrouded and linked in fog, trees I couldn't identify precisely but remembered from the field guide as Engelmann spruce, old-growth western red cedar, giant hemlock, and others: wide red trunks and narrow green leaves cupping tiny mirrors of rain. Breathing steam, I dug my hands into my pockets and walked up the little path, feeling raw around the eyes from the sleepless night.

On the road, under the towering trees, I began to stride. The boots made a scuffing noise I thought every animal within miles must have heard, and I imagined rounding a curve and seeing a moose raise its glistening muzzle from grazing or a grizzly rise to its hind legs. But it felt good to be moving and I was beginning to be able to feel my toes. Above, through patches of fog, the sky was bluing.

How far was I from Alabama now? How far from that ex-wife, the hospital morgue, the incinerator fire? Suddenly I felt detached, as if this part of my life were a narrative, a story where a lonely, unhappy man marries the wrong woman. The marriage fails in a thousand details, scenes like the man slinging his silent wife's puzzle off the table where she's been sitting for days. The man pleading, "Talk to me." The woman standing, looking at the sky in pieces all over the floor. The woman saying, "I'm leaving you."

Then another scene. The divorced man in a hospital morgue, pushing an empty gurney. He takes a rag and wipes the puddle of clear liquid from the black surface. Clear fluid. All that is left of a life, leaked out only a vinyl cushion. He stops. Looks up. Instead of fluorescent lights, he sees the sky, not cracked on a floor but filling his eyes. He is in Montana now. All around him are trees and sky and possibility. He glances up and down the road. He is in the valley. He has come to Yaak, awakened in its myth, and, if only for a moment, been a character in its landscape.

Below, from beside the river, Ken began to strum his guitar, as if signaling that this part of my life had passed, that it was time to roll up the sleeping bag, which would remind me in the weeks and months to come—by the way it felt, looked, smelled—of the Yaak. I took my hands out of my pockets and walked back toward camp, quickly, each long step taking me closer to my mother's camera, where I would take one last picture of the cowboy boots, no longer new, there in the Yaak, before going home.

I got better.

And the Yaak?

CHAPTER 5

AFRAID

By Todd Tanner

I LEFT MY HUNTER—A MAN WITH A BRIGHT ORANGE HAT AND clumsy feet—sitting alone on a rock. As I walked away, I thought about a conversation that wasn't quite thirty seconds old.

"Are you sure it's okay for me to stay here by myself?" he asked.

"Don't worry, you'll be fine. I'm just going to circle around the ridge and try to push that buck back out into the open. If he does come out, take your time and make sure you've got a good shot before you squeeze the trigger."

I didn't mention the obvious. We both knew he'd just missed the biggest white-tailed buck he'd ever seen, and the odds were that he wouldn't get another chance at a deer that size—not in the next couple of days, probably not in the next thirty years.

The hillside was steep, icy, and laced with blown-down lodgepole snags, so I hadn't gotten more than a dozen yards when I heard a short whistle. I looked over my shoulder and there was my client, hurrying after me and gesturing for me to turn back.

A minute later I asked him what was wrong.

"I'm a little nervous about staying here all alone."

"There's no reason to worry. I'll be back in half an hour, forty-five minutes tops."

"Well, what if you're not. I'll never be able to find my way out of here by myself."

"Why don't you relax?" I asked. "Nothing bad is going to happen."

He still looked nervous.

"Just keep an eye out for that buck. He's with a doe, so he probably didn't go far."

I started to turn away, but my hunter wasn't through yet.

"You know," he said, "I noticed that you're not carrying a gun. What happens if you're attacked by a grizzly bear or a mountain lion. You'd be dead and I'd be stuck out here"—he waved his arms around, taking in the whole north end of the valley—"by myself."

What could I say? The guy was obviously uneasy about being alone in the wild. Not quite what you'd expect of someone who'd just traveled twenty-five hundred miles to hunt in the north woods of Montana.

Anyway, I looked down at my feet for a few seconds, trying to frame some sort of reply, but I couldn't think of anything else that might help. If I had told him what was actually on my mind at the time—*Sure, I might get eaten by a bear or a lion in the next half hour, but it's a hell of a lot more likely that you'll shoot me by accident*—the situation would have deteriorated even more.

Finally, after an uncomfortable silence, he said, "I'll tell you what. I'll wait here by myself. But if anything attacks you, I want you to scream, and I'll come running with my gun."

"Right." I said. "You come running if I scream. Otherwise, though, I want you to stay right here."

"Okay."

I turned to walk away.

"Make sure you scream loud, so I can hear you."

Twenty minutes later, just over the crest of the ridge, I sat down with my back against the larch. The bottom of the tree was black, courtesy of some long-ago forest fire, and the ground was covered with layer upon layer of shiny yellow needles.

I closed my eyes and pictured that buck—I'd seen him again a few minutes ago, but he'd slipped off to the north, away from my client—and then I thought about the quiet. It is never silent in the deep woods, but it is often quiet, and if you allow that quiet to seep inside yourself, you might even find a moment of tranquility, of real peace.

I luxuriated in the stillness—and the heady smell of the November forest, and the warmth of the afternoon sun—for a few precious minutes and then, with great effort, I contemplated my hunter, sitting alone on his rock. Sitting there alone and afraid.

As I stood up to walk back, I wondered what it tells us about ourselves when we need noise (and bustle, and roads, and telephones, and televisions, and buildings, and crowds of people who look, walk, talk, and act just like we do) to feel at ease? What, in our pride and arrogance, have we allowed ourselves to become?

CHAPTER 6

PUNGENCY

By Bill McKibben

HIKING IN MIDSPRING THROUGH THE FORESTS OF THE YAAK, I kept stopping short—a branch up ahead would be quivering, as if brushed by the fleeing butt of some surprised creature. Each time it turned out to be the same thing: a tree limb that had been bowed down by the snow's weight and had just that instant been released by the slow melt, stopping my heart for a second as it flung its tip back into the air. What a place! Even the alder boughs were wild.

It's arrogant to announce the character of a forest, and yet in my walks through the Yaak this nearly cartoonish wildness kept overwhelming me. It's not that I saw so many animals—I was with friends, we were chattering, any animal that couldn't have avoided us was due for a date with Darwin. But everywhere, or at least in those roadless areas that the U.S. Forest Service has so far neglected, a kind of rawness prevailed. Great piles of scat, and clumps of feathers, and bits of fur, and the occasional tooth, the odd antler. Time and again I'd think that we'd stumbled across a trail in our cross-country rambles—we'd walk for hundreds of yards down well-graded, needle-covered paths that turned out, of course, to be the work of mule deer or elk neatly walking the contours. No matter where I stood, if I revolved slowly I would see one buck rub after another. And I have such weak senses; I can only imagine what it must seem like to those creatures that can really smell, really hear, really see, to those white-tails that are every second alert and not cursed with the human absentmindedness. It must be as pungent, as bright, as dazzling as the Ginza on a Saturday night.

But not just wild in a Marlon Perkins dart-gun sort of way. Wild in some deeper sense. At certain elevations, dozens of cedar snags recorded a racing, searing fire of

nearly a century before—and the char, the decay, the trees sprouting from the horizon-
tal rot were a reminder that time stretched back and forward into the unknowable
here. That the chain of evidence, as a detective would say, was intact back far beyond
the onset of human assault. It's not bigness that signifies old growth; it's mystery. The
great simplification that is the dubious project of our time on earth has not yet reached
these pockets.

Here is what it means. We stood one day on Grizzly Peak, in an intermittent snow-
storm that every few minutes lifted enough to show us the boundaries of the valley.
This was no pristine place—in fact, the jagged patches of the clear-cuts made it look
more domesticated than the endless unbroken green of my Adirondack home. But we
could see the mountainside just nearby where the biologists tracking the radio collars
swear that a grizzly sow has denned each year, has raised young. So Grizzly Peak was
not the typical American place named for what used to be there, not Fox Run or Buck
Meadow, or Panther Ridge. It was a name in the old-fashioned sense; it referred to the
present condition of the place.

That present is the oddest moment in human history. Suddenly, at the end of the
twentieth century, there is no such thing as permanent wildness on our planet. The reach
of our technology guarantees that each intersection of latitude and longitude also marks
some conjunction of economics, politics, ambition, shortsightedness, need. But there are
places left where the whiff of wildness, the fresh-scat pungency of wildness, remains. Far
stronger even than in the fenced-off grandeur of the national parks, that reek of time-
beyond-counting rises from the melting snow of one more spring in the Yaak.

CHAPTER 7

YAAK AND THE UNKNOWABLE WILD

By   Gregory   McNamee

KAMCHATKA. FOR HOURS I HAVE BEEN TRAVELING WITH THE
arc of the sun, crossing time zones and continents, flying the great circle from Los
Angeles to Shanghai. Between those two huge megalopolises, far below, has passed territory that a Puritan elder, one of those dour thinkers who first shaped—and who continue to shape—American ideas about wilderness, would call a hellish wasteland: the
glacial inlets of British Columbia, the old-growth forests of the Alaskan coast, the tundra of Beringia. And now Kamchatka, a place of childhood dreams nursed by an often
visited globe and by peripatetic parents, Kamchatka, wilderness pure and primeval,
uncut by roads, seemingly unvisited, a russet forested world stretching unbroken from
horizon to horizon.

Just weeks before I had been in another wilderness, the Yaak Valley of northwestern
Montana, tucked away near the Idaho and British Columbia lines. It is but an atom of
wildland compared to the huge landmass of the Kamchatka Peninsula, but it is surpass-
ingly wild nonetheless, a place where wildlife corridors do not run at right angles, a
place through which a Yellowstone-bound wolf might find safe passage on the underground railroad from Canada. Small it may be, but it is largely unmediated by human
presence.

I had traveled to nearby Troy, Montana, to provide desperately needed moral guidance
to a cutthroat gang of musicians who were then touring taverns and trailer parks in the
northwestern corner of the state, but Yaak was the real reason I had traveled so far from
home—Yaak, about which I had been reading for so many years in the journalism and
essays of my friend Rick Bass. Rick is not shy about sharing Yaak, unlike me, who self-
ishly salts away my favorite places, the little wild corners of Arizona, New Mexico,

Sonora. And so on a sweltering July day we set out from the banks of the Yaak River up a spiny knoll in the all-too-evident footsteps of an adolescent male grizzly bear—I say that he was male and adolescent on account of the hormone-charged trail of savaged tree trunks and half-chewed shrubs he had left in his wake, but I have no stronger evidence for his identity—through a tangled association of coralroot, tallgrass, mistletoe, blackberry, lodgepole pine, spruce, alder, cedar, ponderosa pine, an Amazonian density of vegetation bewildering to me, used to the comparative austerity of the Sonoran Desert.

We never did catch up with that bear, although I like to believe with more hope than proof that we saw the barest flash of his tail rounding a draw a quarter of a mile or so ahead of us. The grizzly surely knew we were in pursuit. It is probably to the good that we did not meet him. It is certainly to the good that he had a place in this world big enough that he could afford to tolerate our attentions.

"Among the most sinister phenomena in intellectual history is the avoidance of the concrete," says my one of my great heroes, the Bulgarian philosopher Elias Canetti. Traveling into Yaak—and, for that matter, flying over the reddish eternity of Kamchatka and Siberia—gave mere abstractions about which I had read in books and on maps an unforgettable face. Portions have been ravaged over time, to be sure, but Yaak is one of the few wild places, few *real* places, left in the contiguous United States. It is a place where the processes of nature—growth and decline, decay and regeneration, birth and death—are laid bare before us. Having now gazed into its face, I am even more firmly convinced of its value, and of its being precisely the sort of place that demands our protection—against logging, mining, ranching, and other activities—in those last roadless areas, certainly—that favor short-term gain over long-term good.

We have too few such places. It is time, now and finally, to declare that what we have we will not allow to be taken.

I have been thinking about places like Yaak for years, and that thinking came about by one of those accidental remarks that can forever change lives.

Many years ago, on a train crossing the coastal plain of southern Italy, I fell into conversation with a man about my age who, he was quick to tell me, had just earned a sizable fortune by buying old dockside warehouses in London and selling them as luxury apartments to people who had been busily earning sizable fortunes of their own. He asked where I was from. When I told him Arizona, he smiled and said, "I've been there, once. Quite a beautiful place, really. All that extraordinary land, but"—here he paused meaningfully—"there's nothing on it."

Well, I replied, gazing out at the snarled macchia and tangled drifts of prickly Apulian cactus, by my lights you're off by a word in the chain of cause and effect: all that beautiful land, *and* there's nothing on it.

The Englishman's attitude, neither benign nor malignant, was not at all surprising. The received European vision of the land differs markedly from our own: It defines the natural environment, nostalgically, as a collection of not only forests, rivers, and mountains, but also thatch-roofed farmhouses in sylvan glens, a curl of smoke rising from the chimneys and lambs bleating in clovery meadows full of swarming bees, fair-haired children dancing around a maypole and strong elders smoking their Meerschaums. I am exaggerating that Tolkienesque vision, but not by much, and lately I have been struck by how often it occurs in European nature writing. A land without people, in much of that library, is no land at all.

There can be little or no unmanaged nature in such a conception of the land, and for good reason: Only in lesser-visited corners of highland Scotland and pockets of the Balkans, among a few other places, has Europe left much of its land alone. "It is difficult," the Dutch historian Simon Schama writes in *Landscape and Memory,* "to think of a single natural system that has not, for better or worse, been substantially modified by human culture." Difficult for a European observer such as my Isle of Dogs conversant, perhaps, but not difficult at all from where I sit as I write these words, looking out at tall Arizona mountains that are pockmarked by evidence of human enterprise, to be sure, yet far from substantially changed, still harboring black bears and cougars, ringtails and bighorn sheep, still indifferent to our doings.

That bar-car conversation took place in less chewed-up times. The desert had not yet begun to teem with trailer parks and regional metrocenters, with convenience markets and, improbably, tree-lined lakes ringed by condominiums. Neither did Beijing have a subway, London a Hard Rock Cafe. The solitude of places that have not been severely modified by us busy humans is still close at hand in Arizona—and in just about every other state, even urbanized Rhode Island—for those who take a moment to find it. But that solitude, here and everywhere, is being lost daily, and there is much to be done if it is not to disappear entirely, its loss marked by days on a calendar page.

By now it is a commonplace among environmentalists to say that we need more wilderness. Indeed we do. It is unreasonable, I think, to suggest otherwise—only a few developers, who form the single most powerful political lobby in America, stand to benefit from the destruction of wild places—and it heartens me to see proposals afloat like that of the Wildlands Project, which aims to link undeveloped areas of North America with easements to allow wildlife safe passage from place to place, and that of the Utah Wilderness Coalition, whose projected amalgamation of wildlands around the Golden Circle of national parks holds the promise of making a vast natural protec-torate that would dwarf several European countries. To tender such proposals in these boom-and-bust, go-go-go days is not easy; whereas, for instance, the Utah Wilderness Coalition had been petitioning Congress for an area of at least 5 million acres to set aside from development, Utah's congressional delegation offered only 1.8 million acres—still a vast parcel of territory, but nowhere near big enough for the job at hand. President Clinton's designation, in 1996, of some of those lands as the Escalante Wilderness is just a start.

That job is to preserve something of the American wild as it existed at the time of the first human arrival, to keep safe that fine corner of the world that a Puritan leader indeed once characterized as a "savage, howling waste of wolves." The biologist E. O. Wilson has noted that the number of plant and animal species doubles with every tenfold increase in area, and, while remarking that "wilderness has virtue unto itself and needs no extraneous justification," he suggests that it is a matter of enlight-ened self-interest—extraneous justification of immediate power—to allow that wilderness to prevail. Who knows the potential, for instance, of a new pharma-copoeia derived from plants that are not yet known or studied, the insights into our own beings that might come from observing life not under our dominion? If you set aside a postage stamp of land, you may spare some rare mycorrhizae (the Yaak, for example, harbors a fungus that has symbiotic value for the Pacific yew tree, from which, in turn, is derived the cancer-impeding drug Taxol). Set aside a large piece of territory, however, and you create an evolutionary laboratory—less a museum, as cynics have suggested, than a savings bank with a rate of return that can never quite be calculated.

More wilderness is wanted, yes—or, better, less human involvement with lands already wholly or partially wild. But with the mere fact of more land, mere numbers in a preservationist's inventory, we need to rethink wilderness in the political discussions that have been forming around it so that wilderness is more than just a slogan, what William Hazlitt called "the most airy abstraction," a sinister avoidance of the kind against which Elias Canetti so rightly warned. Wilderness is a place, of course, a tangible thing. It is *real*. It is also a governing idea in the way we perceive ourselves as Americans, an idea that finds expression in a recent *New York Times* survey eight in ten of whose respondents considered themselves to be environmentalists, in favor of substantially more government protection of what wildland remains within our borders.

That is good news indeed for friends of wilderness, who have been having a hard time of it on Capitol Hill over the last few years, but who will, I think, ultimately prevail thanks to friends like Bruce Vento, a Democratic representative from Minnesota who in 1994 wisely warned a gathering of environmentalists, in the language of business, "If you write off Congress, the degradation of existing laws and the defeat of new proposals for environmental protection will become a self-fulfilling prophecy. Remember, the public is with you. Wilderness is a product that the American people like."

Yes, it is, although I dislike thinking of wilderness as a "product." Thanks to our fondness for it, Americans enjoy more real wilderness than do the citizens of most other countries. A wilderness is fundamentally, as in the Anglo-Saxon, a *wild-deor-ness*, a place of "wild animalness," the domain of creatures other than humans; as my friend Doug Peacock has observed, "It isn't wilderness unless something in it can kill you and eat you." (The Irish poet Brendan Behan rejoins, "If God hadn't meant for us to be eaten, he wouldn't have made us of meat.") The operative notion here is that of a fastness in which humans, or at least human societies, have no dominant place. The operative laws are those of nature, of systole and diastole, ebb and flow, birth and death, the order that the singer of Ecclesiastes knew so well.

That wilderness is a place where a falling tree will make a mighty crash indeed without our being there to hear it. I do not begrudge people their sojourns in such places, their residences on the edges, but I would just as soon see wilderness retain its native meaning as the sole domain of wild animals, largely innocent of human encounters. This may seem a curious attitude, and I have more than once been taken to task for airing it. "How can you be a nature writer," an exasperated gentleman once asked me at a writer's conference, "without being *in* nature?"

My reply was then and is now that nature, like the kingdom of heaven, is all around us and within us—especially, I might add, in places with much wildland, places like Arizona and Montana. We need not run with the wolves or dance with the bears to content ourselves with the notion that there are properly worlds that are not ours to comprehend. It is enough, in my estimation, merely to know that such worlds exist. We have overrun quite enough territory as it is. We can, and we must, leave what remains alone.

In his ethnographic memoir *Tristes Tropiques* the French anthropologist Claude Lévi-Strauss remarks that pretechnological societies begin to unravel the moment an anthropologist or missionary sets foot in their longhouses or wickiups. So, too, I fear, do orders of nature sometimes begin to dissolve the minute a Vibram-soled boot crushes a moonwort. I want at least some country about which cartographers can write, as their medieval peers did, only the words, "Beyond here lie dragons." I want places in which the historian who called American history one continuous real estate transaction would for once be proven wrong. I want places where nature knows humans not, or only a little.

I know a few such places. I am happy not to visit them again, to let them go about their ancient business without me. In one, the Gila Wilderness of New Mexico, the oldest federally designated wilderness area in the nation, I once spent a full-moon vigil across a glade from a female mountain lion that studied me with casual indifference, yawning repeatedly to air her lack of concern that I had invaded her place. In another, the Swansea Wilderness of western Arizona, on a fine, warm late-March evening, my only company was a curious kit fox that scampered into my campsite to examine the unaccustomed light of my campfire. He did not know enough to mistrust humans, and I still feel pangs of shame for having disturbed his solitude. In still another, the Yaak, that storied and heartachingly beautiful place, I experienced the next best thing to seeing a grizzly bear in the wild—and that is not seeing a grizzly on its home turf while knowing that he was there, waiting, just over the next rise. I do not have to go there again. The bear can do just fine without me.

I want to know that many more such places exist, that we still live in a world that can imaginatively accommodate this unknowable wild, just as that Yaak grizzly once accommodated a tourist from far away. "The great vice of Americans," the English poet W. H. Auden once observed, "is not materialism but a lack of respect for matter." Working together for more wilderness, I think we are coming to respect matter a great deal more than we ever have. Working to save Yaak—and Kamchatka, and Siberia, and the Mogollon Rim, and all the other wild places that are left to us—will yield our own earthly salvation. In that dawning respect and recognition lies our true geography of hope: the preservation of vast, unquantifiable, unknowable sweeps of beautiful land—*and* with nothing on it.

CHAPTER 8

UP AGAINST OPENINGS

By Janisse Ray

FROM THE WIND-TORTURED SUMMIT OF MOUNT HENRY,
Canada is dark blue and misty, only a few miles away. Leif Haugen points it out,
standing at one of the windows that wrap Mount Henry's creaking lookout. Leif is the
lookie, a young man whose eyes are so blue that they look like the sky itself, shining
through augured sockets.

It's raining in Canada.

But in the Yaak Valley it's plenty sunny, and the sun bores down into the
Purcell Mountains, into the lookie's eyes, into places it shouldn't reach at all, not
in such spates. The sun pierces into these big lime-colored holes in the evergreen
forest.

Clear-cuts.

There are so many of them. Looking due east and using peripheral vision, I count
fifty-two. Sometimes they have a smattering of trees—more recent clear-cuts, although
they're officially called openings—but many of them are wide grass patches, White
House lawns in the Montana woods.

"How big is this littlest one?" I ask Leif, who leans over his rickety widow's walk to
measure the cut closest to us. We could hike down to it in twenty minutes.

"About forty acres," he says.

One of the clear-cuts is six times that big, an entire mountain flank reduced to
stumps and grasses. In fact, on these near slopes, there is almost as much cleared land
as forest, and threaded through it all, like tapeworms, skinny, white logging roads.

On the darker green slopes beyond, more clear-cuts—I don't count those. Behind,
to the west, dozens more, neon green and blinding in the sun. Sometimes only narrow

51

swaths of trees separate them, corridors that look about the size of rope footbridges, and about as secure.

If I were grizzly, I couldn't live in this openness.

A good friend of mine lives here, and he wrestles with the openness too, although *wrestle* may be too mild a word. The cutting rides him hard, because he lives tight in those trees, lodgepoles and Doug firs and larch crowding up around his house so close that you hardly notice the house at all. He lives like any other wild thing in the north woods, which is why I'm not going to call his name. He moves among the trees quick and wary, out of sight in a wink. Many times you don't see him at all, but you know he's out there, in the woods. Like you know the mountain lions are there.

He's been here fifteen years, and every day he wakes up more twined in those trees, his body woven into the bark, into the gray branches. He tells me about the first time he and his wife saw the valley, from a high point on the Yaak Road, coming from Canada: right then something reached out and snagged his heart. He showed me that spot, coming around a curve, and the Yaak laid out like Sleepy Hollow.

"This is it," he said, slowing down, as if wanting it to grab me like it grabbed him and his wife. But his relationship with the place intrigued me more than the place itself. People call it passion but it's more than that. It was that you could not tell where my friend's body stopped and the valley began. The thread separating him from wildness couldn't have kept a spider aloft, it was so thin. It seemed as if before my eyes he might break free of domesticity any second and shape-shift to wolverine. Or lynx. I couldn't keep my eyes off him, wanting to witness it happening.

"I get scared looking at the clear-cuts," he said that day, closer home. "I'm afraid they'll make me sick. I mean really, physically, some disease of bitterness."

My friend's not with me on Mount Henry today. He's working, and his wife and children are off at swimming lessons in Troy.

"Where are the roadless areas?" I interrupt Leif, who has begun his supper, bag of oregano in hand. Immediately south, he gestures, lies only thirteen thousand remaining acres of unwhittled forest in the Basin Creek drainage. He thumbs southeast, toward Roderick, and toward Saddle Mountain, and toward Big Creek.

Maybe 150 people live in the Yaak, 150 of the hardiest people in the country. Snow flies from September to May, and even now, late July, there's a pool of unmelted snow on Mount Henry's summit.

It's a Rip Van Winkle kind of place, asleep a long time, buried. But magical.

About 60 of those 150 people, my hermit friend included, belong to the Yaak Valley Forest Council. Theirs is a logging community and not one of them wants to lose that identity, the character that connection lends. But they're afraid of too many trees being cut too fast, of losing the wolverine like they lost the woodland caribou, of losing the whole damn place.

All total, about 180,000 acres of roadless areas are left in the million-acre Yaak Valley, within the 2-million-acre Kootenai National Forest—not in one big chunk, but in fifteen ragged islands. The Forest Council wants to keep those areas unroaded, unlogged.

I keep looking wistfully into the blue-green mist of Canada, thinking, *There's always Canada, wild and free*, although it's high time we chucked that myth. Canada faces the same dilemmas we do: development, logging, growth. Versus wildness and peace and beauty. Versus grizzlies and wolves.

Once, at a campsite in the upper Yaak, a woman with long, gray hair and wild eyes roared up in a pickup nearly as old as she was. She cut the motor and stalked over to where I sat in the grass talking with a group of college students who were camping beside a little creek.

"A bear lives up here," she said accusingly, glaring. "She's been here for years. You have to be careful with your food, lock it up at night. If the bear becomes a nuisance, they'll take her away. And there's nowhere else for her to go."

"We're being careful," we said truthfully, placating, but the woman was severe.

"If you leave food out, that's not the bear's fault," she said. "This is the end of the road for her. There's nowhere else to go."

That's reason enough to set aside wilderness in the last roadless areas in the Yaak. It's the edge of the country, pushed up right against Canada, and if it gets laid open, made bare and safe and comfortable for people, then we can just about give up on wildness in this nation of fools. That's my thinking.

Some people think the Yaak's already lost. The head of one environmental organization I'm choosing not to name said to me, "Have you seen it? It's been cut to death."

I disagree. I'd like to lay my own place, the coastal plains of south Georgia, up next to this place. We have precious little public land where I'm from, and the forests have been devastated. I'm scared to research what percentage of land cover has been altered from forest to pine plantation in the last century. Some people think southern pines actually grow in rows, naturally.

I do know that ninety-three million acres of longleaf pine once covered the uplands of the Southeast, and 99 percent of it is gone. Only a couple thousand acres of virgin longleaf are left. If I could lay that ruined landscape across the northwest corner of Montana, you'd see why I'm not writing the Yaak off. I'd sure as hell hate to see it looking like south Georgia.

And Jill Duryee of the Montana Wilderness Society disagrees with the other environmental organization. "The Yaak has been hacked," she said. "The roadless lands have been dissolving like ice in water for a lot of years. But I would never want to give people the impression that there aren't places in the Yaak that need saving."

In 1995 Congressman Pat Williams introduced a bill that would've designated forty-two thousand acres of wilderness within the Yaak River drainage, as well as created a seventy-five-thousand-acre McIntire/Mount Henry Natural Area. But wilderness scares a lot of people. They think it means they'll have to pull their finger from the pie, so the bill was defeated.

"What you've got up there is a working landscape," said Hal Salwasser, the tall and gracious regional forester I'd become tentative friends with. Mostly we saw each other in the airport; he always traveling and me picking somebody up. This time we were in his Missoula office, sitting at the boardroom table; he had just returned from a visit to the Kootenai. I'd stopped in to say hi, nothing more, but as usual the subject of the Yaak rose.

He advised against creating wilderness up there. "Why do you need it?" he said. "The Yaak's a perfect example of a landscape that works—you've got logging, you've got grizzly, you've got inland redband trout. You've got all the pieces."

"But will we have them in five years," I asked, "at the rate we're logging the place? Will we have them in ten years?"

"Definitely," he said.

Somehow the wild creatures are disappearing.

Take grizzly bears, for example. By researching mortality records in newspaper and oral accounts, Wayne Kasworm, the Fish & Wildlife Service bear biologist stationed in Libby, found that from 1950 to the present at least sixty-five bears were killed in the Yaak. Most of these died before 1975, when grizzlies were listed as endangered and hunting ceased.

Now about twenty-five bears roam in the valley—maybe thirty-five in the whole recovery zone, which covers the Cabinet Mountains, where there is designated wilderness, and in the Yaak Valley, where, again, there is none.

When Kasworm arrived fifteen years ago, he found the grizzly situation "so tough that unless we did something we ran a risk of losing them." Although four females from British Columbia were introduced into the nearby Cabinet Mountains in 1990, Kasworm would be "hard-pressed to say their population has changed dramatically."

Bears shy away from areas of high human use, clear-cuts and roads. Yet they're phenomenal in their nomadism. A typical female's home range is between seventy-five and one hundred square miles, a male's between three hundred and five hundred.

What happens when animals can't find the stomping ground they need? What happens if they get boxed in?

That's where wildlife corridors come in. Corridors are wide bands of undeveloped areas that allow creatures to roam and to interbreed, so that populations stay viable and genetically strong; that means areas with trees, for forage and cover, not cut areas for easier walking.

But how big should the corridors be? Will the animals use them?

"Thinking theoretically," said Jack Hogg, research biologist with the Craighead Wildlands Institute, "corridors are necessary and good. The question is not whether we ought to aim for connectivity, but work out details of what makes a functional corridor."

Early in 1997 the Forest Service proposed a timber sale in the Mount Henry roadless area, ten million board feet from 850 acres: four miles of new roads that would obliterate Pat Williams' s wilderness forever. They asked for public comment on the environmental impact statement for the timber sale, and comment they got.

"It seems to me that the area should be designated as wilderness rather than logged," wrote Paul T. Crary.

"Whatever the scientific rationale, this degree of resource extraction is, on the ground, shocking," wrote Asta Bowen.

People were concerned about the last stronghold of inland redband trout holed up in the Basin Creek drainage. They were concerned about loss of old growth; populations of lynx, black-backed woodpeckers, and pileated woodpeckers; winter range for elk.

"The nation's highest-ranking forester has boldly directed his agency to focus on restoring the health of the forests rather than on extracting resources," reminded the Montana Wilderness Association.

Always eloquent, resident activist Rick Bass wrote: "Too much on this forest I see biologists substituting the opening and closing of latch-gates on roads an as alternative to true 'core sanctuary,' and I would like to see this trend reversed; I would like to see a commitment to protecting our last roadless cores as the sanctuaries they are, free to proceed at their own biological pace, while we manage the roaded areas."

To the credit of Robert Schrenk, forest supervisor of the Kootenai, the letters received were carefully considered, item by item. The decision: no new roads, but still 4.2 million board feet of timber to be logged.

"Why does a dodged bullet feel like a victory?" Bass wrote afterward. "Wilderness is the only victory."

When Hal Salwasser was visiting the Kootenai someone took him aside and said, "You know, Rick Bass doesn't speak for all of us up here." He referred to Rick's *The Book of Yaak*, a plea for sustainable logging and protection of unroaded areas. Another Troy resident told me that people are picking the book apart sentence by sentence.

Somehow they've confused wilderness with government intervention and with something being taken away, not something gained. For decades they've roamed the land (like the creatures): picking berries, hunting, fishing, gathering firewood. They aren't happy even about a crazy rumor of being driven from it.

"In the last five to eight years, the Forest Service has closed hundreds of miles of roads," said Michael Balboni, district ranger. Some of it is for grizzly recovery, some for elk feeding, some for watershed protection.

In response, residents are destroying gates, the metal ones, ripping them down. On a truck parked outside the Silver Spur in Troy I saw this bumper sticker: IF ROADS ARE CLOSED IN HEAVEN, THEN I'M NOT GOING.

They're that adamant. That angry.

It doesn't matter that they can still walk or horseback ride or bike the roads. Or that thousands of miles of roads are still open.

The Orion Society, a group that celebrates human culture derived from the landscape, hosts Forgotten Language Tours around the country—nature writers reading their work. The tour visited the Yaak Valley in May 1997. Usually the readings are hosted by universities and such, but this was the first that would take place in the small logging towns, in hopes that art might somehow make a difference, might help protect these wild, precious forests. Terry Tempest Williams, author of *Refuge*, would come from Utah; Richard Nelson (*The Island Within*) from Alaska; butterfly expert Bob Pyle from Washington. I drove up from Missoula.

Four nights in a row we read—in the walk-in theater in Troy, in a church in Libby, in the community center in Yaak, in a lodge near Bull River. If the audience in Libby and Troy had been precipitation, it would've been sprinkling, but a crowd of folks showed up the other two nights.

I'll never forget Rick Bass's reading at Bull River. There'd been a big storm that knocked out all the power and he was reading by candlelight, a simple account of his family's life in the Yaak, and a short story called "Swamp Boy," about one child's wildness. Behind his head, outside the window, rufous hummingbirds swarmed a basket of petunias; the light shadowed his face.

He wasn't speaking for anybody, but he was speaking to all of us, and no one left unchanged.

Tour days were full of talk about sustainable development and sustainable logging (a future!), visits to local sawmills and to schools. When Richard Nelson asked the handful of children attending the two-room log school in Yaak who had seen a wild animal that day, not one kept her hand lowered: raven, deer, squirrel. The children took me to the little stream that runs behind the school and showed me caddisflies in their stony wrappers.

One day we hiked with the high school students in the forest behind a little rail-fenced cemetery in the upper Yaak. Someone found a morel growing out of Stan Merritt's chest, in a corner of the cemetery. HE LIES IN THE WOODS HE LOVED, his headstone said.

There was this storm while we were there, a storm so powerful and so erratic, so unexpected and dreamlike that for weeks people would tell each other storm-stories.

We had gone to see old-growth cedars up Seventeen-Mile Creek, all in our separate cars, but our guide hadn't made it. As we milled around waiting for him on the narrow access road, in a stand of thin lodgepole pine, the sky to the southwest began to sulk, darkening. Lightning, still a few miles away but ever closer, spit out across the mountains, gesturing at the puckered sky. It thundered. Thundered again.

By the time the guide, a local guy, arrived with a couple of students the wind had begun coiling through the trees. In a matter of minutes fifty-foot trees were bent double, whipping each other with their crowns, whistling and wailing in the high wind.

"I marveled that the trees were so limber," someone said to me later. "I thought the bending was normal." Isolated drops of cold, high-country rain flew through the pines and hit us, but it wasn't until the first tree cracked—nobody ignores that sound—that we ran for cover. It was as if the storm had come from nowhere, descending upon this odd group of city dwellers and magic seekers. The tree crashed down a hundred feet away. Then we were rushing for our cars, trying to turn them around and get them headed out of the unpredictable.

Trees were thrashing this way and that, falling all around us, and rain was twisting out of the sky in sheets. No sooner were our cars lined on the access road, moving out, than a tree toppled in front of the lead car. By this time hail big as sugar peas was tumbling out of the freak storm cloud, making a tremendous din against our metal roofs. It was the kind of hail that takes strips of skin off you, and when the storm subsided, it coated the ground. Trees were down in front of us, behind us, between us, but nobody was hurt, not a car touched. Most amazing was that something told the driver of the rear vehicle to back up, and he did, seconds before a tree crashed down where his van had been.

Something told me to back up, he kept saying.

My friend, the one I'm visiting, never stops. From morning to midnight he's working for the Yaak, not just to preserve the place but to preserve what it means; to protect the animals, and to protect the people from loss. Writing stories, writing bushels of letters, going to meetings, talking to students, guiding photographers. Even when he's tired he won't stop. Last time I was up there he was coughing, coughing. Not slowing down at all.

"There is just so little uncut country left in the Yaak," he says, "we need places where there are, for once, no stumps—no matter whether horse-logged, heli-logged, tractor or cable logged—just a place for our minds and bodies, our eyes, to rest."

Until then, there's no rest.

The last time I talked to him he was preparing for a community meeting in Yaak. The valley people are getting together to discuss issues of roadless areas and access, to try to reach common ground. My friend knows these ideas will face plenty of fire, and he's not afraid. He's girding his loins, as he joked, not with facts and statistics but with pleas. More pleas.

He's memorizing quotes about wilderness, how we need it when we must turn from the rat race: Bob Marshall and Aldo Leopold. He's arming himself with love, opening himself like the flanks of the Purcell Mountains have been opened.

I have to help him. Something tells me to.

CHAPTER 9

WAITING FOR THE RIVER TO RISE AND THE ICE TO BREAK

By Jeff Ferderer

I. LATE FALL

You have to wonder. The fire from the wood you cut burns before your eyes. The flame burns low, caressing wood like a hand on lover's legs. You watch the flame in the stove, in the darkness of autumn, in the Yaak. Tonight, it is only your valley. And they are only your students. You sit in silent darkness, in the silence of your loneliness and think of them and the Yaak. You pull your old green chair closer. Even the warmth from the fire is not enough.

I have been teaching nine years in the same place. Yet I feel unsettled. In and out of relationships, locations, and jobs. For twenty years I've never had a sense of belonging, anywhere. Never a desire to settle. I've spent nearly the last quarter of my life in this remote corner of northwestern Montana and sometimes the thought of staying in one spot fills me with terror. Usually I move away, but this time I don't. Instead I keep my job in Troy and change houses. Alone, I relocate, nineteen miles from Troy and nine miles up the Yaak Valley; my daughter, a Troy high school graduate, has moved to Seattle, and I am restless without her. I am not sure I belong in the Yaak either or deserve to live in such a place. But I had dreamed of living in the Yaak since I moved to Troy.

"There is more snow in the Yaak," they warned.

I didn't believe them.

Often, I don't believe them—they, who have their own ways ingrained, the mothers and fathers and grandparents of the students I teach. They, who have lived in this area for their whole lives. So when the chance came, I found a place in the Yaak. I had to find out for myself. *And to think things over.*

My losses are no different than anyone else's. I, too, sometimes suffer. Who doesn't, after all, suffer? No one I would want to know. My daughter is gone, but not forever. And this is a pretty good place.

You think and remember. Like the woodpile ants, kids come from everywhere. A hundred or so, from 8:30 to 3:20, fill your classroom. They are sophomores and seniors. Bull Lake kids. Savage Lake and Old Highway 2 kids. The kids who live in town and Kootenai Vista. The kids from the Yaak.

Robin. Krystal. Kevin and Kristi. Josh. Willow and Ian. Audra and Sabrina. Gita. Zack and Edward. All except Willow and Edward have graduated and gone away, and Edward will finish this June. Others, too. Graduated. Gone before you ever met them. At different times two Yaak kids, Robin and Josh, lived with you and away from their own Yaak homes before they graduated. They grew in the Yaak, though, and know it well.

You wait to hear from them. Josh calls and writes from Boston University. Robin sends her newest poems from Phoenix. And a few of the others drop by to see you when they are back, visiting their parents, visiting the place of their past. They all had to leave though. You know.

And Edward. Two miles away, he is one of your nearest neighbors. After school sometimes on his way home from the bus stop, Edward swings by your house and builds you a fire, knowing your own arrival will be many hours later. He wants to surprise you with some warmth. He builds a fire in the stove and walks home.

Later, when you get home, only coals remain. The house is warm, though, and you add wood to the embers. The fire crackles. Smiling, you open the fridge, grab a beer, and think of Ed. He knows the rules of houses opened. He could have helped himself to anything. And maybe he listened to the stereo for a while and opened the fridge too. It doesn't matter. Different rules govern the Yaak, at least for now. It's all right with you, except sometimes, you don't want anything to govern the Yaak. You want the Yaak to be untamed, wild. And unsettled. Like predators' screams. Like mountaintop thunder.

Things change. Even here. Kids leave and don't come back. Newcomers stay. You gulp the beer hard and forget about dinner.

II. Winter

The snow fell, coming early and staying late, just like they said it would. Fourteen, fifteen feet accumulated by May. For Christmas break, I escaped to Mexico while friends stayed in my Yaak cabin, house-sitting and shoveling the roof. But the snow piled once I got back. Light fluffy snow of December, January, and February. And early March. I forgot about the rooftop snow; my jeep easily broke through the highway powder—two, three, or more inches of it almost every morning on my way to school. I did not worry.

Snow. Piling high and reaching upward. Covering seasonal remains. Hiding fallen trees and brown ferns, garden hoses and tire rims, deer carcasses and hibernating bears. Snow. Erasing memories of sudden disappearances. The geese and butterflies. Ospreys and the scarlet of Indian paintbrush.

What was hidden? What was gone? Inches floated down and feet reached up. It continued snowing while I spent the day with kids. I drove the Lake Creek bus in the morning and taught English during the day and before the sun set, I drove the kids back home. The darkness came while I coached preseason track and my sweating kids ran the hallway, narrowly missing collisions with janitors, teachers, and each other. I never saw my house during the daylight hours. The roof was far from my worries.

Drip. Drip. Drip. On the front room carpet. Things changed. A mid-March snow—heavy and wet—fell and warmed, and turned to rain. The ceiling began leaking under the weight of the snow.

So I discover the leak, place a spaghetti pot under it, and call Edward. He comes over and the shoveling begins, thirteen feet above the spaghetti pot. The moon shines through the larch, the spruce, Doug fir, and cedar, and we throw scoops of snow. We shovel and talk.

"*Sometimes a Great Notion* is a better book than *Cuckoo's Nest,*" Ed says with his shovel heaped. "Kesey was really on, in that book."

"On what?" I laugh and throw another scoop of snow somewhere below.

Ed laughs too. He stops to look at the moon. He stretches his tightened back and his hair, a wild display of curl, black and frizzed beneath a motley-colored ski hat, reaches around his face like tree limbs the tree.

I look too. We see the smoke floating from the chimney, a magic carpet rising, and we, the moonlight shovelers, gaze. Smoke floating, twirling and floating to the moon, which appears brightly, this night, between the clouds. The rain stops. Layers of clothing are shed and strewn across the roof. Ed and I stand, each covered by one last layer: hat, T-shirt, jeans, mittens, and a pair of Sorrels. We wish to take the smoke ride, but we don't mind the snow shoveling either.

We don't pause long. We are wet with sweat and we continue. My shovel handle snaps. My back aches, but the leak below must be halted. With my now smaller metal scoop, I stoop low to the snow and throw. Stoop and throw, heavy, wet snow.

And we talk. About the tenth-grade girl Ed kind of likes. Talk about what it will be like for Ed to get the hell out of high school. Scoop and throw. But we don't talk of Ed leaving the Yaak.

I pause again. I stand, smelling the wetness of the moonlight air. I breathe deeply. Puffs of steam rise from me. I, too, am a chimney. My puffs drift and disappear, and I vanish into that fresh cold air.

Before the roof is cleared, I lose footing and slide off the slick, tin covering into an enormous mound of snow. Between the winter's accumulation and the snow we tossed from the roof, I drop only a couple of feet. Ed laughs at me as I climb my way back. He is happy shoveling snow and earning a few bucks. Satisfied, too, being on the rooftop, just beyond the trees and the river, below the moon and stars, with me—his teacher, his friend. We shovel until the roof is cleared. More puffs of steam rise through the humidity.

My body aches. They were right about the Yaak. It is a good kind of ache, *I think.*

All teachers have days when they wish they were anything but teachers. I respect that. But there are some who let those days turn into years. I never want to get to that place. I'll quit teaching and move before that ever happens.

III. SPRING

The runoff rips down the river and from the deck you watch whole trees float past you, like it was almost natural. The trees are out of place, though, swimming in the frigid water, branches reaching and twirling in an outcry of protest and their trunks along only for the ride. You watch and relate. The river roars like never before. At night, you close the bedroom windows to quiet the river roar. But the roar in your head remains. You are lucky to be here; others, who have grown and lived their whole lives here, deserve it more. They belong.

You participate and escape—this silent rage of change and departure, of growth and regeneration—by sitting and watching the trees swim until twilight, until the white-tailed deer approach and the darkness and spring chill drive you to the heat of your stove. You pour a brandy or a Bushmills, stare at the flame, and wonder. Correct a few papers. Plan lessons. And think of the trees. Trees leaving their landscape and entering the cold river, never again returning. Knowing their empty spaces will never be filled in your lifetime.

The roar becomes an echo. You teach.

In the classroom before your students enter, the silence tumbles like the uprooted trees tumble into the whiteness of the Yaak Falls. This echo that calls you a trespasser is lifted momentarily, class period by class period, day after day.

The silence is broken. One kid at a time, a new roar enters your room and your life. And you muffle the echo, keep it hidden in the corner like a classroom dunce. Standing on your ground, you teach subject-verb agreement, the poisons in Hamlet's society, the dangers of alcohol abuse in your society. And you know it's not what you teach that is important. It is *whom* you teach. And it is *they* who help keep you here, in a place that offers you wonderful kids, and lively hardworking people, and sad, out-of-work people. It is they who keep you here, in a scenic land, a land torn by economic strife—a closed mine and fewer and fewer jobs in the woods.

And a land with wonderful torn kids. Kids wanting to stay but needing work. Kids suffering through their parents' hardships. Kids who know about alcohol and abuse. You know it's not easy here and you remember.

One accident and two girls died. Early one morning, a student called to tell me the news before I left to drive my bus. She knew I'd hear on the route if she didn't call. Later, I was asked to eulogize and be a pallbearer at one of the girls' funeral services. For the first time, I did something that I hated for one of my students.

You don't know if you are doing a goddamn bit of good. You would like to think so, but most days you won't permit such flattery. Sometimes it's good enough for you to be standing in the halls, waiting for the kids to enter your classroom, watching their smiles and horseplay, mooching a cookie or maybe a bite of sand- wich, and always giving and getting a friendly hello. Once in a while class goes smoothly, and they learn and develop new interests, and you think you made a dif- ference. But most of the time you can't help wonder if what you are doing is worth anything and, if school and the education your students are supposedly gaining, at all matters.

And to some it doesn't. Some kids will never leave Troy, and it won't make two shits difference if they know geometry or chemistry, know if their subjects agree with their verbs. Some boys will be able to earn a living from trees. They will run a chain saw or a skidder, maybe they'll limb or hook trees. A few, perhaps some girls even, will work at a mill. *They* will bust their backs and asses, pulling veneer—the sheets that become plywood—from the green chain or feeding the veneer to the dryer. Or they'll drive a forklift twelve hours a day making fourteen bucks an hour with two weeks paid vacation. Just like their fathers and mothers are doing. Just like their grandparents did.

But you know that too many of the kids in your classroom are planning on doing that for the rest of their lives even if they, yet, don't know it. And you think that there can't be enough trees left for them all. So you try to make sense and show them they need to think about other ways, that maybe what you teach could help them sometime after the last timber sale has been logged.

You look at the woods as you drive the Yaak highway. There is more space between the trees. You hike Mount Henry to the fire lookout and see the clear-cuts. You hope the kids can make a living here, but you fear they will have to find Microsoft jobs in Seattle or something else, somewhere else.

You try to make sense to them. But you don't know; it doesn't make sense to you. You've moved into their country after you've educated yourself somewhere else. And *they* are the ones who know where to pick berries, picking with their parents since they could walk. And they know where to fish and hunt, missing school to do both. They have a feel and a love for their outdoor education. Knowing how to keep their houses warm. How to fall a snag, split it into cords, and deliver the firewood to your doorstep, as well as their own. They know how to live in the woods quietly and simply. And you live in a cabin someone else built, heated by wood that usually someone else cut. And you are the one telling them what to do.

You suggest and urge them to educate themselves so they can find a "good" job and lead "productive" lives, knowing that for them to do so, they will have to move away.

And you're not sure what a good job is anymore or if being productive has to do with putting in twelve-hour days. Perhaps an hour in the woods is worth six in the classroom. Maybe some of the kids, the ones who most resist their education, are right.

"Work," they say, "when you can. Work when you must. Hunt and fish, gather wood, berries, and mushrooms. Learn about the forest and rivers and their inhabitants. Find someone to share a simple life. Forget the rest. Nothing else matters."

The day is over. The kids have gone home, and you sit behind your desk. You are doubtful, believing you're the only one who learned anything for the day. The echo returns from the dunce-corner and sits on your lap. You correct an essay test on *Great Expectations* and ask, "Is this paper worth the wood it is made from? Is this paper worth a goddamn thing?"

It is to you. At least the kid who wrote it is. And you take the echo home.

One of my students missed what I thought was too much school. So one day when she came to class I said to her, "I've missed you Joanna. Why haven't you been in my class?"

She said, "I missed you too, Mr. Ferd, but I didn't miss being here. Being at this school that offers me nothing but boredom. I was smoking cigarettes on the riverbank by the old bridge. I was writing poetry and watching an eagle look for fish and ducks. I was imagining elephants and sketching. I'm going to do a charcoal of elephants. Give me something better than that and I'll be here."

"I wish you would quit smoking," was all I said.

One spring, the river was frozen yet, in front of my house. On a cold Sunday afternoon, I sat at the kitchen table correcting senior analogy papers. My senior compared herself to a roll of film, and I liked it when she wrote, "just waiting to be exposed." I wrote back in the margins of her paper in my finest handwriting in fine blue ink (red ink is too offensive), "Yes, exposure to and experience in this world is necessary." Then I thought of the world beyond the Yaak and Troy high school and about the other boundaries that keep the school and the Yaak an Eden of isolation. I became afraid for her.

Beyond the papers in front of me and the icy borders of my windows, I saw snow layered over the ice. I stood and stared, careful not to breathe on the window and fog my view. A white-tailed doe emerged. A frozen forest, trees that have been allowed to walk to the river and remain, had hidden the doe. Some trees along the river have been there since before the great fire of 1910. I watched the deer step cautiously on the ice. She wasn't as surefooted, and I wondered how much longer it would be before those great trees fell, before a chain saw or a good wind made new space in the woods. The deer edged her way to the bank on my side of the river where there is far more space between the trees. I stood safely on the floor space in the warmth of my house.

I watched her slip a little, and then wished I were on skis. I wanted to expose myself to what was out there, to ski naked and reckless in the frozen forest beyond. I wanted to leave the world of paperwork and planning, the world of student struggles and sorrows, and ski away, into that same world "my box-of-film senior" so wanted to leave.

I thought of my own analogy. "I am river ice, frozen in place, waiting to break loose."

For a moment longer I watched. The doe reached the bank and waded through the deep snow. I sat and settled again, into cabin warmth with the blue-tipped pen in my hand. I corrected more senior analogies, and I wondered when the river ice would break free.

I am torn and tired. I want to help my students. I want to protect them from the outside world, yet I encourage them to go out there beyond the borders. I want to wrap my arms around them and save them. But isn't it me I save? I am paid to teach English, but in class, our greatest discussions are about life. Sometimes it seems they know more about living than I do. Their lives matter. So I am involved up to my neck with these kids, learning from them, and just waiting for the river to rise and the ice to break. Most of my time goes to them. And I see the river rising.

I stand in the middle of the river with wide eyes and an open mouth.

And you still spend all your daylight hours working. Every morning you pick up the same kids. Every afternoon, Faith, a second-grader, smiles and waves good-bye when you drop her off. You coach sprinters how to start from blocks, how to drive their arms and keep their heads down as the starting gun bangs. And at six-thirty or seven, after the last kid has gone home to her dinner and homework, you put away the starting blocks and go home to the Yaak.

You don't need the extra money anymore, and you know people who do. You think it's time for someone else to drive Faith home. You think maybe you'd like to try fly fishing, hike to Fish Lakes and catch some trout, rather than sitting in the stands on a Saturday, watching those kids drive their arms. You think it's time for someone else to pick up the slack, time for a new teacher to get involved. But you can't seem to let go.

I wrote Edward a letter of recommendation for a Presidential Scholarship at Southern Oregon University. I knew he would be the 1998 Troy high school valedictorian.

But you wished you'd written what you felt. "Ed is the last one left, the last kid in the home of Shamus and Laura. Please, don't accept Edward. He is needed, here, to hike the mountains and bring home venison. Needed to split firewood, write poetry, and argue about books and music and clear-cutting. Where will Ed ski? How will Turner Mountain Ski Area survive without him? Who will shovel rooftops?

"No, Ashland doesn't need Ed. The Yaak needs him. So please, don't recognize his talents and abilities. Must you take him, too, like the other Yaak kids? All the sons and daughters are leaving, and they won't be back. There is all this space. Please, let us keep Ed. Maybe just one more year."

That's what you wished you'd written. But you didn't. Ed got the scholarship.

My school board members, the spokespeople of Troy who also work as loggers and foresters, county road crew workers and drugstore owners, granted me sabbatical leave so I could study writing. Often, I don't understand *them,* my school board bosses and the community they represent. I feel that what I have to offer are things they don't need. And usually I feel misunderstood by them—that I, for some reason, never belong. Sometimes I disliked what they did to the woods and the creatures of the woods. And I don't know what to say to them besides small talk of sports and hunting, of how their kids are doing in school. Most don't care to talk about Nietzsche or Shakespeare. Some think poetry is for fags and reading is something to do once a year.

But these same people have all been good to me. They tease me about my long hair, but they aren't serious. They wave to me without understanding why a man needs to run for exercise, as I jog down the highways and back roads. And *they* gave me a year off and their blessings so I could try something new and come back and teach their children again. They believe in me sometimes more than I believe in myself.

So I missed Ed's senior year. I took the sabbatical and left for Spokane.

IV. Turning

The middle of May the last snow patch disappeared like a whisper. And it wasn't much longer, the yard greened, grass blades replacing snow. The larch needles appeared. Budding larch needles, soft green needles flirting with the black tree moss.

The bird feeder fooled you when the screeching Steller's jays were chased a short flight away by squirrel chatter after it took over the feeder. And it wasn't the squirrel that ate the bread scraps in the feeder the summer before you left for Spokane, but two raccoons. You watched them scurry the tree one night to hide from the porch light in the branches above. And when you quit using the bird feeder and instead used a stump for the scraps so the raccoons would come closer to the house, you were surprised, too, when the scat you found near your back deck was bear. You quit feeding the raccoons, but were overjoyed one late-August evening as the river flowed in calmness and a large black bear sprang by, fifty feet away. You knew you shouldn't have fed those raccoons, but as the bear glanced your way, you were glad you did.

You let the light fade and sit in the darkness of the deck. The year is over and you wait for something different, someplace maybe where you belong. Now there are no papers or lesson plans. The stars fill the sky and you realize your insignificance. You sit in your chair with your feet propped on the deck's railing. And you do nothing but sit in the darkness. And you wonder.

So you leave for a year. *I have to find out.* And you will like writing and the unreal world of graduate school. *I miss the river and the trees.* You will teach but it will be composition for college students. *I am expected back next year.* At grad school, you will find people with similar interests, people you like, people you love. *I miss my high school colleagues. I miss shoveling snow and watching bears.* Your studies will go well, with your time less scheduled. And you will not have to listen to kids who hurt, or have to bury someone you taught, someone you loved. *I can't get so involved anymore. But I just can't stay away either.*

In your folding chair, you sit, hand under your chin, elbows resting on the deck's railing. With your eyes closed, you hear the river moving. And wonder.

CHAPTER 10

IN ONE LIES THE PRESENCE OF THE OTHER

By Ellen Meloy

TO THINK ABOUT THE YAAK COUNTRY IS TO DISCOVER HOW serious a creature of place I have become: a slickrock crustacean and aridity ascetic, bound to the Southwest by fierce love and bone-deep faith. Instinctively, I use the sensory measures of home, my affective ties to the Colorado Plateau, to form and shape the Yaak. Geographically and ecologically, two landscapes could hardly be less alike. Yet each suggests the presence of the other—and of all wild places—so that when you walk through their disparities you arrive at a family likeness.

The Yaak country: rain-kissed, cloud-raked, and mist-blessed, lush waves of earth draped in a dense cloak of trees. The Colorado Plateau desert: drought-prone, edge-sharp, and sky-bared, with high mesas and mountain ranges that float above the broken red canyons like indigo silk. Montana's rivers run gin-clear and pain-cold. My silty rivers carry away the friable landscape in sinuous khaki ribbons. The wet land: malachite, silver, blue-black where one mountain casts its shadow on the other. The dry land: terra-cotta, the alarming green surprise of riverside cottonwoods, sky so deep you fall headlong into it. The northern forests enshroud. In the desert there is less to run into. These spaces shape our line of sight, and how we move our bodies through them. In both places, names on the land testify to loss: Caribou Mountain (no more caribou), Forbidding Canyon (drowned beneath a reservoir). The Yaak's forests grow grizzly, moose, and mink. In common we share peregrine falcons, eagles, and beavers; vast tracts of besieged public lands; isolation and no jobs; rural communities pelted by the slings and arrows of the global economy. Each place bears a layered text of stories. Each place has a wild heart and people who ache for it.

When I lived in southwestern Montana, on the dry side of the Continental Divide, from time to time I traveled to the state's far-flung northwest corner to relish in sheer fecundity—*vertical reality*, we dwellers of the grassland valleys called this magnificent inland forest. Here, in the lungs of the planet, body and soul could be rehydrated. Where the slopes had not been shaved clean by timber mining, the trees grew thick and immensely fixed. Their crowns combed the underbellies of Pacific storms; their roots pierced the thin, granular soils of the Rocky Mountain cordillera. After long hikes beneath a sheltering ceiling of dense boughs, when I came out of the forest into an open meadow, I would nearly lose my balance. In *Song for the Blue Ocean*, Carl Safina found the forest's pulse in a coastal stand. "Among the huge ridged trunks and limbs cushioned thick with mosses, the main impression is of silence so resilient you can almost press it with your hand and feel its flex."

From my shelf I pull out a musty old school geography textbook that I salvaged from a secondhand store. Published in 1935, the book did its duty to propagate stalwart young utilitarians. First it seduced them by piecing the world together in all its alluring beauty. Once the students fell into an aesthetically weakened state, the authors then erected the great anthropocentric filter. At the end of the chapter about the Northwest mountains, an exercise asks the students to "Use these words in a sentence: log chute, timber harvest, flume, strip mine." Come to this land with your axes.

I have now put considerable distance between me and the northern forests. Yet there they lie, up the curve of the globe, fringes of undeveloped land that still afford solace and awe. They are home in the way the entire earth is home. Between the Yaak country and the red desert, the strongest bond is the fattest paradox: the common ground of diversity, the miracle of being exquisitely different, the pressing need to remove these lands from the black hole of greed. Come to these lands with your senses. Use these words in a sentence: *wild heart.*

CHAPTER 11

THE MUSIC IN MY FATHER'S HOUSE

By Pattiann Rogers

JOHN 14:2

Only a music of its own could come
from this dwelling place, formed
as the composition must be by the hallways
of larch and the black columns of lodgepole
pine leading as multiple corridors in all
directions through overlapping shadows
and into the chambers of others.

Entering this open sunroom with walls
of glass, three deer splash through the marshy
grasses, pause as one to look back
at the composers, those scribes who listen
to the measures of their passing.

Themes of osprey, loon, raven in flight,
a skein of ducks reflect off the mirrored
ceilings that ring with depth like bottomless
lakes, like the tolling bells of steel-blue skies.

The stitching of the tapestries hanging
the walls of the highest room is so exact
that the distant valleys in the scene depicted
become sensuous valleys. The threaded notes
of the rivers are heard as rivers, and the finely
sewn mountains are mountains that disappear
into the distance as departure *and* return,
a repeating transition in the score.

In the expanse of forests and fields
comprising this structure, what is not seen
is known by the steady beat and undertow
of its presence—black bear, lion, root, glacier path
and its incantation, the dormant, the conceivable.

Those who are sequestered here
in this house write the music of themselves
conforming to the stone, the seed, the spacious
generations of these living mansions.

CHAPTER 12

UP ON HENSLEY

By Bob Butz

IT SEEMS TO ME THAT BOWHUNTING IS ONE OF THOSE THINGS that you either understand or you don't. If you're not a bowhunter, the whole thing can seem like such an awful business. After all, bowhunting is not neat or pretty. It's mud and dirt and stink and sweat. Calluses, blisters, and blood. It's sneaking around. And yes, sometimes it's killing.

But through bowhunting I've been to places and traveled distances I might not otherwise have gone. And I've seen some things—I've seen the most wonderful things.

I didn't kill a black bear this spring. But I tried to. I've been trying now for three seasons, but something unlucky always seems to happen in those last few heart-pounding moments of the stalk.

To kill a bear with my wood arrows and longbow, I have to be in close—closer than close; fifteen steps is my self-imposed limit. At that distance, you can hear a bear's stomach gurgle. You can hear him fart. Even so, it's not good enough that you be that close with a longbow, any bow. You have to remember that the bear needs to be broadside at the time of the shooting, or facing away; and more than anything you have to be certain the bear is totally, absolutely unaware of you.

Only if the scene is set like this can you even begin to think about shooting. But the trick is not to think about it too long before you actually go and do it. Because the only thing that will betray you quicker than the wind up in the mountains are your thoughts, which, when you're that close to a bear, can pass across the open like a lightning strike.

Last spring a friend invited me to Montana to hunt bears. Up in the northwest corner of the state, the Yaak Valley. Over the mountain to the north is Canada. To the west, Idaho. Both places so near that when hunting, it's possible to wander over the borders without even knowing it. The Yaak is deep woods, a wilderness out of a fairy tale. Creeks in the valley bear the names of old trappers and hermits. Solo Joe. Kookoo Boyd. Less than a hundred people live here today: woodcutters and loggers, mostly, and my friend, Tim, a hunting and fishing guide. Everyone outnumbered by the mountain lions, eagles, elk, and deer. A white moose emerged one day from dark forest and remained here a decade or so. Wolves are commonly heard at night. And occasionally, you might even catch a glimpse of a grizzly bear.

I went to the valley to hunt black bears, last spring. And we looked for the bears on Hensley because of all the clear-cuts and gated roads protecting them.

Even though the gorp-eating tree hugger in me hates the sight of any clear-cut, the hunter in me knows what the Forest Service's work can mean for the black bears. After coming out of hibernation, a bear doesn't give a damn about scenery, only food, which in this case takes the form of the grass and clover that sometimes grows in these smaller sunwashed openings, at least.

But even in this valley where there are too many clear-cuts, it did not at all mean that finding a bear was easy. By midweek, and after some thirty miles walked, I had blood blisters on my feet the size of half-dollars. My head ached from hours hiking under the noonday sun, my eyes from glassing infinite miles of mountainside in that seemingly endless search for that one black spot on the landscape that was not a charred stump but a bear.

My friend Tim and I saw four black bears that week, but I only had one good chance on the third day; one stalk on a big brown-phase black bear that ended almost as quickly as it began when I ran out of cover and could then only watch as he fed down over the mountainside and out of my life forever.

But that's hardly the end, or even the beginning, of this story. There was another bear that day—a grizzly—that we saw on the long hike back to the truck. The grizzlies I've seen at parks and zoos were like images on a television screen compared to this one. If I could, if I had the words within me, I would tell you how small I felt when he stepped from the lodgepole and my crippled, clumsy mind realized what he was.

In heading home, we stopped to glass another clear-cut, an immense swath that had once been a tree-covered mountainside. I took the left edge, Tim the right, and for a good hour or so we just sat there staring through high-powered binoculars, scrutinizing every dark spot, every black stump and log shaped like a bear.

The grizzly appeared for what was only a scant second or two then pulled back in— as if stepping into the open light of the clear-cut and exposing himself had frightened him somehow. Miles away. Still, I know he probably felt my glance. I didn't say any-thing at first because I half thought he might come out again. But my heart was beat-ing so fast the words just blurted out: "Jesus, Tim. I just saw a griz." And then I wished I hadn't.

In this valley—in this whole damn country—what I had just witnessed was on par with a Bigfoot or a UFO. And I felt awful knowing Tim had lived here close to a decade and at the time had not yet seen a grizzly in this valley for himself. We sat there for another hour glassing, panning back and forth along that edge, with me babbling on and on about the size of the bear, the silver color of his fur, the hump. Before long I half swore I had seen his eye. I wanted to hike over there, find his track—anything that might lend proof to what I saw—point to it and scream at the top of my lungs, "There!"

But it would be dark soon, and that mountain was a good day's hike away.

CHAPTER 13

FOR THE KEEPERS OF SECRETS
(FOR KEVIN)

By Amy Edmonds

I HAD HEARD ABOUT THE YAAK FOR MOST OF MY LIFE. VOICES carrying stories of rich forests in the north trickled every so often into the Bitterroot Valley, home of my Montana youth. But they were soon lost in an endless stream of childhood adventures and distractions. Two summers in Libby, playing in the Kootenai River with my sister until our lips turned blue while my father sifted through the history of the Kootenai Indians, brought me closer to the woods of the Yaak. But still those woods lay beyond my knowing. The Yaak.

The name alone summoned images of moody forests in some mysterious world. Even in my adult years, the Yaak remained cloaked and hidden, left alone for another time while I explored other places, other secrets. Then, one rainy spring, the lynx—the legendary keeper of secrets—brought me to the Yaak.

Winter's quiet shrank away, melting into the busy beginnings of spring, and the time to leave my home on the North Fork of the Flathead River came too soon. My reluctance to go was tempered by my excitement over the prospect of spending a few months in the Yaak working for a man I respected and admired, while learning about an animal I knew little about. I was to spend the summer field season in the employ of Dr. John Weaver on his lynx/snowshoe hare study. June and July would be spent doing snowshoe hare pellet transects in an effort to gain a more thorough understanding of the big-footed lagomorph so intricately linked to the survival of the lynx. The later days of summer would be dedicated to running lynx hair collection stations, where the elusive felines would, hopefully, leave soft strands of cheek fur on a tree trunk when marking a territorial boundary or advertising their presence.

My first week in the Yaak was pierced with news of the death of a friend. His passing left me grieving, suspended for a time in a surreal world shaped and made strange by the finality, the impenetrable mystery of death. Kevin's health and youth were torn from him two years ago by the metastasizing grip of a brain tumor. It was a cancer we all struggled to comprehend, invading a healthy man who took better care of his body than most people do.

I saw Kevin only once during his illness, but I won't forget his smile. He seemed to be holding steady a gentle hand on some whispered assurance from his heart, as though he knew something precious. I won't forget his story of how he came home along the path of a dream, where he found courage and strength in his personal relationship with wild nature, where he found the light side of the darkness, where he found life.

He wrote a haunting letter expressing his wish to spend his remaining days "helping Mother Earth." He asked me to please tell Her, whenever I am with Her, that he would be there too, fighting and living for Her.

Kevin entered my thoughts often as I worked my transects in the mountains of the Yaak, wondering about the things he knew, the knowledge and wisdom that grew pure inside of him, allowing him to find resonant happiness as he witnessed the waning of his life. What secrets lay untold in his heart? What lessons for us, we who hurry through our days and nights too often disgruntled over the inane and puny? I miss him. I wish I had spent more time learning what he had to teach.

Kevin's passing told me to slow down and take notice. My work led me to secret places, big and small. I lost myself among ancient giants, huge cedar trees reigning over a lingering pocket of old-growth forest. Lichens hung from them in weeping strands along their bark, secure, in place, while grasses and wildflowers competed for the shafts of sunlight that touched the needle-strewn ground.

The old forest is a place of hidden memories, where time has swept life, climate, and a few random genetic mutations together into living diversity, unfolding into complex, sometimes subtle, sometimes towering splendor. It hits you as soon as you enter the shadows. There is a steady echo from the past in the music made from wind brushing against trees, just as the temporal celebration of spring resounds in the ascending voice of the Swainson's thrush. Together they are timeless, accompanying a liquid patchwork of sunlight and shadows. Easing quietly from within, from unseen places amid guardian trees, water's hushed song reveals a creek's path between wet moss and rock, a stream of miniature rapids and pools, where plant and insect orchestrate a soft riparian symphony.

Yaak's forests are deep—deep enough to help the lynx keep her secrets. It isn't hard to imagine her: silent fluid and strong, muscled stealth moving among the wooden bodies of trees on giant, furred feet, acutely aware of all that crosses paths with her senses. She is one who belongs. Her presence helps shape the integrity of her world— of our world, a world that is rich and clean, with honest places that can freely touch all souls. I felt this place touch my soul, and its fingers opened my mind to some of the secrets that were waiting inside my own heart.

One afternoon I stood high on a mountain where I could see across the Yaak River Valley, over a huge expanse of rolling mountains and sharpened ridges. I watched distant thunderheads build and pile up, high and white into the limitless blue sky. From their flat, dark bellies fell dark sheets of rain, casting steel-gray drapings that hung between them and the mountains. The rain looked motionless from so far away. Overhead, the sky was clear and bright, but the masses of clouds billowed toward me as they climbed higher and higher—impossibly high. Soon my mountain would also be under the hand of the storm. I looked across the valley at the hills of the Yaak. An angular patchwork of clear-cuts, stitched together by rows of roads, glared back. Thunder poured out of the turmoil of cloud and sky, and I saw lightning strike across the valley. The blue above grew smaller, finally disappearing behind unstoppable, wind-driven cumulus.

The mountains stood silent as the rain touched their scarred slopes. They seemed to be patiently waiting. The Yaak is wildness waiting. It bends again and again with the intrusion of man and waits—either for the intrusion to evolve into an intelligent relationship between nature and modern humanity, or for the bending to give way to breaking while the noise from our machines deafens our ears to the crashing in of the natural world.

Four days off took me home to the North Fork of the Flathead, along the western boundary of Glacier National Park, where grizzlies, wolves, and people have managed a relatively harmonious coexistence. The North Fork also struggles a little under the weight of too many people, but it, like the Yaak, remains wild and essentially free from modern ills. Both are cherished and rare gems, still home to the same predator and prey species that roamed free before the arrival of white culture. The lynx lives in the North Fork also, sometimes leaving a faint track among crystals of snow that sparkle with hidden stories of her travels.

I drove home over Trail Creek, a route traveled so many years before by the Kootenai Indians as they set out for the plains to hunt buffalo. I drove through a narrow break in the mountains, over purple rock and past avalanche chutes tilled with alpine grasses and shrubs, still short in the latent high-mountain spring. The rocky pass echoed with the endurance and spirit of a people who knew the land, loved the land, listened to it. Their culture harbored intimate knowledge of how to live with nature, not against it. They were well acquainted with her secrets: where to hunt and gather, what plants to eat or use for medicine, how to find the way through the mountains. So much of the knowledge that lay in the hearts and minds of the Kootenai is now lost to history and technological arrogance. The secrets they kept are gone. Perhaps one day we may rediscover them.

The beauty of a secret lies in how it can unfold gently before us, without force, quietly lending light to our reflections, bringing depth and dimension to our perception. There are no limits to the secrets that live inside of a person, a culture, a forest. The tragedy lies in our own deafness and in our own reckless destruction of the keepers of secrets. The lynx will not tell her secrets to those who do not stop and listen. The forest will hide her, along with secrets of its own, for as long as it can. And like Kevin, when the lynx and the forest are gone, they will be missed. And their secrets will lie cold and still while our hearts ache for the knowing.

CHAPTER 14

GUNSIGHT MOUNTAIN

By Steve Thompson

I USUALLY APPROACH THE YAAK VALLEY FROM THE EAST, ACROSS Dodge Summit and into the headwaters of the East Fork, which houses Montana's most impressive array of public lands clear-cuts . I don't like that route much, but in some ways I'm an outsider, a Flatheader who comes to the Yaak for its unique spark, and this is the fastest route.

The East Fork Road passes quickly enough through the barren headlands and into the shaded hush, past the enchanted McIntire homestead, where every summer evening the McIntires waved a lantern good night to the solitary keeper of the Mount Henry lookout. By the time my truck passes the McIntire homestead, the mystery of the Yaak is once again upon me.

The first time I entered the Yaak was up and over Pipe Creek Pass, down the winding road into the South Fork. Equally dramatic, but impressive in a positive way. My first hike—flirting on the edges of this different valley—was from this pass, scampering onto a rocky outcrop and rolling saddles. This first trip sparked my vivid, enduring image of the Yaak: swirling in power magic, a world apart, a threatened relic.

And I've rolled up the Yaak River Road, against the flow instead of with it.

But what I want to tell you about is Gunsight Mountain. It's barely in the Yaak. Driving, biking, and hiking to Gunsight's rocky top with my friends Rick and Susan, I'm not even sure where we entered the hydrologic boundaries of the Yaak River Valley. Of all the gateways I've used to pass into the Yaak, it's the sneakiest. Gunsight is the most subtle corner of the most out-of-the-way valley in Montana.

Gunsight Mountain is so obscure, in fact, that the Kootenai National Forest failed to include this wild place in its inventory of roadless areas in the 1980s. It was added years later, only after wildlife advocates noticed the omission.

Obscurity is not a favorable trait for wildlands in western Montana. For years the U.S. Forest Service has taken advantage of obscurity by dozing roads and clear-cutting mountainsides, areas that hunters and anglers and hikers hoped would remain wildly obscure forever.

When massive clear-cuts started appearing throughout the Yaak Valley, those hunters and anglers and hikers were powerless to stop the destruction. Only after they started to appeal to outsiders—Flatheaders like me, or activists four hours away in Missoula—did the forest service begin to respond. But still dominated by timber dollars, the Kootenai National Forest didn't stop the clear-cutting. Instead, they just looked for quieter, more remote, and less visible pockets within the folded layers of the Yaak.

In the winter of 1994–95 Gunsight Mountain must have appeared to fit the mold of quieter, more remote, and less visible. It was difficult to find and even more difficult to get to. A fire had burned across the flanks of Gunsight Mountain, in the southwestern nook of the Yaak Valley, and the agency cried "emergency fire salvage" as if it were a patriotic battle cry.

There were many "emergency fire salvage" sales proposed that year, and only a couple could be explored. Perhaps it was the proposed 344-acre clear-cut with a new road up the middle of a roadless area that caught our attention. For some reason, our little three-person committee chose Gunsight for a field visit.

On a hot August day, we rode mountain bikes behind a closed gate. We found the old hiking trail, which had been cleared and used by firefighters as a fire line. We got to the edge of the burn, but progress through the fire area was slow. Huckleberries had survived the creeping fire and, fueled by the flush of nutrients, had produced whopping hucks. Our hands were dark and juicy when we discovered the first morel mushrooms. Morels in August? Our eyes adjusted for the fungus among us, we suddenly found them in abundance, large and grotesque and oh-so-tasty in our hungry imagination of hot-butter sautés.

The going was slow, but with our packs overflowing, we broke from our splendid harvest. Following fresh elk spoor, we refocused on the task at hand. Was the proposed 344-acre clear-cut in the middle of a roadless area justified? There certainly were dead trees: black, bulbous, twisted, short, and not worth a dime. Towering overhead, however, were beautiful granddaddy larch, which surely had survived past fires much like this one. They had survived this fire, too, and had no doubt been boosted, just like the hucks and morels, by the nutrient-and-ash picnic. If the forest service had its way, this would be the last fire these larch would survive. They were already marked for loggers to cut.

Reluctant to leave this enchanted and threatened forest, we nevertheless were driven down the mountain by an afternoon cloudburst, wet and happy and mad and purple as we loaded up on more huckleberries for tomorrow's pancakes.

As much as we would have preferred to keep Gunsight's delicious and wondrous secrets to ourselves, we understood that this was not an option. The Montana Wilderness Association organized a bigger field trip with elk hunters and loggers and wildlife biologists and the media. We invited the Forest Service, too, to reexamine its previously obscure project.

A month later, beneath the granddaddy larch, the forest service stood alone and confused in defense of its proposed clear-cuts. Loggers shook their heads, embarrassed for a government caught with its hand in the public cookie jar. Montana's elk biologists muttered unhappily among themselves, peeved at this sham invasion of wildlife security. The newspaper reporters scribbled furiously. As if to douse the whole notion of a 344-acre clear-cut, the clouds let loose anther volley of rain.

Revealed as a scam for all who cared to notice, the Gunsight Mountain salvage sale did not survive its passage from obscurity to spotlight.

The final and decisive blow, ironically, was struck in a pique of frustration by Montana's leading timber executive, who had declined our field trip invitation.

Upset with newspaper comments attributed to biologists he considered uppity, the timber executive demanded that "salvage" sales in roadless areas proceed as scheduled. Instead of asking the forest service to protect elk habitat on public lands, he recom-

CHAPTER 15

LIVING ALONG THE ROAD LESS TRAVELED

By Scott Daily

*...if one advances confidently in the direction of his
dreams, and endeavors to live the life which he has
imagined, he will meet with a success unexpected in
common hours.*

—Henry David Thoreau

IT IS MOTHER'S DAY TODAY AND SHERRIE AND I WALK NEARLY
a mile to the telephone to call our families. The road leading to our cabin dead ends
just beyond our driveway and our nearest neighbor along the road is a quarter mile
away, so traffic of any kind is rare. The road is narrow with trench-like ruts and puddles that could swallow a small car were the driver foolish enough to attempt visiting
us. It is not the type of road one takes for a Sunday drive.

As we round a bend a wood duck lifts out of a pool in the middle of the road and
flutters out over the aspens in the meadow. Sammy, our golden retriever, charges into
the brush and rejoins us a half-mile later looking battered and muddy. Duckless and
defeated.

In the soft wet silt we track deer as they meander along, traveling from the forest
down into the meadow along the river. Suddenly Sammy forgets the duck and is off on
a new trail, her head to the ground, pivoting right to left down the road. At times
when we walk the road we find the bones of deer lying about with traces of fur and
blood and flesh still attached, and we know that it was not our dog that was cunning,

patient, and nimble enough to bring it to earth, but rather something much larger and wilder. Once I viewed through tracks in the snow an entire predator/prey scenario laid out for me to bear witness. For me it began with a patch of blood in the snow and from there unfolded backward.

I was at a high point along the road overlooking the meadow. The angle of the dull winter sun cast the perfect shadow within the tracks and I could see them in meandering line cross the meadow for at least two hundred yards. From there they crossed the river and came out of the forest on the other side. The tracks I viewed could have taken an hour or more to be made as the doe scratched the frozen, snow-covered ground in search of browse. I stood at the point where the tracks merged with those of a mountain lion, which lay crouched near a Douglas fir waiting for its prey with the patience of the seasons. The cat leaped and struck the deer, which fell broadside onto the ground. The deer struggled on spindly legs for purchase but the cat was on it again and tooth met flesh and a trickle of blood emerged and fell to the snow. The doe broke free, kicking wildly. It ran a short distance up the knoll, but the cat lunged again with its pads touching earth only a few times. Another puddle of slushy blood, this time much larger; the cat struck the jugular and all around it the snow was fanned and kicked by the hooves of the deer. The carcass, now limp, was dragged several yards to where I first encountered the sign, the largest blood smear of all where the cat released its grip and panted and surveyed the landscape. I found the carcass tucked up under another fir tree. It was covered in brush with only one hoof poking out of its grave. Ravens circled overhead squawking at me. Had the snow not been present, I would have perhaps only noticed the ravens and nothing more. I continued my walk.

Our road is wonderfully shabby—a shock jammer, an insatiable devourer of mufflers. When people drive the three-quarters of a mile back to visit, they usually leave a piece of their rig lying on the road when they leave. I collect these things—mufflers, tailpipes, pieces of plastic trim, an occasional hubcap—and keep them in my truck for the owners to claim, but they never do. It is like a big lost-and-found box of forgotten rust and rubber that ends up at the county dumpsters. One man on a search for the fabled peaceful getaway left a ten-pound mud flap from a proportionally large pickup lying in the spot where he turned around on a heavily rutted section of the road. It must have been like performing a five-point turnaround on railroad tracks without a crossing. The property he was venturing back our way to see, and perhaps purchase, is along the river and across the road from my driveway. It is a piece of land I have been saving money to buy. Rumor has it the landowner is desperate and will accept almost any offer, so I was pleased to see the prospective buyer leaving truck parts in his wake. He never came back. The "for sale" sign remains hidden in the brush. The road served me well that day.

The road is a double-edged sword. I once lost my entire back bumper once from my old white Toyota just by driving out in a slight hurry. I stood ankle-deep in the muck. A family of deer watched from the brush, their jaws rotating, grinding their browse, their black eyes fixed on me as if ready to run should I fly into a tantrum. I wanted to kick the truck, shout a few vulgarities, and then wallow a bit in the mud, but remembered how the road had already saved our asses from the guy with big mud flaps. Instead, I shrugged, put the bumper into the truck bed and continued on, sliding and bouncing down the road. The deer resumed eating.

The road runs parallel to the river. Talk at the tavern is about how the river is going to flood because of all the snow in the upper elevations. The local paper that comes out twice a week says that up high it is the second deepest snow pack on record. Some say the flooding will be more severe than in '97, the year Sherrie and I arrived, the year most of the valley was part of the river.

My friend, Fishburn, tells me that during high water he and Porcupine canoed across cabin porches, waving through the windows at the people inside. Fishburn says that some of the people were not too pleased with this, but since the river is owned by no one there was nothing the people could do but wave. Some of them screamed as if startled, then waved. One lady waded out of her front door with her nightgown hiked up around her knees and chatted a bit about owls that had been hooting from atop her roof all night until she lit a fire in the stove and smoked them out. After awhile she sent Fishburn and his friend off with a paper plate of brownies that made them feel funny after they'd eaten them. Downriver a naked man holding a trumpet called them sons-a-bitches and hollered for them to get out of his pasture. Fishburn, being kind and generous, paddled over to give the man their last brownie, all the while trying to avoid eye contact with his shriveled member dangling as best as it could in the misty air. After some uncomfortable small talk about unpredictable weather and the history of the man's tarnished trumpet they pushed off from the top step while the man stood nibbling the edge of his cake and eyeing them suspiciously as they drifted away.

They canoed over split-rail fences where ants gathered at the tops of the posts like sinners fleeing the flood. They canoed through horse corrals with the horses just standing there on the high ground watching them pass, with their ears perked and their tails erect as if worried that their world was forever changed. Some, he says, just trotted in circles on their little islands. With all the lowland outhouses and horse corrals, I imagine the river took in a lot of nutrients it didn't really need that year.

We make our telephone calls and walk home with the road squishing underfoot all the while, discussing what news we have learned from the place that used to be home. For the most part it is the same news as the last time we spoke with them. My mother's car is falling apart and Aunt Dorothy would have won $250 at bingo but five other people went bingo at the same time so she had to split the money. Sherrie's mother is still taking care of her grandmother who is still gaining weight and not doing anything about it except sneaking Coca-Colas and Hostess Ding Dongs from the pantry when everyone else is in bed. But they're on to her, they say. A whole plate of shoo-fly-pie disappeared during the night last Sunday and they found a sticky fork and plate under the old woman's bed on Tuesday.

Similarly, we offer little new news to them because not much has changed, at least not things that I want my mother to try sleeping on. I consider telling her about the mountain lion kill I found during the winter but decide against doing so. When they ask how we're doing, we say things like, "As well as can be expected," and, "Pretty good now that the snow's melting." Neither of us bother telling them that our one reliable vehicle was blown up in the fall by a long-haired man with *Jesus Saves* tattooed on his arm, who hollered *"Repent!"* over and over as he sped off on a red scooter with our gas tank exploding behind him. Sharing stories of mountain lions, deer blood, and exploding trucks wouldn't do anyone good. For now we decide to sit on the facts of our lives. They worry about us enough without us telling our truth in its entirety.

The snow has finally melted outside the cabin. The land looks trampled because of the trash that was hidden under the snow, all of which are remnants of last fall's projects lying there on the soft brown earth uncovered at last to face the sun again. These are some of the things I had forgotten about because the snow hid them from us: sections of water line, a sagging cardboard box from something once new, sloppy pink wads of insulation like cotton candy tossed aside at a carnival, a rusty hammer, a coffee can full of range nails, a mound of bark where we chopped a woodshed of firewood. All these things remind me of our autumn stress and rush and hard work to make the unfinished cabin we had purchased livable for winter.

I think of Ernie, Sherrie's father, late last summer during their visit. It was the first time he had seen our cabin. The year prior, they visited us while we were renting a place with all the amenities they are used to, and even then they sighed and shook their heads as if their daughter had either finally lost all good sense they had instilled in her, or more likely she was somehow living there against her will. "Pretty far from the real world," I remember him saying.

We later decided that they thought us crazy to live in a place so far from Wal-Mart and the rest of the real world, here in a place where mountain lions still carry deer off into the forest ("The poor things, they don't deserve it," I heard her mom say).

And now they are faced with this: no running water, no electricity, no insulation with winter coming on quickly; an outhouse that made Linda, her mother, cringe as if it were unimaginable and somehow backward. "Well, I'm just glad we're staying at the lodge where there's toilets with water," she said, in her central Pennsylvania way of cutting off the ends of words and running others together. She said this while smacking herself repeatedly even when there were no mosquitoes on her. I didn't bother reminding her about the mountain lions.

Our families' concerns over winter mirrored my own in many ways, but I didn't let on. Rather, I told them the good things, like how quiet and still winter is and how we can ice fish for cutthroat trout in the lake, just over the ridge, and even earn meat by packing moose and elk out of the forest when a friend's hunt is successful. In reality, my worry as autumn waned was all-consuming: Snow, the road, having enough money to keep the road plowed, keeping our rattling truck running well enough to take us down the road should we find the money to have it plowed; having enough firewood, enough insulation in the roof, what we would do about the east side of the roof that had no insulation at all. It was my first experience relying on a generator for power, but all we had to power was our well pump that would burn up, freeze up, or otherwise leave us with no water at all and a repair bill that would total every penny I had made in the past year if we didn't run it properly.

Later, after all the whining and worrying, once the snow came and the temperature dropped to twenty below at night, frosting mugs set on the windowsill inside the cabin, and bursting trees with the sound of a lever action 30-30 being cocked, we would get letters from our folks asking if we had enough wood to keep warm and enough money for food, and somehow we always had both. And somehow we never really seemed to mind how cold it was, perhaps because we knew spring was only a few months away.

I look back now and shake my head, wondering how I did not die of some stress-related illness or, more likely, get run over by a logging truck while crossing the road from the Dirt-Tee-Shame Yaak O' Mat to my pint of Moose Drool waiting for me at the tavern. My mind was so noisy and distracted that if breathing were a voluntary action, I might have suffocated. Now, with our first winter in the new cabin behind us, I'm not certain what the fuss was about.

I meander about the yard for an hour with a plastic bag picking up trash and piling fallen branches into a swelling brushpile. When finished, I admire what is left: rising crimson shoots of wild sarsaparilla; lupine with a drop of dew nestled in the transect of leaves; a wad of false morel, orange, crumpled and rubbery. There is no grass. Come summer, the green on the ground is a low canopy of sarsaparilla. By then the leaves are wide and strong, providing a foot-high canopy above the earth. Among it will grow Oregon grape, Solomon's seal, twisted stalk, bunchberry, club moss, Queen's cup bead lily, fairy slippers, and other moist habitat forest natives. Above them all rise the three-hundred-year-old larch trees, at the top of which the ravens perch, watching us.

It has been raining for what seems like a month. We have forgotten what it is like to be outside and dry at the same moment, much less warm and without the clunk and bulk of oversized boots and jackets. The river is within inches of spilling over its banks into the meadow where a pond is already forming from the highland runoff. We head for higher ground, walking through the forest around the cabin. We discuss someday buying the lot next to us so that we don't get neighbors. We'll do this, we say, after we buy the meadow property because the meadow is more affordable and because it is listed on the market and the forestland is not, and because people are already looking over the meadow like a used car on a lot. We devise a plan to take photos of the meadow once it is under water so we can show them to any prospective buyers we might meet. Instead we stick to the old routine of making Sammy speak incessantly and target shooting when we notice a prospective buyer poking around down there. It takes a lot of bullets and dog biscuits, but we hope that in the long run the effort pays off.

Our home and the land around it is a wild corridor used by bears, both black and an occasional grizzly, as well as deer, moose, and mountain lions to reach the river and all the food sources that are found there. I take a break from tidying the yard and head under the trees where crusted snow remains in patches. While walking I find another lion-killed deer to the north of my cabin, its legs sprawled in the snow—hindquarters here, skull there, front legs gone altogether except for one hoof. The vertebrae lay aloof, curved into a question mark and stripped of most of its flesh. I stop, hold my breath, survey the blood-blotted snow, wonder for a moment if I might be next, reach for a stick, call for my dog who runs up panting. She stops, sniffs, and immediately drops to her back and rolls in the blood and bone, grunting and kicking the air.

"Knock it off," I say in a harsh whisper. Sammy stops in mid squirm, her ears lying flat on the ground, the pads of her feet pointing to the trees. "Get up, please," I say as if talking to a child. She kicks once more as if to squeeze in a last word, and then gets up, shakes, and slinks over to smell the spine. I crouch there for a long time surveying the scene, turning over pieces of bone and tufts of coarse hair, retracing the tracks and signs that detailed again, the death of one creature sustaining life for another. All this, here in my own backyard. At times I know for certain that I am blessed, and feel doubly blessed when I realize that the kill scene is at least a day old and that the big cat is most likely far away.

It is a powerful thing living in the womb of a forest. I find myself each day increasingly molded, emotionally and physically, by my landscape, and living within the valley's natural rhythms and cycles: birth, growth, proliferation, death, sustenance. I pick up the skull and consider placing it on the stump in my yard where I have gathered a collection of such things, but decide against it for no reason I can explain other than that it is too fresh. The ravens will find the remains soon and feed from the meat left on the bones, and the cycle and rhythm continues.

I climb to the top of the hill behind my cabin and watch a crescent moon rise over a snow-laden Mount Henry miles away, its lookout tower glowing orange from the sun setting behind me, while Sammy lies beside me working the rib bone of the deer.

A short time later Sherrie and I are creeping through the night, bouncing and spinning and sloshing our way along our road toward town. Sammy is in the bed of the truck getting jostled and drenched as we maneuver the pits and puddles and trenches of slick silt. She stands looking out around the cab with her front legs positioned on the tire well and her tail stiff as if on a mission of dire concern. Back and forth she moves from side to side, at times by her own will, and at others by the will of the road as we spin sideways, madly, as if on ice, and as if the road has its own plans for us. Sammy, like us, tries to stay grounded and in control but the path is unpredictable and at times she loses her footing.

When we hit pavement life suddenly seems simple, and we flow easily and with grace to the tavern only four miles away. The neon lights hang in the windows and smoke rises from the chimney. They are the only lights in town. The mercantile, the Dirty Shame, and the Yaak-O-Mat are closed. There are only three vehicles in the tavern lot and we know who owns them, so we decide before even entering to buy a six-pack for home where we won't have to listen to political tirades firmly grounded in imagination of the ugliest sort.

Driving to our cabin, we stop at the meadow. The rain has quit and suddenly the sky is only mottled with clouds. Shining our headlights across the meadow we see water from the river seeping over the bank into the growing pond. Ducks, startled by our intrusion, make their way to its safety. We turn off the headlights and shut down the engine. A loon calls as it wings its way through the air above the river, probably checking out the scene as well before banking eastward, over the ridge, to the lake for the night. In the distance we can hear the river gurgle as it rises slowly, and powerfully, coursing toward the Kootenai, then the Columbia, and then to the sea. The moon reflects off the pond and we see the trails of ducks shimmering on the water.

Shortly after, we are sitting in our own cabin. Our fire, like fifty or so others in the valley, is crackling and popping in the stove. Candlelight dances on the log walls and Sammy perks her head up and lets out a muffled bark. Sherrie found bear scat in the road yesterday while taking a walk, and we talk about how we hope our composting bin is safe now that spring is creeping in.

We borrowed a movie from a friend earlier in the day, but decide against threatening the night with our roaring generator. The night is too peaceful for such commotion. From our cabin we cannot hear the rustle of the river, or the sound of water rising over the bank to flood the land. Instead our conversation drifts like smoke into the fog, talking first about our plans for the garden and finishing the cabin, and then moves at its own rhythm to our families in Pennsylvania and how hard it can be at times, especially at their age, and how sometimes we wish we could be there for them now, as they have been for us. The rain starts again and it patters on the tin roof and the gas lantern hisses into the night, eventually growing dim. Sammy lies on the floor, twitching, perhaps dreaming of running off into the rain and trees in pursuit of something untamed.

In the morning, after coffee, amidst raven chortle and thrush song, we carry our canoe down to the meadow, which at some point during the night became a sprawling lake community of ducks and geese clustered in groups of dozens, honking and quacking, ascending and landing on the water. It is like a flower that was a bud the day before that has blossomed with the dawn. We launch the boat and paddle over places where yesterday we had walked.

In one place there is a long, narrow strip of high land between this ephemeral lake and the river, which acts as the divider between water raging and water calm. The river carries an entire tree past. We watch its sprawling branches float by, rising above the bank in a rush. Somewhere, upriver, the forest has become smaller. A pileated woodpecker wails in the distance and hammers at a tree. Chickadees *phee-bee* and flutter from tree to bush as we drift past the bank, the water swirling around our paddles.

A beaver tows a cottonwood branch ahead of us making the water shimmer behind him. Sammy's ears perk. She growls. The beaver dives when it hears her. Sammy grows anxious. She jumps out of the boat, swimming, chasing after the branch she thinks is a beaver.

CHAPTER 16

GHOST PRINT

By Laurie John Lane-Zucker

ON MAY 30, THE NIGHT BEFORE WE ENCOUNTERED THE tornado in the cedar grove, The Orion Society's Forgotten Language Tour read to one hundred people at the Yaak Community Center in the remote Yaak Valley of Montana. Richard Nelson, one of four readers that evening (the others were Terry Tempest Williams, Robert Michael Pyle, and Janisse Ray), read from *The Island Within*:

> *The world never seems more alive than during a storm.... It has all the power and beauty of a wild animal—a bear in the backyard— unbridled, tempestuous, feral, petulant. ...I love to look into the throats of storms, feel their wet breath, their tension and strength. Being out in a storm is like standing on the back of a living whale or running under a trumpeting elephant.*

That very next afternoon, between the shadows of tall trees, we stared deep into the throat of the Yaak.

The rich humid scent of cedar filled our nostrils with a thick urgency. We looked up to see a dark cloud bank rumbling up the valley toward us at great speed. One shaft of lightning after another was shed then quickly swallowed. Then the wind came. Gale-force winds lashing out, pulling and pushing the tall cedar and fir trees, bending them to impossible angles across the road. Branches fell. Then the hail came. Marble-sized hail turning to the size of walnuts.

We ran to the vehicles, hoping to drive out to the main road beyond the grove. But a tree had already fallen in front of the first car and we could go no farther. At the rear, in the minivan, we watched helplessly as the storm worsened. Hail raged down on the roof and windshield with a sound that made the world crumple. Chunks of ice fell from the sides of the van, accumulating in layers on the ground and turning it as white as Ahab's whale.

We waited. Then, for a reason still not clear, we shifted the van into reverse and drove backward ten feet. We applied the brake. And then we watched as a tall Douglas fir tree fell from left to right across the ghost print the van had just left.

The Forgotten Language Tour had spent most the previous week visiting small towns in the Yaak Valley. Several months before, Rick Bass had invited us to come. "Please help the unprotected Montana roadless areas," he wrote, "... before these lands, and their importance to us, are truly forgotten and lost to the future."

We agreed to take the six-year-old barnstorming tour to four logging communities in this far corner of northwest Montana to speak on behalf of the Yaak's remaining roadless areas and to visit with local people who are wrestling with complex, troubling issues.

The Yaak is a deeply-polarized place, scraped raw by a diminishing economic base and a disappearing wilderness. Like numerous other places visited in the tour's travels, from the polluted Anacostia River in our nation's capital to the fragile canyonlands ecosystems of the desert Southwest, the Yaak reveals what happens when nature is seen merely as a resource and not as an actual member of a given community. The Yaak wilderness, rich in diversity and hidden beauty, has been forgotten rather than cared for in the same way care should be bestowed on a child or the elderly, with unquestioned respect for the value of its life and a sense of humility before the things that it can teach and give us.

In bringing the Forgotten Language Tour to the Yaak Valley, we hoped to witness the kind of dynamic interaction that took place at the previous year's Watershed conference at the Library of Congress, where three thousand grassroots activists from forty-two states joined fifty leading writers, poets, and educators for a week of dialogues, readings, and workshops. Beyond all else, what we witnessed there was the power of people from many places speaking in one voice on behalf of home places and wise stewardship. The Yaak appeared to be in dire need of that kind of magic.

Through Watershed and our other travels, we have become convinced that this work—work at the grassroots level—could well be the work that secures the long-term health of the environment and our communities. Sadly, this kind of activism has heretofore been undervalued, underfunded, and the most visionary and successful of these efforts have been undercommunicated to others in the field.

In recent years, we have expanded The Orion Society to serve as a support and communications network for grassroots organizations and have opened our membership to local and regional groups that are undertaking groundbreaking, often heroically back-breaking work. Furthermore, we have created new opportunities to highlight and aid this work, including publications like *Orion Afield*, online resources, training institutes, conferences, and the newly focused Forgotten Language Tour.

In Yaak we were hosted by individuals and organizations who are working toward building consensus, like the Kootenai Forest Congress. This community-organized think tank of logging and environmental "interests" comes together twice a month to discuss, and try to answer, the grave environmental and economic pressures that are making the Yaak's future so cloudy.

During our stay, we had the opportunity to attend a Congress meeting, gaining perspective on the complexities of the issues and their urgency. Afterward we spoke briefly with Ellen from Libby, the wife of a logger and mother of two. With exasperation in her voice, she told us that her husband had tried other jobs, such as bagging groceries, but with each attempt he grew lethargic, depressed. "He—we—love this valley and will do anything to continue to live here," Ellen said, "but Ed's true spiritual home is in the forests. That's his love, where he's whole, and logging is the only way he can make a living in the forest right now. It's been that way for generations. We can't stand the clear-cuts either. But what are we to do?" It's hard to answer statements like this with aphorisms. And it's tough not to feel the weight of the struggle. Yet we came away from the occasion heartened. These people come together twice a month to hash it out, sometimes raising their voices to each other, often leaving frustrated. But they do it, fearlessly, or in spite of their fears.

The next night, at the public reading in the town of Yaak, Terry Tempest Williams read:

> *The web of life in the Pacific Northwest is rapidly unraveling. We are seeing*
> *ourselves as part of the fabric. It is not a story about us versus them. That is too*

easy.... Nor is it a story about corporate greed against a free market economy. It is a story about healing and how we might live with hope.

Once the storm passed, we left the vehicles cautiously, not quite believing the worst was over. The tornado left the cedar grove looking like it had passed through a shredder. Along the road, an orgy of branches and pine needles mixed with hail under a shroud of mist. The tall fir tree lay heavily across the road. We approached it warily, as one might a coffin or an angry local deity.

This tree and the one that had fallen in front of the first car had locked us in. Someone found a small handsaw in the cab of his truck, and another took the saw in hand and began cutting through the fir tree. It was exhausting business, and after thirty seconds of sawing, with minuscule progress to show for it, the saw was passed on to another. And so it happened: One sawed for a short time, then passed it on to another who sawed until he or she began to tire, and then passed it on. Slowly we sawed through the tree's many rings. Each hard draw of the blade and the imperceptible progress of the cut seemed to reinforce the fact that in one brief moment this tree had been denied its many decades of life in the ground. At the same time, each stroke represented a process of redemption. For when we had sawed enough, we placed a strap around the tree's trunk and managed to pull it from the road, freeing ourselves from our predicament.

Looking back now, I see in our experience of the storm and this collective act of sawing a reflection of human enterprise and destiny. We are destroyers but also healers, much as the Hindu god Shiva represents at once the forces of creation and destruction. We use the world, blemish our landscapes, and harm our communities. And we have the ability to re-envision the world, protect and restore our rivers and forests, and reknit the fabric of community life. Each of us—logger, activist, writer—must struggle with these two faces. We must, as Pattiann Rogers put it recently in *Orion*, "reconcile our 'egoistic concerns' with our 'universal compassion.'" Doing so requires many human attributes, not least among them hope. But there in the cedar grove, one late afternoon in the Yaak, we glimpsed grace in the form of a falling tree and a van's ghost print outlined by hail. And where there is grace, there is hope.

CHAPTER 17

THE COMMUNITY OF GLACIERS

By Rick Bass

I HAVE BEEN THINKING FOR THE LAST FEW MONTHS, OFF AND on, about glaciers: reflecting on how slow change has been in coming to northwestern Montana, regarding the preservation of our last few remaining roadless areas as wilderness, and at how resistant we've been as a culture to reforming the dominant land-altering management practice in this region, forestry.

A glacier isn't just a chunk of ice, static, frozen in time. We know that glaciers are like rivers, sliding through time, up one valley and down the next, with the laminar grace of wind or flowing water; that it is only when we try to compress the life of a glacier into the scale of our own short lives that the life leaves them, and they cease—or so it appears, to our blind eyes—to move.

They are always moving. Who dares to say that they are not: that because we cannot see a thing happening, it is not happening?

The common definition of a glacier is any patch of earth where snow remains present year-round, with a depth of ice accumulating across time—but what interests me is the point where a glacier, having invested decades in patient endurance, finally gains enough overburden and ceases to act as what it was up until that point, and metamorphoses instead into a slippery, living fluid, and begins flowing down the mountain: carving a new world, finally, and setting new rules.

I cannot help but think that efforts to protect the last roadless cores of public land—zero acres protected in the Yaak Valley, nothing achieved, since the national forest system was created up in this corner of the world—almost a hundred years without wilderness—is exactly like the formation of a glacier; and this is a thought that gives me solace.

I used to have a certain vision with regard to environmental activism in this part of the world. I used to think that up here, it consisted of the tedious, enduring stonework of a mason; that the activist's duty, in such a situation—outnumbered twenty or even a hundred to one—was to stay calm and to be enduring; that even the greatest and most skilled artisan could never be anything more, from a historical perspective, than a laborer, laying down stepping-stones across some river over which those who would come later might pass.

What I think now is that it is *not* like laying stones across a river, or stacking one's stones, one's words and deeds, in an ongoing, eternal rock wall, but rather, that it is like being snowed upon in winter: that one's life is not nearly so significant or dramatic as a rock wall, but is instead far more silent, made up often of a lifetime of snow; that our lives and work are nothing more and nothing less. I have begun to think that the conceit of our lives, our hearts, as hot furious maelstroms of passion is but a romantic's fancy: that what we really are is nothing more than windblown snow, swirling, beautiful yet ephemeral when measured flake by flake.

We would like to think of ourselves as hundred-pound slabs of mountain: square-cut, durable, and imminently useful. I think that the opposition—those who would kill and eat the wilderness—are the stoneweight, and that we, and our works, however passionate, however intelligent, are but snow, melting unto vanishing in poor years, though in good years beginning to accumulate in skiffs and ridges, drifts and mounds.

For a long time, nothing happens. It's just snow: silent, beautiful, monochromatic, relentless, heartless—or so it seems. Twenty feet might fall in the mountains, one winter; by summer's end, nineteen feet might have melted.

But then winter—the time of beauty, the time of work—comes back around again. Twenty feet might fall again, and once more, beneath summer's broil, nineteen more feet might vanish.

Nothing is happening yet. It's just a bunch of old crusty snow and ice. But something is getting ready to happen.

For a long time it seems to be for nothing—seems to be as but snow, silent, stacking up, changing nothing: luminous, elegant, but frozen and forceless. But that is only because we are looking at it using the scale of four seasons, or of a lifetime, or even two or three lifetimes.

Depending on slope and aspect and density—usually a function of moisture content—it takes about sixty feet of ice to make a glacier come to life.

Once that proper load weight is established, the glacier begins to move—begins to
flow continuously, behaving now as a plastic or a liquid, rather than as the brittle solid
it had heretofore been, trapped and frozen for so long.

I've often wondered what it must feel like to the mountain when the long-building
glacier first begins to move—or rather, what the inhabitants on that mountain think.

All those years of waiting. All those years of close-but-no-cigar: For under the laws
of physics, it makes no difference if there is 10 feet of ice, or 50 feet of ice; it's not
until that 60th foot is achieved that movement begins.

You can be real close for a long time, but still not go anywhere.

Surely there must be an audible, tangible release of relief, in that interface between
glacier and mountain, when the glacier does begin to move. What must it feel like,
for the glacier at that point, as it finally comes to life?

Some of the ice at the bottom of certain glaciers has been measured to be twenty-
five thousand years old.

I do hope we get the last roadless cores on the public wildlands protected—permanently protected—before that kind of time, but if not, we will keep doing what we do,
will keep saying what needs saying, even if for all intents and purposes it seems as if we
are speaking in silence, season after season, with nothing happening.

I want, or perhaps need, to tell a story about my glacier.

For decades, this region of northwest Montana has been the place to come if you've
given up on government, and if you've even given up, more or less, on people. And
across the years, a handful of corporate strawbosses (some true believers, crusaders, others of them in it merely for the money) have spent their lives building high walls around
the island of this strange, dark, lush rainy region of the world: demonizing the outside
world and all its admittedly vapid iniquities, while simultaneously promulgating this
ridiculous myth of independence, self-reliance, and a purer integrity within these walls
than without.

Anyone can stop something. Building something is the real measure of a community, a man or woman, or a government.

I know of many people in my community who support the idea of, and even desire, wilderness designation for the last little islands of roadless land in our valley—our valley has about 150 year-round residents, scattered on private lands among nearly a million acres of national forest; there are more bears than people, more owls than people, more lions than people, more elk, more coyotes, more deer, more ravens, more moose than people . . . Such are, or have been, the ingrained social pressures of this corner of the world, however, that it is hard for a person in the valley to dare to admit that desire: the need, the yearning, to know that a few wild places will remain forever wild in the valley, free to grow old, rot or burn, grow young, then grow old again, in a forest's natural cycle.

I'm not asking for much—just a little. All I want to know is that some places will be safe forever. I'm not trying to stop logging—in fact, I'm a proponent of certain kinds of logging. I just want to know these last little wild corners and ridges will remain the way they are, wild forever. Wilderness designation is the only permanent protection; all other classification systems are fraught with loopholes.

Can you imagine how long and how fierce, how *cemented*, has been the cultural opposition to wilderness, for some grown men and women to be afraid to admit such a thing—to be afraid to even say one word, the w-word, because of all the hatred and fury the word will arouse? Particularly amazing to me is the fact that this is so in such a remote and rugged land, one that is supposedly inhabited by big old, tough old independent thinkers: loners, rugged individualists. But it's weird; it doesn't work that way. Instead it's the opposite: Because of the remoteness, and the loneliness, it seems to me that people really, really want to be liked—or at least not to be disliked.

And for several generations, industry has been pushing the fear button, prophesying that if roadless lands in the natural forests are designated as wilderness, then the private landowners next to those national forests will be evicted.

So very few people say the w-word. We talk about bulldozers, talk about hunting and fishing, talk about the basketball playoffs; but then sooner or later I'll mention the w-word, just to keep the idea of it from being forgotten.

My neighbors try to make it easy for me. I've had conversations of varying lengths with almost all 150 of them, at one point or another in my fifteen years in the valley, and I don't think it's inaccurate to say that roughly 99 percent of them would agree, they'd like to see the valley stay just the way it is, and keep the roadless areas roadless. But why call it wilderness? Why not just leave it alone?

Because I'm tired of fighting, for one thing. When I moved up here, I used to be a fiction writer. I loved that craft, that calling. I've had to all but abandon it, to speak out instead for another thing I love now just as much as language—the woods. These woods. And I need it to be designated as wilderness because frankly, I, and the other activists up here, are the ones paying the dues, fighting back sale after sale in one unprotected roadless area after another. By and large, there's not a lot of marketable or accessible timber in these last roadless areas—it's why they never had roads built to them in the first place—but all I can surmise from recent activities is that they—industry and Congress—want it all.

In the last seven years there have been at least eight timber sale proposals in the Yaak's last roadless areas; each time, public opinion has been able, so far, to turn them back, or aside, for a little while longer.

These are stories that most residents of the valley aren't aware of. They look out their windows every morning, or drive up and down the Yaak Road, admiring the view, and they tend to their gardens and live quiet lives and wonder, *What's all the fuss? Why does this Bass guy like to fight so much? Can't he see that things are better—that logging practices are improving, and that for the most part the forest service is leaving those roadless areas alone?*

Opponents of wilderness designation up here sometimes try to make it easy for me, but of late I get the feeling that they are growing weary with my inability to take the olive branch. What would you think about calling it a natural area, instead of wilderness, they ask—or how about "heritage forest," or "roadless core," or "primitive area," or even "national roadless monument?" What about "National Recreation Area"? How about an eighteen-month moratorium? How about a ten-year cease-fire? What about other kinds of new designations?

To all of these, I have to say no, it's not enough; I have to stay firm and stand my ground, asking for wilderness, which is the only complete and permanent protection a forest, or a watershed, or a mountain, can obtain: All the others carry various loopholes for helicopter logging, snowmobiles, motorcycles, gold and silver and copper mines, hydroelectricity projects . . .

I'm not even saying that I'm against those activities, nor even that I'm opposed to them being executed on the national forests *in certain places.* All I'm saying is that I need to know that these last little roadless islands will be protected, permanently. I do not want to have to be traveling down to Troy, or Libby, or Helena, or Missoula, or Washington D.C., week after week, year after year, to keep trying to turn back the road building from those last little refuges. I want my life back, and the frustrating irony is that many of the opponents to wilderness would be happy to offer me my life back, if only I will discard my beliefs, my needs. If only I will think of myself, and the present, and sell out the future, which is so suspect in any event ...

As long as there is ice, and snowfall, there is hope. Once the adequate load or pressure has been achieved—fifty to sixty feet—and the ice begins to flow, a second kind of movement occurs, at even greater depth. In addition to the flowing of all the ice resting beneath that sixty feet, the entire glacier itself begins to slip from its contact with bare earth, with bedrock: sliding now like a wet tennis shoe on ice. You can imagine, once this phenomenon is achieved, how very hard it would be to stop it. You can imagine how the glacier would begin to write its words, its sentences, its stories, in stone, with claws of ice, upon the previously implacable mountain. You can imagine how such etchings might finally—after thousands of years of waiting to be released—begin to get the mountain's attention.

These glaciers—lying so patient upon the stony, intractable mountain—will, in the end, have their say almost completely: They will carve and shape and scour all the way down to the core, the bottom, cutting the mountain itself—the very thing that, in some instances, birthed the glaciers by creating those weather systems that gave rise to the snow and clouds.

It all started out as only an inch of snow, two inches of snow, upon a great mountain range. Just a skiff at first.

Just as exciting, to one whose heart is increasingly emboldened by the patience and strength of glaciers, is the unexplained, unpredictable phenomenon of glacial surges, in which the slow advance of some glaciers is characterized by periods of extremely rapid movement. A glacier might be moving along in its normal manner, only to speed up for a relatively short time before returning to its normal rate again. The flow rates during surges can be as much as one hundred times the normal rate. No one really knows why such surges occur. The thing to remember, of course, is to gain that sixty feet that's required to get things started...

I have never seen the Rhône Glacier in Switzerland, but would like to someday. It is the site of a classic study of an alpine glacier that measured the lateral and vertical currents of a glacier's flow. The study discovered that the glacier moved not like a grinding, ground-eating tank—not like something our crude and clumsy hearts might have created or imagined—but with the grace of a river, complete with eddies and currents both lateral and vertical. Glaciers are different from human communities in one respect, in that it is easier to mark or measure them. In 1874 the scientists at the Rhône Glacier simply pounded stakes into the ice at fixed points, and then watched as some of the stakes crept downslope, still upright, in patterns and distances different from the other stakes.

By 1878, four years later, the stakes were stretching out to form a tongue, much like the pattern of a current in the center of a river; and in only four more years, the stakes had stretched farther, into an intricate ellipse, giving away the telltale movement that to any other previous observers would have seemed static, hopeless.

There is nothing about glaciers that does not give me hope. Even more exciting than the graceful, riverine movement of things that appear to be immobile chunks of ice is the miraculous news that even with glaciers that are having a rough time, with the ice front retreating, the old durable ice *within* the glacier will often still be advancing, like a riptide running in reverse. It is as if, once that momentum has begun, the glacier is its own living entity, its own organism, intent upon and committed now to a destiny that seems more biologic than geologic: one that seems to radiate a force of will.

And surely, seen from some great distance of either space or time—from a hundred miles up, or across the span of ten thousand years—the movement of the glacier would seem like a sinuous galloping thing, sliding across the landscape with an elegant gait, leaving behind tracks etched in stone and spoor the size of small villages.

Believing deeply in Wendell Berry's advice that "To enlarge the areas protected from use without at the same time enlarging the areas of good use is a mistake," and in an attempt to demonstrate to my neighbors that I care for them and their ways of life, as much as I do for the wilderness—believing as I do that they too, like me, are of the wilderness—I put aside my wilderness advocacy for a while and found myself dedicating the autumn and winter of 1998, and the spring of 1999, working with a small local group, the Yaak Valley Forest Council (YVFC), to lobby hard in Washington and Missoula and Helena, in Troy and Yaak and Libby, to secure one of the nine pilot programs authorized by Congress in Montana, Idaho, and the Dakotas.

In these pilot areas, a new style of logging would be practiced. Rather than the old paradigm of focusing on how many board feet a unit could yield in a single cutting, two new objectives would be paramount: the desired "end result" of the forest, and full community participation in the planning process.

A logger would be awarded a contract based on the quality of work he or she could perform, rather than the amount of timber he or she could scalp in the shortest amount of time. As well, the program would favor the employment of local workers who, working on their own home ground, would have more motivation to take the weaker, lesser trees and leave the strongest and the best; and the emphasis of sites selected for this program would be on the restoration of damaged landscapes and watersheds, rather than the further invasion and liquidation of healthy ones.

After six months of hard work, our little pro-roadless group, the Yaak Valley Forest Council, was able to secure a much-coveted position in this federal program.

At a community meeting, we found nine volunteers willing to serve on a steering committee that would help implement the program. Three of those volunteers were pro-roadless advocates, members of the YVFC who, "despite" being pro-roadless-protection, had done the work involved in bringing the stewardship logging project to the valley. This one-third membership on the steering committee frightened and upset the others in the community—they didn't trust us, had been listening to gossip—and so the Forest Service assisted in an awkward reconstruction of the steering committee, a weekend's downsizing that resulted in only one YVFC member remaining on the committee.

The stewardship project didn't have anything to do with roadless cores, or wilderness—the logging and restoration projects would take place only in areas that were roaded—but so stark and polarized a dividing line has the issue become in this community that here, too, it was used to cleave.

Nonetheless, the YVFC agreed to go along with the hastily reconstructed downsized committee in order to bring the project to the valley—and from there, we've limped forward with it, trying to find common ground on these projects, logging units and land management prescriptions on which we can all agree: on which we can reach consensus.

Clearly, such agreement is not possible everywhere—but just as clearly, we believe it's possible to find some areas where that consensus can be met, and we're looking for those areas in which to work, rather than in the more sensitive and controversial places. That's our vision of future land management by the forest service.

I still believe that in the Yaak, there is opportunity for sustainable forestry. The valley has been turned upside down: It was once 50 percent old growth, but in the last half century the rampant clear-cutting, and taking the best trees instead of the weakest, has converted the valley to a young forest of overstocked, crowded, weaker trees. Nearly two-thirds of the forest now consists of trees less than seventeen inches in diameter at breast height (DBH). There is, in many of these postharvest units, opportunity for the restorative work of thinning, both commercially and precommercially.

Even after the YVFC brought this new logging project to the valley, to put local people to work, opponents of our needs—opponents of the protection of roadless areas—continue to spread the rumors that the YVFC therefore is against all logging, and furthermore, that the YVFC, wants everyone—ourselves included—evicted from the valley.

Maybe it's part of the glacier's process, to lose some of your fire. Or for the nature of the fire to change, as if metamorphosed under the pressure of time and distance traveled, or not traveled: so much labor, with not one singular gram of tangible difference. It is not a giving up or even a wearing thin, but instead a reconstituting of desire. In some cases, fire is too quick an instrument for the work that needs to be done. In some instances, ice is the tool that is called for—the ice of decades, or the ice of centuries. If you cannot, even in your best efforts, attain speed, then perhaps you can gain solace from images and models of power: the great sheets of ice that sculpted many of the wild places we find ourselves fighting for. The great masses of snow and ice that scribed their direction into every ravine and peak and cirque of these stony landscapes, and which laid to level the resistant landforms, entire mountain ranges of obstacles.

In the various defeats conservationists have met up here, and in the static or even backward-moving attempts of our goals, I have been taking solace in the patterns and history of glaciers. It is a pleasure to know of the nature of crevasses—cracks appearing in the zones of tension that are created as the glacier creeps across irregular terrain. Though the jagged fracture of these gaping cracks may reach as deep as fifty meters, for the most part the crevasses are merely surficial, even cosmetic expressions of the struggle below and, as such, insignificant in the flow of things. At depths down below that sixty-foot mark, the plastic flow of the glacier remains relatively unperturbed; seamless, with the hidden and earnest momentum of its mass and, I like to believe, its desire.

You think things are moving very slow, or even not at all. But you must not forget those shiftings and releases of built-up, buried hydrostatic pressures, little understood, wherein one day the glacier surges, suddenly like a skater free and clear, traveling as much as 180 feet in a day. And beneath the glacier, at its base, are runnels of gushing water, creeks and rivers honeycombing through the ice in myriad and unmappable, unknowable braids, like the convolutions of a brain's folds. It's theorized that, like the miracle of lock-and-key, these shifting braids of river tunnels beneath the ice one day click into such a combination as to provide an immense hydraulic lift to the project, and the whole glacier is fairly catapulted down the mountain.

I take solace in the agony of the glaciers, and their sloppy detritus, their tortured yet elegant residue. A glacier rasps, roars, grinds, hisses, gushes, and spurts as it moans and hollers its way down and through the mountains. It spreads before it, like the rimed breath of some advancing colossus, the clattering terminus of boulders deposited as till and outwash. Sometimes this breath, this terminus, has been carried vast distances, and once deposited in a new land, these deposits can play a significant role in transforming the physical landscape. Particularly dramatic are the glacial erratics—the igneous boulder from Canada that is finally found millennia later in the wheat fields of Nebraska. But sometimes the wheat fields themselves are but the abraded, ground-up, wind-tossed remains of glacier-gnawed mountains that had once towered so far to the north. The fires are what we notice, but the glaciers are what change the world.

A glacier often plucks some rocks, like ideas, from the mountains over and through which it travels, while discarding others. It leaves behind a legacy of troughs and drumlins, arêtes and horns and tarns, cirques and kames and eskers, kettles and moraine. A glacier is transformed daily, even while seeming to represent the very heart of consistency. It adapts, shifts, flexes, readjusts itself like an animal bedded down in a straw nest or daybed, turning around and around, seeking the right and comfortable balance or position. But always moving. A dry paste is often deposited across the land by glaciers, the grist of all that work, all that grinding, which is called rock flour; it exists briefly, where it separates from the rivers draining from beneath the melting glaciers, then is whirled away by the wind and cast across the globe, having been visible, measurable, for only a moment . . .

Within a glacier, there are different kinds of ice. Even as the whole of the glacier is moving, there will sometimes be pockets of stagnant, motionless ice within it, which deposit nothing, and in other places pockets of faster-thawing ice, which collect dust and gravel of a different density than that which the rest of the glacier is either depositing or picking up, as it glides across the land . . . No one can predict what pattern a glacier will leave behind until after it has already passed, and despite the glacier's great force, it occurs to me that perhaps even the glacier itself does not have as much say in the pattern or scribing of its passage as I might have earlier suggested. Perhaps for all the elegance of its residue, it is still nothing but gravity in motion, ultimately uncontrollable, blind brute force rather than calculated rhythm. But effective. More effective than any force I know.

We don't even know where glaciers come from, really. One theory that was once prominent, then fell out of favor, but which has been embraced again is that glaciers are the result of a wobble, a hitch, in the earth's rotation. An imperfection, if you want to think of it that way, but what a beautiful imperfection. A Yugoslavian scientist named Milutin Milankovitch theorized that the climatic changes that give rise to the buildup of glaciers occur due to slightly cockeyed variations in the shape, or eccentricity, of the earth's orbit around the sun—as if, in some great and vast gearworks, a tooth in a cog were chipped or missing—as well as changes in *obliquity*, which is the difference between the angle of the earth's axis and the plane of the earth's orbit—and, additionally, from the simple, charmed, wobbling in the earth's axis, like the spinning of a water balloon, which is called *precession*.

To put it crudely, these factors make the earth a moving target for receiving the sun's radiation—sometimes we receive more, other times less, as if dodging some of it, in our wobble. The glaciers get built, or not built, simply, miraculously, because the earth is canting a single one-trillionth of a degree in *this* direction for a long period of time, rather than in *that* direction.

When I am alone in the woods, and the struggle seems insignificant or futile, or when I am in a public meeting and am being kicked all over the place, I tell myself that little things matter—and I believe that they do. I believe that even if your heart leans just a few degrees to the left or the right of center, that with enough resolve, which can substitute for mass, and enough time, a wobble will one day begin, and the ice will begin to form, where for a long time previous there might have been none.

Keep it up for a lifetime or two or three, and then one day—it *must*—the ice will begin to slide.

I do not mean to dismiss our little fires, nor our fiery hearts. I mean only to remind us all that our lives, our values, are a constant struggle that will never end, and in which there can never be clear "victory," only daily challenge; and that after the glacier passes over, all it will leave behind will be sentences and stories written in stone, testimony not to winning or losing but rather, simply what path the glacier took, while we were here, and whether we were the mountain or the ice.

CHAPTER 18

UPRIVER UNTO THE CHURCH OF THE DIRTY SHAME

By   William   Kittredge

RISING THROUGH THE VALLEY OF THE YAAK RIVER WAS A WAY
of ascending, maybe *floating* is the word. Overcut Montana timberlands turned to rain
forests. Riverwater tumbled, white and energized, breathable and thus alive so the fish
tell us. Or so fisheries scientists tell us the fish tell us.

But the Yaak didn't seem to be a place that was crazy for scientists. It seemed to
be a place for mushroom hunters and wildflower naturalists, for wolves and grizzly
bears, and blackpowder gunsmiths and bowhunting deerslayers and old men of the
mountain, old women of the other mountain, and pine-smelling scents on the
breeze.

We're talking constant encounters with primordial, evolving glories—splendidly
green ankle-deep mosses over the almost-decayed-back-into-the-topsoil crumbling
hulks of what were once crowned-out imperial cedar trees. But no empires. No so-
called performance anxiety. Nobody in the Yaak seems to be interested in empire
building. Or in the trappings of empire, except for occasional first-rate pickup
trucks.

What interested people in the Yaak seemed to be freedom, and the state of their
connection to fecundity and friends. Annick and I gave a reading in a roadside
church/community center, and were gratified that it was attended by barefoot children
and dark men in heavy backwoods boots wearing camo gear, and gray-headed citizens
who might have been retired stockbrokers or lifetime hippie jewelers, who could tell?
What did they want from us?

Mostly, we decided, a communal evening out. Some of them, like us, were obviously anticipating some bar hopping later on. People were finessing the evening, old-timers catching up on the likelihood of a dry summer (high), and impudent children were dancing and chanting playground songs. A handsome young man, new to the community, asked if anybody would tell him where he could find morel mushrooms. There was a moment of silence. Then we went on talking like he'd never said such a dumb thing. Except for the pretty girl who touched his arm. Later she drew him a road map on the palm of her hand with a ballpoint pen.

Afterward, down the road in the village of Yaak, two taverns across the road from one another, we worked the evening arts of communality. We'd already spent some time in the "new bar," the Yaak River Tavern, enjoying the late-afternoon fall of sunlight through the big windows, so this time we headed right for the old Dirty Shame, a refuge of the kind our ancestors inhabited during the flint-chipping ages.

Some of our communal work in the Dirty Shame consisted of singing along on choruses while Bill Schreiber played and sang "The Prostitute's Waltz" ("I'm living on the first floor. Up the stairs is a French whore"), ordering another round for the house trading semi-articulate quips with the owner, Rick Carsello, and hugging his wife, Willie. For me, it worked. I'm a western boy and my churches have oftentimes been taverns, where heedlessness and intimacy are encouraged, and foolishness is forgiven. Our loneliness is the actual Dirty Shame, but curable.

CHAPTER 19

THE BEST LAST PLACE

By   Annick   Smith

THE HILL ISN'T MUCH, JUST A SLOPE IN THE TALL GREEN OF THE
Yaak Valley, a cleared patch marked by sentinel larch maybe two hundred years old,
maybe twice two hundred. The trees are arrow-straight, tempered by fire. Their
branches, feathered chartreuse with new growth this June afternoon, rise in gossamer
light like souls seeking release, which is an easy notion, for the roots of these trees are
nourished by the bones of the dead.

"Hug a tree," says young Scott, a recent Yaak immigrant who is working to keep the
roadless forests wild. My arms encircle less than half the girth of an ancient giant. My
cheek rests on its bark. I breathe the perfume of sap and decaying needles. Looking up
through evergreen lace to a sky fractured into bits of blue, bits of pearl, I laugh because
I would rather be walking this teeming earth than aspiring to heaven.

I am a tree hugger, not a tree chopper like most of the folk who lie in the Boyd Hill
Cemetery, people who fled when the going was rough into a nearly impenetrable corner where the maritime rain forest meets the Rockies. The Yaak is not on the way to
anywhere. You must arrive here on purpose. To hunt, to trap, to fish, perhaps to
scratch out a garden in the meadows along the river, but most of all to log. What a paradise it must have been for those first loggers—a seeming infinity of trees. The forest
called. They cut a hunk of it down. Now they *are* the forest.

Within the fenced enclosure, hand-chiseled names are hacked into blocks of stone.
Families go back to the 1880s. There are veterans of World War I and World War II all
in a row. There is Froy, and Wife of Froy—no first familiar name to mark her passing.
Some metal grave markers once held pictures, but the oval frames are empty. Even

119

these nameless are not forgotten. I see flowers fresh from Memorial Day and plastic bouquets, electric blue, shocking pink. One plot is set apart by a white picket fence— perhaps to keep predators away from the babies. So many little ones dead in one family. This is not child-death from the influenza of 1923, which is a common sight in old burial grounds, but death that came in 1985, '87, '89. You could weep for that mother. Weep for your good luck.

The rat-a-tat-tat drumming of a pileated woodpecker breaks the silence like a chain saw. *Time to go. Time to go.* We pile into the four-by-four and head for the crossroads called town. *Yaak*, according to a Kootenai story, means "arrow."

"The Kootenai River is curved around our valley like a bow," says Scott's wife, Sherrie, who makes her living massaging tourists. "The Yaak runs straight down the middle."

I like to imagine life is a river. If life is a river that curves like a bow, stories are its arrows, and we are the slingers. When the stories of the living are joined with the stories of the dead, what you've got is a culture, a place that holds meaning, a home.

In Boyd Hill Cemetery, I was touched by a world larger than the sum of meadows and mountains, grizzlies and trout, old-growth cedar, waterfalls and white-starred bunchberry dogwood. I cannot know the stories a trout knows, although I am sure each trout has a story, as do the migrating eagles, the wolves come down from Canada. I will never think like the mountain lion or moose, but I can know the stories of humans.

There are people in this valley descended from the pioneers whose remains nourish larch on Boyd Hill. There are communal hippies who settled here in the 1970s, foresters, teachers, nurses. I chat with a tattooed trapper and a white-permed retiree, a survivalist gun-toter and college-bound teens.

We are sitting in the Dirty Shame bar, which holds more stories than the graveyard. I recall one stone I saw there inscribed PISS FIR JIM. The image of a chain saw was etched into marble and enameled red. Jim died not long ago, and must have been a regular at this watering hole.

Downing my beer, I order another. When twilight fades, I will go out beyond the small perimeter of light into the dark woods. I will follow a dead logger's implicit advice about how to grieve in the Yaak. My plan is to squat beneath an old fir, hold up my glass for Jim, pull down my jeans, and piss.

When I'm on my journey, don't you weep after me . . . lines from a folk song that we sang over my husband's grave come back to me. We are graced with this remnant of a verdant world. The best we can do while we have breath is to sing its sad songs, the jokes, love songs, and nonsense that root us deep as any tree to the wild and fecund earth.

CHAPTER 20

DIVERSIONS

By Tim Linehan

I SAT DOWN AN HOUR AGO WITH THE INTENTION OF WRITING this story about why Yaak is so dear to me and thought I'd probably end up using memories of particular moments throughout the year that define my life in this little valley. I had in mind to re-create images of daily activities like fishing the river on a July evening, woodcutting and grouse hunting with my dogs in September, or maybe even fixing burst pipes in the attic of my cabin on a subzero winter night, in an effort to show that these are things I've come to know well as a result of living here.

I'd be lying if I said I enjoy every one of them (I'd rather leave frozen pipes to the plumber), but they're part of what makes living here what it is . . . the essence, if you will, of being in a place like this. But the list of things I love about my life here is infinite. And as I was trying to narrow my focus and gather my thoughts, something caught my eye.

Just now, outside the picture window of my cabin, an immature bald eagle shattered the stillness of the pond attempting to kill a hen mallard.

Mottled brown with just a hint of dusky white showing up in its head and tail, the eagle appeared from out of nowhere. Judging from the steep angle of its attack, it must have been sitting high in a tree above the pond. I was surprised by its speed, and as always, by the extraordinary size of these birds.

Although it was flying fast, a brown blur really, I could clearly see its feet, bright yellow against the gray of the day, and even its talons, exposed and angled slightly ahead of its thick body as it aimed for the duck.

At the last second it pulled up, flaring its wings for stability, and smashed into the weeds. Several mallards vaulted from the water around the small island in the middle of the pond. Quacking loudly, some of the ducks ran across the water, still unsure of the situation, and paddled around in tight circles near the far bank. The airborne ducks made a pass overhead and continued down valley. I watched them go out of sight, a small V against the sky.

The eagle sat on the island, its bright eyes and hooked beak clearly visible now, while a few feathers floated in the water next to it. I couldn't tell if it had the hen mallard or not. There was no struggling underneath it, but perhaps the impact of the eagle alone would have killed the duck. I don't know.

Finally aware of danger, the ducks at the far end of the pond started jumping for the sky. Green-heads at first, and one at a time. Then the hens, having moved out of the weeds in a tight group of five, lifted off together.

The pond was quiet now save for a few ripples moving across the surface. Still the eagle sat in the weeds at the edge of the island, motionless except for the almost mechanical movement of its head—first left, then right, then left again.

I had time to get up and go into the kitchen for the binoculars. Just as I centered the field of view on the bird he looked right at me. Maybe I imagined it, but it appeared he knew he was being watched and seemed to hold my gaze for a moment before leaping into the air. Flying low over the alders, he finally disappeared against the heavy timber across the valley floor. There was no duck in his talons.

CHAPTER 21

TININESS

By Sue Halpern

IF IMAGINATION IS NOT JUST INNATE BUT LEARNED, MINE WENT
to school in the East. I did not realize this until I spent time in the Yaak, where the
trees are so tall and dense, so numerous that every human thing—the houses, the
school, the two saloons, the community center that doubles as a church, the store—
is revealed to be as small and as impermanent as human things really are in this
world.

Elsewhere—the elsewhere where most of the people who live in Yaak came from,
and not that long ago—human desires make the landscape into cities and strip malls
and suburban housing tracts. These give the mistaken impression that people are the
permanent feature while the natural world is mutable, shrinkable, and ultimately dis-
pensable.

Yaak, though, challenges this. The people who live here know their place in the
landscape because they can feel it. They are surrounded by trees that dominate them
and put them in their place, not reductively, but in a way that is honest, and chasten-
ing. As much as the trees themselves, this is what they want to preserve. Not a way of
life, but a consciousness, an understanding, which is purer here than anywhere I've
been, of how the world (the world of phyllum, genus, and species) really is.

Not everyone feels this way. There have been fistfights, and unhappy grumblings
about "damn environmentalists," and suspicions on both sides—which is to say that
there are two sides. But here, unlike most other places, it's not a fight between insiders
and outsiders, or between those who consider themselves locals and who consider
everyone else to be "flatlanders." Almost no one in Yaak was born there; everyone is an
outsider. They are united in that.

The school brings them together, too, as schools often do. Eleven children ages five through thirteen, with a teacher and an aide. (The aide is the mother of two of the eleven students.) It is a multiage classroom, where the big kids help the little kids, and where they all play together, and share lunch, and openly welcome strangers into their midst. When people talk about "living in community," it's a place like the Yaak School they mean.

"You mean there is forest in New York?" the kids asked me and my husband, when we said we lived in an isolated hamlet like theirs. And though we said yes, we lived in the Adirondack Park, a forest bigger than Yellowstone, Yosemite, and Glacier National Parks combined, I was starting to doubt it myself. In "my" forest, one has the sense of cohabitation, and of human rootedness. In Yaak, where a sincere and diverse group of people are fighting to keep the roadless areas roadless, and thus to preserve the forest intact, people are fighting for their own irrelevance, all the while understanding it is the most relevant, the most permanent, thing they can do.

CHAPTER 22

THE SYLVAN LADY

By Lynn Sainsbury

I FIRST GLIMPSED IT OBLIQUELY—THE BLACKENED CAT-FACE carved to depth. A third of the base of the tree was gone, eaten away by fires that had overrun the country over hundreds of years. Given the location of this tree, surrounded by boulders, it must have been only during screeching fire-years that the bark was scorched, when flames bit into the living cambium, partially killing it. Perhaps a snag had fallen against it sometime in the late 1800s, and during August 1910, when millions of acres burned across northern Idaho and Montana, that fallen snag, then a log, had bridged the rocks and channeled the flames against this giant. As my eyes moved from the scar to the remaining bright bark, I shivered; the girth was breathtaking. I have rarely seen trees so stoutly massive, and I've seen, touched, and measured a helluva lot of trees. Above the cat-face, heavy bulbous protrusions marked this larch as a granddaddy, as did the broken-off top, which lay twenty feet downslope. Woodpecker holes marched up and down the trunk—defining the rotten pith—but this old man is still among the living, and probably will be for decades to come.

Three species of larch constitute the sole genus of western North America's native deciduous conifer. Western larch, *Larix occidentalis*, is the species commonly found in Montana and Idaho—the species' stronghold. Soft, frilly, kelly-green tufts of needles spray out from spurs along thin, infrequent branches by early May. Over summer the green deepens, until larch become indistinguishable from Douglas fir and lodgepole pine from a distance. By October needles turn brilliant yellow, then shower down to form a silent carpet between naked trunks just before snowfall, sometimes just after. Giant larch trees once stippled valleys and hills alike, all across western Montana. Most are gone now, turned into plywood and two-by-fours long ago. Good-sized pockets still remain up through the Swan Valley, where the co-champion larch tree—a double-topped giant—stands out even among its ancient cohorts. Like ponderosa pine, larch is a fire-resistant species. The common ecological history of both species' landscapes, before Smokey Bear, was frequent low-intensity ground fires that killed most seedlings but left the big trees alive. "Cat-faces," those blackened cavities that triangle up from the base of a tree, are often the only evidence that a big tree is a veteran of a large, hot blaze.

Approaching big trees is a deliberate act. I imagine the loggers of yesteryear, their well-oiled and freshly sharpened misery whips slung over their shoulders. They must have felt the same awe I feel as they studied the chosen tree, trying to gauge the best way of toppling it. Did they reach out and let their hands hover just above the bark, hoping to feel the living presence as I do, or nuzzle the clefts between plates of bark, seeking that vanilla scent? Or did they immediately throw their tools into action, carving out a space for the springboard—beginning the work?

This colossal western Montana larch was only lightly vanilla'd, and I was too excited by the cat-face cave to wait long before clambering inside and staring up into charcoal stalactites. It appeared to be the perfect roosting spot for little brown bats, or others in the *Myotis* genus, though perhaps they avoid the black chalky dust. While not large enough to stretch out in, the tree-cave would be perfect shelter during a brief violent summer hailstorm or a good blind during November's deer season. Looking upslope, I glimpsed another giant larch beyond the crest of the hill. Elizabeth must have followed my gaze, as she asked if I wanted to continue our walk that way.

I had come to the Yaak for a visit: to see Elizabeth and Rick, their two daughters, and the country that has sunk its hooks so deeply into Rick that you can see the ache in his eyes whenever he's forced to travel somewhere else—out of the valley. Elizabeth had written me about the tree and a snow-free, southern-facing slope she had reconnoitered earlier in the week. The snow had not melted in my territory yet, though the bare patches below the trees were beginning to coalesce. The winter had been cold, and every flake of snow that fell in November remained until March. I was thirsting for a bare slope to plant my winter-tired feet on, to be free of snowshoes or heavy pac boots.

My first visit to the Yaak had been a very brief one the prior summer. I was recovering from a major illness, and just managed a slow walk on a trail routed through old-growth riparian stands that had escaped the 1910 fires. What primarily stuck in my memory from that visit was the prickly bite of tree bark on my cheek when I gave a wide-arm embrace to an enormous Engelmann spruce. On this, my second trip, the larch wonders came to light.

I have a continuing love affair with big old trees. Maybe they got under my skin before I even knew they could, while I watched the wind buffet the ungainly branches of ponderosa pine trees through the window—lying crib-bound during nap time. My hometown, in the foothills of the Colorado Front Range, is still surrounded by thousands of old-growth ponderosas that were spared the ax that felled so many for mine timbers near higher-elevation mining towns. Though old, the genes of these particular trees have guided them into a life of squatness and medium girth, at least compared to those majestically huge beauties found in eastern Oregon or northern Arizona.

My work, too, has put me in direct contact with trees and sometimes with the critters that depend on them. In the Cascade Mountains of eastern Oregon I searched for the much-maligned northern spotted owl. If our nightly hoots were echoed back to us, we searched out these ostensibly tame birds the following day. Auditory clues were generally more useful than visually finding the white-speckled brown owl. The dark, deeply furrowed bark was the perfect camouflage and the multilayered canopy, hung tinsel-like with lichens, offered a million hiding places. Once spotted, we offered the owls white mice, which they would carry off to their children hidden away in a cavity nest. The cavities are formed when huge limbs pull loose from trunks of giant Douglas fir trees. Because owl habitat consists primarily of old growth, chasing after the mice-carrying owls meant scaling huge logs, or if the log was headed in the right direction, running along its wooden trail. Forest highways—these fallen trees are the fastest, easiest way to negotiate rain-drenched, brushy forest types.

In Arizona, where another subspecies, the Mexican spotted owl, dwells, I clambered up and down the deep canyons where the Doug firs and western white pines grow large, and the canopy closes around you like a glove. The heat-sensitive birds seek these cooler areas for roosting and nesting. Here, too, the owls make use of cavities when they can, but will more often use witches'-brooms—large blossomings of small, upright branches created by the parasitic mistletoe. The common thread tying these two sub-species together is habitat: dense, multilayered canopies with a sizable component of large-diameter trees.

The other bird of concern in the dry Southwest, the northern goshawk, frequents ponderosa pine habitat. Though they hunt over a wide variety of forest-structure types, they nest in areas of greater-diameter and denser-than-normal stands, often in draws, swales, or canyons. At the nest stand we would hunker down in the bits of cast-off bark and needles, pressing our backs against a stately pine, and remain as still as possi-ble—knowing the raptors' keen eyes could spot any trace of movement. Branchless trucks rose in groups of three or four; eight or ten, and the early-morning light bounced back—a brilliant, deep orange—from the thick plates of bark. Above the thirty feet of clear trunk, thick crooked limbs elbowed each other, forming a loosely interlocking canopy. We'd watch for the comings and goings of secretive hawks amid these "pumpkins," hoping the birds would choose to raise young another year among these particular orange-barked trees.

In the temperate rain forests of Alaska few conifer species grow: mountain and western hemlock; Alaska yellow cedar; and the granddaddy of them all, Sitka spruce. These straight-grained, towering trees were the chosen masts stepped on ships crossing the seas during the age of sail. They were made into spars for aircraft during both world wars and today are still sought after by master violin makers. Valley bottoms are the best growing areas for Sitka spruce. There the alluvial fans build up; these well-drained soils allow tree roots to remain above the water table, and the trees grow big. Very big. Colossal black trunks veiled with curtains of dark green, spiky-needled branches form vast cathedrals of pure Sitka spruce. Individuals produce wondrous pitch balls that protrude yellow from the dark scaly bark. Our lunch break often began with a search for this pitch that magically and quickly starts warming fires even on the wettest day. Some days when we traversed the upper hillsides, we were lucky enough to find a large spruce complete with deeply hanging branches. We would huddle between its buttressed roots, hang up our rain gear, and steep in the heat of the little fire—steam rising off our fleece clothing as if from a piping-hot cup of tea. Leaving our cozy shelter was loathsome; donning our rain gear to head back into the dripping world outside required all of our gumption.

The flip side of forest work is not so wonderful. I've traversed thousands of public acres on foot, and thousands of acres in Forest Service green trucks, land that was subjected to the 1980s' trickle-down economic logic. The stands where we found spotted owls were often isolated, squeezed between clear-cuts strewn across whole landscapes. Roads built above these cuts to access timber are prone to "puke-outs" in the rainy Northwest. Whole sections of road peel off the steep-sided mountains and pour down over the stumpy ground like hot fudge on an ice cream sundae. Stream buffers designed to filter sediment transported from an intact clear-cut fail to slow the puke-out debris, which ends up choking the streams below. I've witnessed several buffers that are not even adequate to contain "normal" amounts of sediment coming off clear-cuts.

Many ridgetops saddling owl-containing canyons where I worked in Arizona experienced *OR 9 prescriptions*: overstory removal of *all* trees greater than nine inches in diameter at breast height (DBH). This same prescription, or ones like it, degraded the habitat of the northern goshawk throughout much of the Southwest. Critters that lose their preferred habitat don't thrive, thus goshawk numbers dropped, and the bird became a species of concern.

In southeast Alaska hundreds of thousands of holy, grand Sitka spruce trees were transported from their native valleys and turned into pulp—surely one of the greatest sacrilegious acts humans have yet perpetrated against Ma Nature. Sitka spruce trees ended up, in part, as ice cream filler and rayon sport shirts. Entire valleys, miles long, were stripped of their tree cover during four and a half decades of frenzied cutting. Loopholes in environmental regulations, specific to the Tongass, were routinely passed into law at the urging of Alaska's congressional delegation. For years clear-cuts marched right over streams; no buffers were left, thus threatening the loss of phenomenal native salmon runs—the last ones left in the United States.

What's downright heartbreaking about woods work is stump encounter. I first happened upon it in Oregon while working as a tree planting inspector. The best view of the clear-cut being planted was from atop a large stump. Once you're there you can't help but try counting the rings. It's hard to get a good count when the rings are so tight it seems they've been squeezed together with a God-sized vise. The highest I got was somewhere around 550. Think about that age: five hundred and fifty years old. I have stood on five-foot-wide stumps in Oregon; three-foot-wide stumps in Arizona, South Dakota, Montana, and Idaho; two-foot-wide stumps in Wyoming and California. In Alaska I have crawled, crashed, tripped, fallen, and cursed my way through clear-cuts hoping to come across stumps tall enough to see above the higher-than-head, tightly woven wall of brush. My varied contacts with stumps have been far more numerous than a person should have to go through in a dozen lifetimes. And every time I meet another huge stump, I know that there will never be a tree that large allowed to replace the missing elder. Never. Old growth is not a renewable resource in a global economy.

The Yaak came to my attention far earlier than the day I entered the valley. In 1988 large wildfires burned through many parts of Montana. Yellowstone got all the attention, but the Yaak burned, too. At the time, I was working for the forest service in South Dakota, on a helitack crew. The helicopter and three crew members went to Yellowstone; Lance, my coworker, and I stayed behind. We were helitack rookies, and instead of fighting fire that infamous fire-year, we built fence and cleared saplings from firebreaks along ridges in the Black Hills. Eagar to load cargo nets and direct helicopter bucket drops, we hungrily devoured stories sent home by our crew, dreaming of the next year when we'd have enough experience to go work the big fire complexes in far-away places. The next year, and the one after that, then ten more, witnessed slow fire seasons. Sure, there were big fires here and there, but the entire West didn't burn up again until the notorious season of 2000. By that time firefighting was part of my past.

Winter stories told in forest service offices invariably come around, at some point, to fire—about two-hundred-foot-tall roaring walls of flame, or the time that blobs of slurry knocked the hell out of you because so many fires were burning that there wasn't enough time to mix the fire retardant properly. Sometimes tales of the country filter through the adrenaline-laced fire descriptions. So it was that in January 1995, during a lunch break gathered around a woodstove in northern Arizona, I heard of the Yaak. Forest Service employees are pretty hard to impress. Most move around from forest to forest and live in some of the most beautiful, wild places in the West. Summer seasons offer ample opportunity to stalk the most inaccessible and glorious areas, all while getting paid for everything from measuring trees to looking for endangered species.

When Jon, the youngest member of the timber shop, started telling of the fires he'd worked in the Yaak in '88, a kind of smoke drifted across his eyes, like he was still there, squinting against the heat. "The Yaak, now that is some country," he said. "Right up there by Canada. Wild. Big trees, rivers. Remote; it's remote—a place you could go and not come back from. Not want to come back from." And he told of the fires, and of getting dropped off at a helispot and being left there for some time because another fire broke on some other ridge and the helicopter was needed for bucket work there. But he didn't mind; the crew had a good view and the spot fire they were working was easy to control.

Later in 1995, I moved to Montana to go to graduate school. Before I left, Jon often brought up the Yaak, telling me to go up there and take a look around. It took me five years to make it.

And as wild as it is, with its grizzlies, wolves, lynx, and beefy larch trees, the Yaak Valley didn't escape the slaughter. In fact, the Kootenai National Forest—home of the Yaak—was touted as "the working forest." A series of aerial photos meant to brag on this fact was pieced together, but the result was a painful outcry by the public. Clearcuts march across million acres. Within the valley, around 40 percent has been cut. But there's also a lot of unroaded, stumpless ground. Unfortunately, though it contains such charismatic carnivores as grizzly bears, not a single acre of the Yaak Valley is protected as designated wilderness. With the roadless initiative under attack by the Bush administration, and without permanent protection afforded by the Wilderness Act, more granddaddy trees could end up as stumps.

Rick, Elizabeth, and I had begun our quest for the giant larch less than ten miles downstream from the wide-spot-in-the-road town of Yaak. We deserted the truck next to the Yaak River Road and climbed the crumbling road cut. Once above the road, we clambered over and around glacially sculpted rock outcrops. Nearly the entire valley was buried under Pleistocene continental ice sheets that pushed south, softening the outlines of mountains and polishing their exposed roots. Unlike valleys that have been under the influence of valley glaciers, and possess wild-eyed steep side slopes, the Yaak country comes across like a gentle pat on the shoulder. It's maneuverable.

Giving the giant larch a last, fond pat, I pushed off and followed Rick and Elizabeth up the hill. The snow cover was greater on this more westerly slope. In my early-spring optimism, I'd left my boots behind, and I zigged and zagged from one open spot of ground to another. We could just see glimpses of more reddish trunks ahead. The area hadn't burned in decades, and Douglas fir—a species very susceptible to death-by-fire—had moved in, effectively hiding the more scattered well-built larch. A hot fire now would wipe them all out. Even larch or ponderosa, built to resist low flames, could not withstand the kind of crown fire that could easily fly through these denser forests. Old cat-faced larches populated the ridge. At the top it was snowier than not, and my friends took pity on my tennis-shoe-clad feet. As we turned back to the south, I spotted an odd larch.

Most cat-faces are triangular. This one was not. Instead, a sort of oval-shaped wavy frill set the black interior apart from unscorched bark. It was as if the tree had recently given birth and it lay still open. The char did not extend far into the wound, though a space had developed between the bark and trunk near the brow of the oval. Again, I checked for bats, even though I knew it was too early to expect the migrant insectivores. Just a tad of vanilla scent wafted from the bark. My friends were ahead of me, but some oddity kept me lingering. There seemed to be something missing, gone from this black oval space. It was as if the rim were outlining a palpable absence.

As I finally turned to go, I realized that what the space cried out for was Our Lady of Guadalupe—the patroness of the Americas. In a miraculous appearance, she made a promise to a poor Mexican, in 1531, that she would listen to lamentations of the people and remedy their miseries, afflictions, and sorrows. She promised love and compassion, help and protection. As I stared at this blackened space a ghostly three-dimensional mirage shimmered in my imagination. I could picture her there—bright rays

flowering from her body, one outstretched arm beckoning lost souls, the other holding
serpent-demons at bay with a long staff. The sheer weirdness of this vision teased me,
yet I could not shake it.

I was reminded of a time while hitching a short distance while in Baja, when my
friend and I were picked up by a Mexican family on a mission. Three generations had
piled into a beat-up old black Ford pickup and set off as custodians for the various
shrines to Our Lady of Guadalupe on the road to La Paz. As each small shrine
appeared, the patriarch driving would suddenly swerve off the road, and the family
would tumble from the truck. They removed the worn-out candles and scraped off the
built-up wax; arranged the shiny tokens left by other wayfarers and swept out the little
enclosures.

No one had left offerings in the cat-face of the larch—not a penny or a candle or a
scrap of food. Not even an oddly shaped larch cone or a squirrel-chewed branchlet.
Why should they? But then again, why not? Why not covet a miraculous Sylvan Lady
who looks out for unfallen trees, or gives eternal hope to the stumps? The big trees
have abundant reasons to hope for a savior.

CHAPTER 23

NERD SCIENCE AND MIRACLES IN SUPRATROPICAL MONTANA

By Douglas H. Chadwick

THE YAAK IS A FAR, GREEN, LOVELY, LONELY REACH OF THE
Columbia River watershed. Like portions of the Pacific Northwest closer to the ocean,
many of its valley bottoms and lower slopes grow woodlands that naturally culminate
in towering western red cedar and western hemlock interspersed with spruce, fir, cottonwood, alder, and birch. They are temperate rain forests. To be more exact, they are
interior temperate rain forests, a version found in swaths and patches along the
Rockies' cloud-catching western slopes from Montana, Idaho, and northeastern
Washington well north into British Columbia.

Most people assume that the richest ecosystems on land are tropical rain forests.
Nope. Temperate rain forests, which occupy less than a thousandth of the planet's surface, are about as biologically diverse and even more biologically productive. In the case
of old-growth stands, they generate and store one and a half to two times more organic
material per acre than an equatorial jungle does. The corollary is that the Yaak qualifies
as one of the true hot spots of creation. And mind you, that's on the basis of just one
kind of forest in a place that also supports a variety of others.

This sounds more than a little stretched, doesn't it? Especially if you feel that envi-
ros are always cooking up arguments to the effect that their favorite spot in need of
protection is the Serengeti of western Ohio or something. Cool, conifer-spiked mountainsides in the middle of Nowhere, Montana, on a par with the flowerlit Amazon or
New Guinea? But yes. Yes, it is the case. Facts are facts, and those that make the Yaak
ecosystem a rare and globally significant lode of animate wealth are neither too fancy
nor too good to be true. Rather, they are as follows:

Most of the biomass of a tropical woodland exists in its overarching canopy of branches, leaves, and vines, bulging skyward under the strong sun. The amount of living material up in a temperate rain forest's branches is also considerable, once you add the epiphytes such as mosses and liverworts to the many millions of needles that every single mature conifer holds. The older the forest, the greater the number and variety of epiphytes it supports. I don't know a precise figure for the Yaak, but coastal rain forests in the Pacific Northwest harbor hundreds of species of arboreal lichens alone.

Lichens gather some nutrients from passing dust particles and synthesize others. Through a process just shy of alchemy, several common genera fix nitrogen directly from the atmosphere. Rain and melting snow wash these compounds onto the ground, while storms and limb breakage send lichen fragments and sometimes whole mats tumbling earthward. One way or the other, tree-living lichens supply between one-quarter and one-half of the nitrogen that fertilizes the forest floor. Which is where the real action takes place in this woodland—not high overhead, not around you, but underfoot.

A rain forest floor in the Tropics has virtually no humus layer. It wears only a thin skin of litter from the treetops, and that material is rapidly broken down by microbes, scavenged by surface roots snaking around in search of scarce nutrients, then transported right back up into the canopy. Below the litter lies little but lateritic soil, a sort of hardpan clay leached of crucial organic elements by the frequent rainfall. In contrast, the temperate rain forest floor is a deep, absorbent jumble of fallen debris: tree trunks, branches, epiphytes, cones, needles, and leaves. The crisscrossed heap can build several feet high because decay takes place so slowly in temperate climes in comparison to equatorial regions.

This latticework of dropped wood and duff, of cellulose and lignin and softer tissues all basically built from carbohydrates, is home and dinner for countless decomposers. A supposedly dead, fallen tree will be livelier than when it was upright, for it becomes packed with burrowing beetles, millipedes, ants, springtails, mites, nematodes, and so on through levels of decreasing size and increasing numbers to microscopic fungi and bacteria. Together, they soften the downfall decade after decade, crumble it century upon century, and steadily load it with their excretions all the way to compost. The end products are granules of mulch and nutrified soil, the earthly goods in which the forest structure is rooted.

Now we're in the domain that hardly anyone sees and everything depends upon, the component of the system that expands and, I think, finally explodes our basic notions of how living communities operate. Am I overdoing this? Selling a little too hard? Probably. But the really pivotal organisms, the true engines of the temperate rain forest, could use some hype. After all, they are the epitome of obscure science: invisible subterranean fungal threads, universally overlooked except by specialists and stuck with the nerdy-sounding name of mycorrhizae.

Temperate woodlands in general host an astounding assortment of mycorrhizae. Temperate rain forests contain the most recorded anywhere. Whereas a typical equatorial rain forest might have a few hundred species of these filaments, a cedar-hemlock forest will include three thousand to five thousand and possibly more. In fact, the mycorrhizae largely explain how temperate rain forests can rank so high in biodiversity, as measured by the total count of unique life-forms in a given area.

Here again, an old-growth temperate rain forest such as you might walk through in the Yaak resembles an equatorial rain forest turned on its head. While the richness of tropical species hums and flits and unfurls high in the green dome above, the cool forest's variety of life just keeps increasing as you move down through the moldering, woody tangles on the forest floor and continue underground.

It isn't easy writing about what drives an ecosystem. If you're rolling ahead telling grizzly stories or describing the silver path of a trout stream, you can be fairly sure that readers are coming right along with you. Discourse about lichens or mycorrhizal fungi for more than a paragraph, though, and you begin to feel as though you have to start turning around to tell folks, "It's just a little way farther now," or "You're going to love the view around the bend." "Look! I brought chocolate bars and gourmet sandwiches. Let's go on to my favorite place, and I'll pass them around, okay? Hunh? Okay?"

Okay. In terms of the ecological role they play, mycorrhizal fungi far overpower griz and outshine trout. They form symbiotic associations—joint ventures—with the root hairs of most of the trees and other plants, effectively extending their reach by an order of magnitude and extracting water, minerals, and other nutrients from crevices in the soil too minuscule for the plants themselves to reach. In return, the fungi sip a bit of the starch and other energy-laden carbohydrates manufactured by the green vegetation through photosynthesis.

Picture the fungi as gossamer cells with slightly more opaque walls made of chitin, the same tough but flexible material that covers insects' bodies. Now picture the fungal cells elongating into fibers. Go on and imagine highways of those. Starburst networks. Delicate interlacings. In the end, you might be able to at least glimpse the immense fabric underlying the woodlands of the Yaak.

There are miles and miles and hundreds of different kinds of fungal filaments in one small pinch of temperate rain forest soil. The dirt is practically saturated with them. They comprise close to one-third of its volume and more than 90 percent of its biomass. Consequently, you will find more of the forest from the ground (with its fallen debris) on down than from the ground up—more organic material, more life-forms, more of the green plants' metabolic activities, and more of the interactions that sustain the habitat as a whole. People walk through the woods trying to figure out what's going on, looking all around, when the heart of the ecosystem is beating straight under their boot soles. Like the saying suggests, you can't see the forest so long as you keep staring at trees.

Lichens, too, are symbiotic relationships between fungal threads and photosynthetic organisms; in this case, single-celled green algae and cyanobacteria (formerly called blue-green algae). These partnerships produce an impressively long list of chemicals, a number of which show promise for pharmaceutical products. The antiviral properties of usnic acid, from one of the hair lichens commonly called old-man's beard, would be an example. Similarly, mycorrhizae manufacture their own broad spectrum of compounds. Some act as plant growth hormones. Others defend host plants by repelling pathogenic fungi and bacteria that attack roots. Many render organic soil constituents into forms that root hairs can more readily invade and absorb. Still other chemical inventions of the mycorrhizae break down solid minerals for use.

Having a network of symbiotic fungal threads makes a plant more resistant to disease and to other stresses such as drought, injury, natural toxins, and man-made pollutants. By the same token, mycorrhizae allow a plant to thrive in more marginal locations than it otherwise could. Overall, they improve the plant's vigor, promote faster growth, and thereby boost its ability to compete for space and sunlight and to successfully reproduce.

Certain plant species are linked to just one or two varieties of mycorrhizal fungi. Many plants' roots will be tied to dozens or hundreds. The number and type of mycorrhizal species involved often change as the plant matures. And while most mycorrhizae wrap around the outside of root hairs, quite a few invade the roots' cells and merge with the plant internally. The list of relationships goes on and on, because this symbiosis is very old—it may have promoted the colonization of land by plants around four hundred million years ago—and wonderfully complex. To its many qualities, I would add the potential to revolutionize our perception of nature.

Lichens have been described as fungi involved in agriculture, since they more or less farm algae inside protective nests of fibers. Given the predominance of mycorrhizae in temperate rain forest soils, you could almost view trees in the same way as the symbiotic algae, insofar as even the grandest cedars or firs amount to chlorophyll-containing plants within a network of fungal threads.

Not only do mycorrhizae dramatically expand the reach of each plant's root system into the soil, but they also run between one plant and another, connecting them underground. They do this between individual trees of the same species, and they do it between trees of different kinds, between trees and shrubs, between shrubs and herbs, herbs and grasses, and so on.

As a result, fungal webs can tap the resources of one plant and selectively funnel some of them to another plant. They can jump-start a cedar sapling by linking it to a thousand-year-old titan, or tie a spruce rooted in an impoverished site to the nitrogen-fixing roots of an alder bush. They bind the flora of a woodland together in more ways than we've ever conceived of. In so doing, they challenge our assumptions about the workings of a forest and the way we define organisms. You tell me: Exactly where in this myriad of cross-stitched symbionts does the individual life-form leave off and the community begin? It is like trying to separate strands of yarn or drops of dye or one design element from the sweater they constitute.

As a temperate rain forest ages, both the biomass and the biodiversity of the community's subterranean portion increase. So does the intricacy of the underground relationships. All achieve their greatest expression in undisturbed old growth. Conversely, the number and variety of mycorrhizal fungi and their activities markedly decrease in logged sites, where most or all of the canopy is removed and the ground is compressed, scraped, and exposed to the drying effects of wind and sun. We all know how little emphasis there has been on sustaining ancient forests in the Yaak. I think it is safe to say that their underground dynamics have received even less attention, if any at all, even though they are in many ways the ultimate source of forest riches. Managers have hardly budged beyond the old style of focusing upon large species, mainly as commodities, one at a time.

Yet trout require mature forests to cool the waters in which they grow and to filter the runoff sediments that flow toward their spawning beds. Amphibians, invertebrates, mosses, liverworts, and molds need the moisture stored in spongy, rotting logs and in the boles of massive trees and their foliage; it represents millions of gallons per acre that can be slowly released and held as humidity under the dense canopy through dry times. Wintering deer, elk, moose, and grouse prosper where old-growth branches intercept so much snow that they leave haloes of bare ground as shelter and easy traveling routes through the lean days of winter.

I could call up a hundred more examples to show why an ancient rain forest or other mature forest in the Yaak is far more than the sum of its obvious parts—why it is anything but a mere collection of plants and animals. The underground fungal web-work that binds the plants to intimate reaches of the soil and to one another remains perhaps the most potent illustration. Those monumental conifers rising far above our heads are merely the visible part of a superorganism, a meta-life-form powered by an underground jungle as mysterious and exotic in its own way as any tropical realm. It's all in how and where you choose to look.

The more I contemplate the Yaak, the easier it becomes to envision the interior temperate rain forest as a continual flow of energy and nutrients back and forth, up tree trunks in solar-powered pipelines of sap and back down in the form of falling leaves and wood; scurrying from branch to branch in the form of flying squirrels that eat truffles—the fruiting bodies of mycorrhizae—and other mushrooms and distribute new fungal spores in the soil through their droppings; walking on long, lithe bones in the form of deer foraging for nitrogen-rich lichens fallen off tree branches; piercing layers of dirt and duff and crusted snow with spears of tender new tissues in the form of sprouting trilliums; hatching from rows of eggs in the form of wood-boring ambrosia beetles that cultivate fungi and carry seedstocks of spores with them from tree to tree in special pouches on their exoskeletons of chitin.

There at last, within and among and under the trees, is a Yaak forest. Although someone else might call it a bottomland cedar-hemlock stand or maybe prime pileated woodpecker and pine marten habitat, we can see the place more clearly now as an inextricably united, unimaginably elaborate system of circulating vitality. Nature. It may be expressed in the multitude of shapes and sizes that we identify as separate plants and animals in different stages of growth—the members of the wildlife community. Yet each is a process enmeshed in myriad other processes. Only some of those are visible. All are at once ancient and eternally renewed. All are a source of boundless discovery leading forward and backward in time. And that—the forest in its largest, most miraculous sense—is the forest we want in our lives.

CHAPTER 24

INTO THE YAAK

By Robert Michael Pyle

YAAK. THE NAME ALWAYS AWAKENED IN ME AN IMAGE OF A
high, practically barren landscape, I suppose because of its aural associations with the
woolly butter-bearers of Tibet. Of course I knew better. I knew this valley and its peaks
lay above the old High Line, route of native exchange, fur traders, and the Great
Northern's *Empire Builder*. My own work with butterflies had taken me into the Pend
Oreille country of northeastern Washington, not far geographically (or ecologically)
from Yaak. And I knew from Rick Bass's eloquent stories and dogged entreaties that
there was timber here, big timber for inland forests, though much had been felled; and
diverse wildland still without roads. And truth be told, I knew that one thing the Yaak
was *not* was barren—that life teemed here, in abundance and variety unmatched by
many western valleys.

Of yak butter tea there may be none, nor windswept pebbled plateaus nearly four
miles high. Of the stuff of western myth, life, and logic, there is plenty. I knew these
things. But when I finally went to see for myself, I was unprepared for what I found.

My excuse for finally doing it was The Orion Society's Forgotten Language Tour. In
the hope of showing the breadth of care for the place while getting to know it better
ourselves, several writers from around the country converged to share poems and prose,
butterflies and Bigfoot, questions and ideas with the people of the Yaak. We came also
to be informed and instructed by the wild voices of the valley's high surrounds, and to
give something in return if we could.

On the last day of May 1997, I awoke to the soft, sifting sound of snipe winnow-
ing over the wet meadows outside the lodge. It was only seven, and several of us had
sat up until two after the previous night's reading in the Yaak Community Center and

the subsequent pool and beers in Yaak's tavern, talking over the things that tear apart people who should be natural allies. So I felt I should turn over and sleep another hour before this packed day began. But I was awake, and I hadn't yet had a morning's walk across the river, as I'd promised myself five days before, and this was our last night at Tamarack Lodge. So I rose and crept out the side door into the gray and dewy day. I noticed a small log cabin beside the stream, and walked down to it. Part of the roof was gone, and you could climb a ladder to a loft and sit in it with your head out, as if in a wildlife blind. I lurked there for a while, watching the high water tug the long grasses and willow wands, and thinking over the tour so far.

Monday we'd hiked a wild creek trail full of windthrow with a film crew, often repeating our steps for additional takes, laughing at one another being movie stars. That afternoon we rode horseback, and when my palomino Blondie galloped, I laughed again, and didn't get as alarmed as last time. Then Gary Nabhan had insisted on a dawn Forgotten Language Ride on Navajo ponies in Monument Valley, and when I yelled "Whoa" to my galloping pony it obeyed abruptly, almost pitching me onto hard red rock. This trail was probably no less dangerous but, being grassy, the landing looked soft.

Tuesday we visited with Prescott College kids on a camping-and-writing field trip to the Yaak; then with the children of the valley and their teachers, first through eighth grades, in the log, two-room Yaak School. Placing blue butterflies on small upturned noses, sharing tales of Bigfoot, hearing their astonishing stories, essays, and haikus, I wondered how any larger school could ever be a better place to be. Little Tad, self-assured Haakon, and an eighth-grade girl reading a story of abuse all bound us in spell.

That night's reading took place in an old movie house with a tin false front in the nearby town of Troy. The audience included some timber and forest service folk, and our readings looked for common ground. I opened with "Countrymen and Naturalists" from *Wintergreen*, in which I tried to come to terms with the differing but related reasons we have for dwelling near to the heart of things. Richard Nelson and Janisse Ray read stunning narratives of place: Nels, the powerful conclusion of his new *Heart and Blood: Living with Deer in America*, and Janisse her strong poems out of Georgia's longleaf pinelands. Afterward, among the sounds of pool and poker, with pitchers of Guinness and Rainier, we'd shared converse in the Club Bar with loggers, latter-day settlers, and a jet-boat skipper who'd worked on Meryl Streep's *River Wild*, as irony took a night off.

The next day we tried to fly the Yaak's diminishing roadless areas with Project Lighthawk. The film crew made it up, but when Janisse and I went aloft for our flight, the little Skyhawk had to turn right around as the weather closed in, and a good thing. Even so, we still had no idea what the weather had in mind for later.

Instead, we all attended a meeting of the multi-interest Forest Congress in Libby, with a retired timber executive, a massive Indian short-logger with a great smile, and a logger's wife who had grown tired of everybody being mad at everyone else. It reminded me a little of the Willapa Alliance's efforts to sit everyone down together back in my area at the mouth of the Columbia River, except that the options in the woods are still much greater in Yaak. Its mountains are not yet all logged off like the Willapa Hills of southwest Washington. And that was much of the point of being here. The longtime participants in this ongoing conversation accepted our band of scribblers politely, if with obvious curiosity. Then to the local mill, such as it remains, to see how pickup loads of short-logs and value-added specialty products are taking over from the vanishing union jobs and big sticks.

Wednesday night, in a pretty Methodist church in Libby, I sat out while Janisse knocked our collective socks off with her essay of growing up in a Georgia junkyard; Rick Bass told his own scary, amazing, and moving grizzly mom-and-cubs story from the Yaak; and Nels read the stilling encounter when he actually touched the doe's nose in *The Island Within*. I was struck that each piece turned on a particular encounter with a specific organism (grizzly bear, pitcher plant, mule deer). The modest audience was deeply appreciative. Each person there, I suspect, could have shared an equally intimate story.

Thursday, we went afield with the Troy high school kids of the writing club known as Railroad Ties, who were our shadows and alter egos for the whole visit, making our introductions in the evening. Nels and I took a few to the West Fork Falls, where we spoke a little and set them loose to write words of personal perception. I was amazed and thrilled to see Willow and Brook using their own plant press to learn more about local wildflowers; and to hear the general knowledge and curiosity of local natural history among the whole group. These kids were cheerfully anarchic and wholly good-natured, and wrote some remarkable words of close encounter, sensory stimulus, and thoughtful response. I took on more hope from them than I'd felt in a long time.

Rick and Elizabeth Bass's home lies out a long gravel road, beside a marsh, under high peaks: a comfortable place, with no visible power or phone lines, only solar panels. Between them, they have made two sweet little daughters, who greeted us as Elizabeth laid out a comely feast. Rick showed Nels and me the cabin that he had moved next to the marsh and rebuilt, where he writes by hand. The winter wind gets in between the caulking. His "to be filed" pile, a great overflowing sediment in a lobster trap, made me feel a little better about my own. Wishing he could be a hermit here with his family, Rick has written and elicited thousands of letters trying to protect the last roadless areas in the Yaak, besides a dozen-plus books of fiction and essay.

That night, in the log-built Yaak Community Center, Terry Tempest Williams joined us along with Jeannie Kim of the Lannan Foundation, a supporter of the Forgotten Language Tour. I shared travels in the company of migrating monarch but-terflies, Janisse "surrendered to Montana" at Wildhorse Island, Richard told wonderful Inupik riddles, and Terry gave an intense and moving reading from *Refuge*. Later came shooting pool with the film crew and drinking Slow Elk Ale with the friendly folks at the Dirty Shame Saloon, and then, all too soon, this sleepy morning.

I left the cabin loft and strode off across a bridge toward the far woods, where our lodge host had told us he'd seen great gray owls more than once. I stopped to feed pulls of long grass to a pair of big white draft horses. Some of the other horses came over, too, but not Blondie, probably afraid I'd climb up on her back again. Birds were vocal but high and largely invisible in the aspens and pines and larch under the mountain. The great grays did not show. Ravens hooted, then gronked, and audibly flapped close overhead. Nels's beloved whitetails stirred and trotted off, flicking their vast cottony banners back and forth as they bounced. I was glad I'd gotten up, though sightings were subtle. The wet clean air purged the saloon-lungs, and the great looming Yaak put my personal concerns in their rightful little cubbyhole. On the way back, a pair of killdeer and a couple of spotted sandpipers screamed at me and finally skittered off the path, as I lay a sheaf of timothy inside the fence for the Percherons.

In the handsome lodge's dining room all were there for breakfast, a pack of humans arrayed beneath the heads and hides of a creationful of large mammals, birds, and fish. Just as well the breakfast was hearty, because a hell of a day was about to unfold—one of the most bizarre and memorable I've known in a long time.

First, we each had to be talking heads for Haydn, Mark, and Andy, the camera crew filming a short prior to making a full-length film on Orion and the tour for PBS and other uses that might carry our themes to lovers of land and literature far beyond where our barnstorming jaunts can take us. Then we were off from Tamarack, with hugs from the maids and kitchen crew, who were also the moms of the kids we'd been with. The day's plan called for a float trip on the runoff-swollen Yaak River and a visit to an old-growth cedar forest before heading south for our final reading. We met up with several of the Railroad Ties lads and lasses at a tavern and put in beside the Yaak River. Three rubber rafts, an inflatable kayak, a rowboat, and Rick's open canoe waited to take us down the river. Only one of the kids, Cliff, was an experienced rafter, and he had checked out the high-water stretch a few days before. The rest of the show seemed a mite loose to me. On my thirtieth birthday, I had drunk too much Coors with my big brother Tom, and we'd tubed the Chutes on the North Fork of the South Platte in Colorado's pink-granite Front Range—a fairly stupid thing to do. This time, not long before my fiftieth, I declined my counterpart Adam's kind offer to take me in the row-boat in favor of a secure place in the bow of Cliff's raft. I guess that's aging for you.

The day was the brightest we'd had, sunny and hot, and we all hoped to get a little wet. We floated gently but swiftly through a mile or so of broad, straightish river, then heard the rush and tumble of rapids ahead. Our raft went first, with Jeannie Kim and me in the bow, and then Janisse in the stern, after Cliff insisted she leave the canoe and join us for the rapids. We bounced through and got a little wet as the nose dived into troughs and bounced back onto the lips of standing waves. Fun, fresh, nothing scary. Everyone got through okay. The second rapids, a little farther on, were rougher and we got a little wetter. All three rafts came through, then held position so we could watch the others. Nels shot through adroitly in the kayak, as much at home in cold water as an Alaskan surfer ought to be. Then came Rick and Laurie in the canoe. They took the course well, but a rock or a big riffle threw them sideways and over they went. Rick shot out and swam to shore. Laurie stuck with the canoe. When he got to us, his face shocked with the cold but unafraid (and truth to tell, having a ball), he shoved his paddle on board, clambered up himself, and then he and Janisse wrestled the canoe onto our stern: great work! Nothing lost but the other paddle.

Into shore for a lunch stop, a challenge for all to land against the current. We put Laurie, Janisse, and the canoe ashore first, where Rick was, then dropped on down to where the others had taken out. Soon we looked up to see the canoe crew coming down-current—in the water again! Attempting to load, they had upset in the fast flow. All dragged ashore, but the canoe was caught under willow roots. We had to rope it, push it loose, then claim it back from the current with the rope wrapped around a stump.

At last all were ashore and resting with lunch in the sun, or so we thought. Petite Jeannie Kim had never done anything like this; exhilarated, she was poking among the fern, moss, and lichen gardens growing out of blackened stumps. Then someone noticed the rowboat was absent. "Shit!" said Cliff. We were getting worried, since in or out they should have come past, when all of a sudden the rowboat appeared around the bend, riding very low, with Adam and Jason yelling, ecstatic. They had been swamped in both rapids, and nearly gone under but for wild bailing. Witnessing their exuberance, at first I was sorry that I had turned down the invitation—their wild ride would have been more fun than my mild one, if not quite the Chutes. But then I realized that I had at least eighty pounds on Jason, and would surely have sunk it. We might have lost the rowboat altogether, and had a job getting to shore at all, with the big Yaak waterfall not far below.

But now I asked to switch with Jason. So for the rest of the journey, I rode up at the front of the regatta in the stern of the rowboat. There wasn't much more action, a riffle and splash or two, in and out of a few waves, but it was a fine way to ride a wild river. Well, fairly wild; as we got farther down toward U.S. 2, there were more houses. Finally, beyond a bridge, came the take-out. Fighting the current, Cliff nearly missed it, and whether another landing would have presented itself before Yaak Falls is an open question. Laurie was scintillated by his dip, and all were glad to be out there and alive. Little did we know that the river's gentle threat would soon be bettered.

Drying off, we laughed and relived the damp action. Silvery blues, anglewings, and mourning cloaks came to our salty drippings in the dust. Once the craft were loaded, we drove to a place in the forest where we were to meet the Railroad Ties—Cliff, Adam, Ed, Sarah, Jason—who were to lead our hike into the old growth. Waiting for them, we noticed the sky quickly cloud and heard thunder not far off. Time was a little short, and we'd just decided to give the hike a miss when the kids arrived in their trucks from the other direction. Just then, a great circular wind came up and began whipping the trees all around us like fern fronds in a gale. In mass confusion, people dived for their cars,

No one could turn around or get out of the traffic jam at the forest junction. I was with Jeannie in her rented sedan. She yelped, "Look! They're falling!" just in time for me to look right and see a whole row of Douglas firs go down like dominoes. Then they began crashing down all around us. At last we got the automobiles sorted out and started to drive toward the highway. But soon the lead vehicle stopped, blocked by a fallen Doug fir. Just then, for some reason, Laurie moved the Orion van in which he and Marion were sheltered—moments before a foot-thick fir crashed to earth right where they had just been. It struck between their van and Richard and Nita's truck, missing them all by a short yard.

Now we had no choice but to wait it out, sitting ducks, not much more protected in the vehicles than if we had gotten out and run. The wind whipped high and all around, like a tornado. Then heavy hail commenced to fall. It wasn't Thunder Tree hail—the grapefruit-sized iceballs that broke cattle's backs and almost got my brother and me in a devastating Colorado hailstorm in 1954. This Yaak hail was "only" cherry-sized, but it was heavier and more violent than any storm I'd seen in the forty-three years since Tom and I dived into the hollow tree that saved our lives.

Jeannie and I, hunkering in the cave of her car, just looked at one another. "Should we be scared?" she asked. "I think so," I said. Not only had she never been on a float trip, she had never been in a hailstorm, and certainly not a tornado. The hammering was deafening on the metal roof. I thought of putting our seats back all the way to get away from the roof, but if a tree had hit us, it would have just killed us supine instead of upright. We said nothing else, mesmerized by the drumming and the curtain of falling and bouncing ice. Ed was running between the cars, trying to see if everyone was okay. Janisse jumped out, unclear as to what was going on. And then it was over, and we all emerged, slow and shaky except for Nels. Thrilled at the display of raw power, he ran back and forth with an unbridled glee he was neither willing nor able to quell for hours.

I too was excited by the force of the storm, but I was also sobered by the recognition of how close we had come to disaster. Sure, one of the flights in the little Cessna could have crashed (the first flight was half an hour late returning); one of us could have been tossed off our horse on the mountain path where we shouldn't have been running, and someone could have been drowned earlier today. But those were all modest risks that came out just fine. Here, minutes ago, we had been surrounded by falling trees that really could have killed any of us at any minute. It was a genuine close call, and it dimmed my pleasure in the exuberance of the weather. Another sign of turning fifty?

The next thing I saw was Rick Bass walking past holding a little George Washington hatchet. He also had a hacksaw, and that's the best we could do. No one seemed to think of the cameras until I mentioned to Hayden that they were missing some great footage. So they got out the gear, and caught the chaos, the larch and fir foliage covering the road, the penned-in cars. They couldn't record the thick sweet smell of all the thrashed evergreens that filled the air. But they did get Rick, sawing away at a thick fir with his hacksaw, and interviewed him as he did so—"That's what these so-called shelterwood selective cuts are good for," he told the gray woolly mouse of a mike, "they lay 'em wide open for the first breath of air to knock 'em down." Someone else commented on the oxymoron of *shelterwood:* "It sure as hell wasn't much shelter for us!" And to think that if the kids had come earlier, we'd have been hiking through it.

By yanking on the weakened, partly cut logs with a canvas strap hooked to his truck, Ed was able to break enough off that we could get all the vehicles out to the highway. Once we reached U.S. 2, we saw cars and trucks stopped in both directions, and trees down everywhere. But the loggers going at the sticks with their McCulloughs made quicker work of it than the nature writers with their hacksaw and hatchet. One of them said, "Just goes to show! You need to cut 'em *all* to the ground, then this wouldn't happen." Hayden tried to get him to say it on camera, but he declined, laughing.

Once traffic moved again, we passed big yellow-bellied ponderosa pines snapped off midmast, and structures smashed by downed trees. No one seemed to have been hurt. Nine tornadoes had touched down in the region that day. It was unclear whether we would even make it to the Bull River Lodge, south of Libby on 56, where we were to stay, or to the historic Bull River Ranger Station where we were scheduled to give our last reading of the tour by campfire. Even if we did, we doubted many people would come after such a storm.

We got to the lodge after all, in the rain, and found our beds—too few for our numbers, with the women sharing beds and me out in the hallway on a divan. This place too was beautiful, with high vaulted ceilings and a huge fireplace, and it held at least as many dead animals as Tamarack. As there, a great big puma perched in perpetuity over the end of the room. But the folks here had shifted from big-game guiding to harvesting botanicals and herbs for folk remedies and yew tips for Taxol. Terry had read to us about Taxol and cancer just the night before.

In the powerless aftermath of the storm, the reading was shifted from the ranger station to the lodge, and people began showing up even as we were sitting for dinner. Inez, the innkeeper, managed to feed us splendidly despite the absence of electricity and the water out, too. By the time the meal was finishing, dozens of people were milling all around the great hall. We were dining on display. And then the reading began. In the absence of lights, candles and kerosene lanterns glimmered all around. A small galaxy of candles placed on the reader's table, with one up high on a tripod, illuminated the page. The rain pelted the outside walls, but rufous and calliope hummingbirds still attacked the petunia baskets and feeders with crazed shrieks and whizzing, and would do so until hard darkness, an irreverent and ecstatic Greek chorus to our main stage.

Rick opened with an essay on the rural mail and a short story about a bullied kid, "Swamp Boy," in which he played both sides. Then my shadow-rower Adam introduced me, saying I was brave for going in the rowboat, but omitting that I only did so after the dangerous part was past. I read a poem called "Life and Death in Yellowstone," for the bison that died outside the park that spring. By then the thin daylight was gone and the setting, all candles and firelight, was perfect for scary Bigfoot stories.

When Terry read, I could really look around. There were some 150 people present, when we'd expected maybe 30 or 40 *without* a tornado. They had come from three states and many counties, and they packed the room and the balcony. Those faces! Their eyes were illuminated by candlelight, looking out between every second or third space in the railings up in the gallery where I would later sleep. It was fair to say there'd never been such a night in the Cabinet Mountains. Many had no doubt come to hear Terry, and she did not disappoint. She read an essay I love about her family's construction business and threatened desert tortoises; and one about her breech-birthed, "special" uncle, who arrived feetfirst. "The Mormons say you should be buried with your feet to the East," Terry said, "to greet the second coming. I want to face West."

Then it was over. Marion Gilliam, Orion's chairman and publisher, gracefully called the tour to a close, thanking the powers that be for the storm that brought us safely there and caused the need for candles. With kind comments about an evening likely to be remembered for some time, all the folks drifted away. At last the Railroad Ties departed for Troy, without a horse, but with a life-sized stuffed lion they'd found by a Dumpster after the storm. Liberated, christened Cedric, and bungeed to the top of Sarah's car, the lion led the charge into the damp and worn-out night.

Left to ourselves, sprawled in green leather armchairs before the dwindling fire, we were a little numbed by the whole thing. The last of the beer and wine appeared, then a phenomenal German chocolate cake that Inez had made for us, then another one after the first quickly disappeared. Haydn produced a blues harp and we sang, cracking up on most attempts, but not half as much as Terry cracked up over the Mormon Sunday school songs she essayed for us, including a march supposed to be accompanied by an Indian tom-tom. Finally Laurie, throat sore from the snow-fed river, said, "Hell, let's just sing 'Amazing Grace' and be done with it." Haydn and Nita conjured a remarkable harmony, bested only by Nita, Janisse, and Terry's rendition of a slow and slinky Motown groove, girl-group dance moves and all, to "Scotland the Brave" on my harmonica.

Reluctant to finish a day and a week that could truly be called remarkable, but all pooped out, all language forgotten, maybe for good, we dispersed to our rooms and hallways in the glow from one lantern and the embers of the great fireplace. I couldn't sleep for a while, as motion pictures and stills, in bark black, foam white, and all the colors of the undiluted wild, jostled and grappled over which would become the new image in my mind whenever I heard that strange and magic name like a syllable of raven's, like the chock of ax on a cabin-log, like the laughter of parnassians over the chink of boulders on the high and yet-wild slopes: Yaak.

And then, guarded by four pronghorn antelope and a sage grouse mounted over my couch, I slept about as hard as I know how.

POSTSCRIPT

I have been back to Yaak once since the time of the tornado. It was a hot and sunny pair of days last summer, one in from Glacier, one out to the Pend Oreille. Thea and I camped beside Pete Creek, beneath nighthawks. In the morning we explored the meadows beside the Yaak River for butterflies. The buttery groundsels were thronged with crescents and fritillaries, the wet meadows overflown by glittering blues and gilded skippers. In forty years of tracking butterflies around the West, I have very seldom stepped into a morning's habitat of such diversity and abundance. And as I consider that fact from the cool distance of summer's end, I see no reason to be surprised. Everything I know about the Yaak concurs in the basic condition of its phenomenal richness. As I left the Yaak for the second time, I felt that I finally understood how it must be seen to be treated as it deserves: as wholly remarkable, as completely protected, and as one of the utmost jewels of our entire forest patrimony.

CHAPTER 25

YAAK MAGIC

By Jim Fergus

MY FRIEND GUY DE LA VALDENE AND I HAD BEEN HUNTING chukars on the breaks of the Grande Ronde river in eastern Washington State late one September. It was country of enormous grandeur, of vast benches above winding canyons, shadowed hills rising to mountains, deep canyons falling away forever to the river below. Where we hunted up high, it was the kind of big, open country that gave you a kind of pit-in-the-stomach thrill, nearly a queasiness.

We each had our own vehicle and had driven in tandem straight from Washington, where it was hot, dry, and bright, to the Yaak Valley, which has the feel of a Pacific Northwest rain forest, and where a cold front with rain and fog and low dark clouds had settled in over the lush, dark-timbered woods. It was the first time either of us had ever been to the Yaak. We had come to visit and bird hunt with our friend Rick Bass.

Sometimes going too quickly from one country to another can be unsettling, as if the afterimage of the country you have just left behind is still burned upon your mind's eye, and the new country seems somehow alien and inhospitable or, worse, malevolent. At the same time, for those of us sensitive to country (and most hunters are), certain topographies and climates can serve as triggers to the imagination and memory. In this manner a deep sense of dread had fallen upon Guy as pervasively as the black storm clouds that hung over the woods of the Yaak. "I don't think I can stay here long," he said to me shortly after we arrived. "I don't like this country; it makes me uneasy."

The mountains hereabouts did seem a bit close, tightly set, and heavily forested (that is, where they haven't been scalped on top in vast bleak tracks of clear-cuts). In fact, it was hard to see why they even called this a valley, and I must say I, too, found it a bit claustrophobic at first, especially with the low dark sky closing in from above.

"It is a little gloomy," I admitted. "But you can't leave yet. We have a date to hunt with Bass tomorrow."

"I'll see how I feel in the morning," Guy said. "But I may have to get out of these woods."

"Maybe it'll clear up tomorrow," I said. "A little sun could make all the difference in the world."

But it didn't clear up, and the next morning's late dawn was even gloomier—colder and darker and still drizzling steadily. Guy was staying in a bed-and-breakfast on the edge of the tiny town of Yaak, little more than a crossroads, with a couple of bars on either side of the street and a mercantile, and I was camped out back in the Airstream. First thing that morning he knocked on my door. "I'm leaving," he announced. "Are you coming?"

"Gee," I said, indecisively, "I don't know, I came all the way up here to hunt with Bass. I made a date with him. I just don't feel that I should leave."

"I understand," Guy said. "But I really have to go."

It is said that the Yaak is a place of magic, and where there is magic must also lurk its evil twin, black magic, and perhaps this is what had so affected de la Valdene; I had never seen him spooked like that, almost frightened, and he is one of the bravest men I know.

"I hate for us to split up now," I said. "It's only for one day. We can leave together tomorrow."

"I'm sorry, I have to leave right now," Guy said. "This country reminds me too much of Switzerland." He hesitated, and added almost apologetically, "It looks just like the place in Switzerland where my father died."

I understood; certain country holds our ghosts, and sometimes we just have to get in the car and drive a couple of hundred miles to escape them. So Guy and I said our good-byes; I was sorry to see him go, and right after he left, as the black clouds descended even farther upon the forest and the rain ticked steadily against the aluminum shell of the Airstream, I wished that I had gone with him; I envied him the big open plains of eastern Montana toward which he was headed. I turned the furnace up higher, poured another cup of coffee, and went to scribbling in my notebook.

The rain had abated to a misting drizzle by the time Rick Bass met me at the Airstream for our hunt. Of course, the Yaak is Bass's home country, and just as it filled Guy with apprehension and dread, so it fills him with wonder, reverence, and joy. Indeed, the same sense of mystery and import that is palpable in the damp, dark woods and mountains of the Yaak seems to inhabit Bass's fiction, where magical occurrences become commonplace, where characters, both human and animal are capable of feats of strength and endurance possible only in an alternate world, the "other world behind this one" as the Cheyenne called it.

Bass had his German shorthair, Colter, with him, and they piled out of a small, incredibly littered truck, from the bed of which Rick extricated a beat-up shotgun from beneath his chain saw. We all loaded up in my Suburban and headed for the first covert of the day.

There was still plenty of green in the woods, but the aspens and cottonwoods were beginning to turn various shades of yellow, orange, and red. The snowberries were white upon the bush, and the berries on the kinnikinnick a deep red. There were larch trees and alder, fir and spruce, a diversity and lushness to which I was unaccustomed. And there was a strange stillness about the forest, the earth lying somber under its shroud of clouds.

I liked hunting with Bass right off. He's a walker, a careful, attentive hunter, who seems to absorb the land as he moves through it. And he knows his country. Sweetz and Colter worked well together, too, Colter ranging a good deal farther out, Sweetz working close. "Do you ever get lost in the woods around here," I asked Rick, because it struck me immediately that this was the kind of country in which I'd have been instantly and hopelessly lost if hunting alone. To be honest, I'm a little afraid of the deep woods.

"Oh sure," he said. He paused, and seemed to consider the question. "Sometimes I get so lost," he added, "that I don't know where I am." I had to think about this for a moment, and then I knew just what he meant: There's lost, and then there's *lost*.

Just then Sweetz got birdy—nose to the ground, snuffling, tail wagging stiffly—and suddenly she put up a ruffed grouse. I mounted my gun and fired. The grouse vanished in the woods. "I sure shot hell out of that tree," I said of the tree that stood between me and the unscathed bird. I rarely hit anything when hunting in the forest, either. We hunted on. Every now and then I would look over at Bass as we walked through a covert. He was always smiling to himself, as if in pure conscious joy at being alive at this moment, to be right here in the country that he loved so, doing what we were doing, a smile of pleasure and gratitude that couldn't help but make the visitor feel hopeful about things.

We hunted on, working out each of Bass's coverts, and then going back to the vehicle to drive through the woods to another. Sweetz and Colter were hunting well, and put up several birds for us. At one point Sweetz flushed a spruce grouse, but it only fluttered up to the nearest tree branch, allowing me to walk over and look it right in its red eye. Spruce grouse was one of the handful of American upland gamebird species that Sweetz had not retrieved in her career, but of course, we don't shoot birds out of trees. We hunted on.

The drizzling rain continued. "Look at that," Bass said of a bank of thick clouds drifting over the mountainside. "It's so beautiful." It was as if he was seeing the country for the first time, seeing it through the eyes of his visitor. He told me a story about a mountain lion chasing his dog, his own sense of fear, anger, and exhilaration in witnessing the scene. He told me bear stories and wolf stories. This is clearly a man who spends a great deal of his time in the woods, and pays attention.

It's an odd thing, but I remember how well Sweetz and Colter hunted that day, I remember very clearly the grouse they pointed or flushed as the case might be, and even how each bird flew through the woods. I remember the country and the weather, and sitting in the steamy Suburban in between coverts as the rain fell outside and filling our coffee cups from a thermos. "Doesn't that smell great?" Bass said. I remember that my other dog, a part dachsund/part terrier mix named Betty, who is Sweetz's and my frequent traveling companion, and Colter struck up a little innocent flirtation in the back of the Suburban. All this I remember, but I can't remember if we killed any birds. I don't think we did, but I just don't remember exactly. I do remember that we had one of those rare perfect days, when the dogs were brilliant, and the country revealed just enough of itself to keep things interesting.

And I remember this: We were driving out on the highway after hunting our final covert of the day, headed for the tavern in town (both taverns, actually, as Bass can hardly patronize one without also crossing the street to have a beer in the other). We were driving through the forest and I turned to say something to him, and in that split second before I turned my eyes back to the road, a deer had materialized directly in front of the vehicle. There it stood, a doe, ears pricked forward, staring at us in frozen silhouette as we bore down upon it. I slammed on the brakes and the Suburban came to an immediate halt. I don't mean that it screeched to a stop, I mean, it just *stopped,* right there, dead in its tracks. The doe bounded across the road and disappeared into the forest.

"I was certain that you were going to hit that deer," Bass said. "I've never seen a truck come to a stop like that."

"I just had the brake pads replaced," I answered lamely.

But we both knew that new brake pads had nothing to do with it. It was a simple case of Yaak magic.

CHAPTER 26

WHY WE NEED THE YAAK WILD

By Doug Peacock

SOMETIMES I DREAM ABOUT BEARS, OCCASIONALLY I HAVE A dream for them. The bear of my dreams, the recurring one, is white, though not a polar bear. The dream-bear comes to me most often in winter, when real grizzlies are sleeping—a convenient time for me to work out my fear of bears before I bump into real ones in the spring. The white grizzlies are alternately mesmerizing and horrifying and I spend much of my dream time breathless from fear, trying to scurry up trees or onto the roofs of cabins just out of reach of the marauding beasts.

It seems odd that the fearsome white bears of my dreams often threaten me on the fringes of civilization, in cabins, outbuildings—human structures oddly out of place out in the wilderness. I try not to make too much of these coincidences; this fearsome mixing of wild beasts and human cultural edifices seems a natural and metaphorical confusion (from which my unconscious is not immune) of an urban people who blindly fear what they no longer know—the beasts of the night beyond the concrete barriers. Yet that's how we live these days and the last grizzlies, as in the dream, must now stumble about on the outskirts of our settlements to make a bear living.

The dream I have for the bear is the opposite; it concerns a homeland big enough for them to survive in. This means wild country; the wilder the better. Roadless wilderness is best. And I want this for the grizzlies south of Canada. It's not that bears in Canada or Alaska aren't important or not having problems of their own. They are. It's just that I've always considered the lower forty-eight the real battleground; whatever we do down here we'll probably do up there, except faster. We need to secure a place for the griz in the contiguous states. If I were a real workingman, I'd consider this my lifelong job. It's my notion of patriotism.

I now live less than a mile from the Absaroka Wilderness north of Yellowstone National Park. For the better part of two decades, I tracked grizzlies from April to November in Montana or Wyoming, migrating to the desert during the winter, trying to raise and support a family until it all fell apart a few years ago and I moved into an abandoned whorehouse back here on the edge of what is now called the Yellowstone Grizzly Bear Ecosystem.

The nut of my dream for the grizzly would be to create a safe linkage—a series of wild cores connected by bear-safe corridors—that would allow a bear in my backyard to wander up to the Canadian border and shake hands with a grizzly living in the Yaak Valley.

If we could accomplish this linkage—a simple, though not necessarily easy task—we would more or less ensure the longtime survival of grizzlies in the lower states. At present, their future is far from secure.

The reason the future looks dim for grizzly survival south of Canada is that its six ecosystems are isolated; an ancient predator called man has carved all remaining grizzly habitats into shrinking, fragmented ecosystems. The Yellowstone grizzly, for instance, is marooned on an island ecosystem, surrounded by a sea of human activity.

Modern conservation biology tells us that the Yellowstone ecosystem can never, by itself, support a self-sustaining population of grizzly bears. Because immigration is hindered by isolation, large, rare carnivores survive poorly on islands; extinction is common, especially on smaller islands, and the greater Yellowstone area loses bear habitat every day. Conservation biologists today generally agree that the best way of ensuring the long-term survival of grizzlies in the northern Rockies is to restore migratory corridors and link Yellowstone with other island ecosystems to the west and north, all the way to Canada.

To secure an area big enough that it approaches a self-regulating wilderness, including sufficiently wild corridors to physically and genetically link up the isolated bear populations south of Canada, is a tough but not impossible model that we should at least consistently hold before us as an attainable ideal. Today the modern conservation movement has reached a critical juncture. While we are yet beset by staggering threats to wild habitats, great hope and optimism also lie on the horizon. For the first time in memory, there is extensive discussion, study, even groundwork exploring the possibility of restoring wild nature—of re-creating linkages and corridors of isolated islands of wild animals, of blowing Glen Canyon Dam, reversing what was once considered the one-way road of the taming of the wild, repatriation of regionally extinct species, restoration of cover and riparian areas—of putting back together the wild pieces.

Reconnecting the islands challenges some of the most sacred tenets and assumptions of our industrial culture. The grizzly is a lot of trouble; no other American creature so awakens our most primal of fears—the lions and bears at the mouth of the cave of our origin. It is also a beast of great beauty that instills, like no other, compulsory humility in the most imperious species on earth, ourselves. It is the weight of expense versus value to human beings of retaining the source of this organic fear that lies in the balance.

Providing wild-enough corridors from Yellowstone through the Yaak to Canada will require removing a network of obsolete logging roads, providing passage over or under freeways, and, insofar as we have created these fragmented island landscapes with our settlement, facilitating passage through this landscape: grizzly bears marching across golf courses and ranches; past whiskey bars, squat-and-gobbles, and shopping malls.

Only by reconnecting these islands of wild habitat can we assure our so-called wilderness indicator animals, especially the big, mobile ones—grizzlies, wolves, wolverines, woodland caribou, lynx, bull trout—a reasonable shot at surviving beyond the next century. Here in the Rocky Mountains, these creatures live marooned in a necklace of isolated habitats, arching through Yellowstone and the Bitterroot, a wild archipelago whose northernmost islet south of Canada is the Yaak Valley.

Looking at a map of the northern Rockies—as I used to gaze in my youth at a globe of Africa and South America—there are two or three seemingly logical ways for a grizzly to get from my house to Canada. The most likely and practical route ends up in the Yaak.

Fortunately for me, I have a friend who has methodically studied these routes. Dr. Lance Craighead, second generation in the most eminent family of grizzly researchers, has teamed up with Richard Walker, a geographer, to see how Yellowstone grizzlies might reach other grizzly areas, like Glacier Park or through the Bitterroot to the

Cabinet-Yaak. Using landsat photos, the two put road and human densities along with habitat factors into a computer to produce a map of the best migratory route for grizzlies and other mobile animals. Two possible corridors run north, one past my house; a third route, the best one, goes west out of Yellowstone into historic grizzly country then swings north toward the Yaak.

The biggest obstacle to wildlife migration are interstate highways, I-90 and I-15. All potential corridors from here to Canada must cross both. I live at the northern extreme of a long finger of wilderness known as the Absaroka, which dead-ends less than ten miles from I-90 by Livingston. Bears don't cross the freeway here, but they do just west of Wineglass Mountain along Trail Creek, hitting I-90 near Bear Creek. The researchers found a spot on the interstate where a black bear is hit almost every year.

"They'll continue to show up," says Craighead about the place, "so knowing that, we could make it easier for them to get through."

He means that we have to look into the technical engineering and biology necessary to get animals like grizzlies over or under things like freeways.

But this route would lead to another problem—crossing the Missouri River near Canyon Ferry Lake, then a subsequent hop over I-15 and west toward Roger's Pass. No grizzly to date has been known to use this route.

Another possible grizzly route studied by the scientists would lead northwest of Yellowstone into the Gravelly and Tobacco Root Mountains and cross I-90 around Butte. Grizzlies have been sighted in each mountain range, but the crossing remains a problem.

If reconnecting the islands is indeed the answer to long-term survival of the grizzly in the lower forty-eight—and I believe it is—the most obvious and logical linkage would be to hook up Yellowstone with the largest wilderness area remaining south of Canada, the Selway-Bitterroot of western Montana and central Idaho, which in turn could link up with and augment the besieged Cabinet-Yaak ecosystem adjacent to Canada.

The problem, of course, is that the Bitterroot Ecosystem (BE), a fifteen-million-acre wilderness ecosystem, contains few, if any, remaining grizzlies. As almost everywhere else, we shot them out of there to make the West safe for European immigrants.

There are two ways to get grizzlies back into the BE (the U.S. Fish & Wildlife Service has produced a draft environmental impact statement, or EIS, on BE reintroduction): to reintroduce transplanted bears from other grizzly ecosystems, from Canada; or to allow natural recolonization of the BE from Yellowstone or, from the north, the Cabinet-Yaak.

There's all kinds of circular reasoning here: In order to ensure survival of Yellowstone's grizzlies, we need to hook them up with bears adjacent to Canada; the Yaak appears to be the best shot. In that case, the problem of the empty Bitterroot Grizzly Ecosystem has to be solved first; if the Cabinet-Yaak (C-Y) had a larger population of grizzlies, which depends on securing yet unprotected habitat, the grizzlies of the C-Y could migrate into the BE (one grizzly was known to have crossed I-90 west of Missoula and den south of the freeway). If Yellowstone's bears could migrate into the BE, they could, in time, augment the tiny population of griz in the C-Y. It blows my little mind.

The fact is, we can't sustain any one of these areas without securing the others, a daisy chain of wild but precarious dominoes. The YE needs the C-Y by way of the BE the way the Yaak needs viable Canadian grizzly populations.

I must admit that, although I would like to see grizzlies back in the BE more than anything, there are big problems with reintroduction. Where would these "surplus" bears come from? The draft EIS lists two existing source populations in the United States and from Canada, in cooperation with Canadian authorities, where "grizzly bear populations are healthy enough to sustain removal of a few bears per year over a five year period." Only bears "with no history of conflict with humans" from similar habitats would be translocated. Supporters expected most grizzlies to be transplanted from southeast British Columbia.

But early in the summer of 1997, a group of forty-three Canadian environmental organizations announced their opposition to removal of grizzly bears from Canada for use in the proposed recovery effort in the BE. They wanted assurances that these bears would not only survive but also make a meaningful, long-term contribution to recovery. The last phone message from Victoria, British Columbia, in the wake of the salmon-controversy blockade, was that use of their bears "was entirely off the table."

That leaves, under the draft EIS, the Yellowstone and Northern Continental Divide Ecosystems as the only potential sources. The "bears with no history of conflict" troubles many conservationists, who think that "problem bears" have mostly to do with notions of human control, that "good bears are the ones that conform to our wishes." Baloney. Most bears that get in trouble with people have been the victims of human failure and stupidity; agency reluctance to offer these doomed bears a second or third chance has more to do with their chickenshit fear of litigation than good science.

And is it ethical or wise to transplant any wild, healthy bear out of its native habitat? Though individual grizzlies are broadly adaptable, I don't think so. Grizzlies spend a long time—two and a half years just with their mother—learning a home range. No spot on earth has surplus bears. A few years ago, when another group of citizens were looking into a way to augment the tiny population of grizzlies we believed still survived in the San Juan Mountains of Colorado, we discovered that unwanted grizzly cubs were born into captivity every year. These bear cubs born in zoos are a possibility, like wolves bred and raised in wilderness halfway houses.

At the present time, however, all talk of reintroduction in the BE is passé. Regional politicians have killed it by gutting the funding. It has always struck me as sadly curious that the most beautiful, vibrant territory on the continent—the northern Rockies—is represented by the densest concentration of partisan spit-dribbling assholes in the United States.

Representative Helen Chenowitz (R-Idaho) characterized grizzlies as "manic depressive animals" and compared reintroducing grizzlies into the BE to "introducing sharks at the beach." She sniveled on another sound bite for the press: "The only practical purpose grizzlies would serve is if they ate gray wolves." Governor Phil Batt of Idaho joined the antibear bandwagon after it seemed safe and wrote, in all his courage, to Secretary of the Interior Bruce Babbitt, that ". . . reintroduction will pose a significant public safety risk for Idaho's citizens." Finally, for two straight years, Senators Craig of Idaho and Burns of Montana have blocked wildlife officials from spending any money on BE reintroduction.

The second way to get grizzlies back into the Bitterroot is to encourage natural immigration of recolonization. This process would be much slower than just parachuting in a bunch of griz from Canada. But the arriving Yellowstone or C-Y bears would have the advantage of falling under the full protection of the Endangered Species Act (ESA). Consider Yellowstone:

Yellowstone grizzlies have been moving west toward the Bitterroot for decades. Mothers with cubs have been sighted halfway down the Centennial Range, about twenty-five miles from I-15. Grizzly tracks have been documented in the Snowcrest Range only thirty miles east of Clark Canyon Reservoir, a drowned-dead section of the Beaverhead River. In the summer of 1998 a three-year-old male grizzly was captured and subsequently killed by wildlife officials in the Sweetwater Hills, a mere twenty miles southeast of Dillon, Montana. The official line of the state and federal wildlife people was that the bear may have killed some domestic sheep, was outside the official "Recovery Zone," and was therefore expendable.

This, of course, is horseshit. This subadult grizzly is exactly the kind of far-ranging bear needed to accomplish corridor recovery and link up with other ecosystems. As long as we allow our government game managers to kill these animals, Yellowstone will be doomed to remain an island ecosystem, and true recovery of the grizzly will never be achieved.

This same bear, of incalculable value to long-term survival of the Yellowstone, was also sighted (and trapped) near Gardiner, not too far upstream on the Yellowstone River from my house. This could have been the bear that went all the way—from here to the Yaak. We will never know.

The government wildlife officials who murdered this bear proceed on the unproven and dangerous theory that grizzlies that wander outside the invisible, political boundary on the map demarcating the Recovery Zone are unwelcome and must be trapped and killed or moved back to the park. Additionally, sheep shouldn't be there. Domestic sheep are an irresistible temptation to any carnivore; the whining, bleating, and endless run of excreta of these domestic animals, which have been known to die of fright during light-ning storms, drown in heavy rains, or run unpursued off cliffs, seem to trigger the pred-ator instinct wherever they roam; they are born to die. Domestic sheep are totally incompatible with bears. All grazing leases in occupied or potential grizzly country should be canceled. Sheep have plenty of other places to graze outside of grizzly country.

The heart of this argument is human control. All state and federal management plans are predicated upon intensive management of grizzlies: snaring, tranquilizing, and GPS-collaring of bears, which are then tracked by satellite; or helicoptering in a captured griz from Glacier to Yellowstone to prevent genetic isolation; or trapping and returning grizzlies that naturally wander during lean food years beyond the artificial boundaries of the official Recovery Zone, instead of allowing bears to recolonize their historic habitat on public land. This sort of thing—which costs millions in taxpayer money and puts a premium on control of grizzlies—is itself a contradictory undertaking.

Down in the Bitterroot Valley, humans are debating if and how to have bears rule these mountains again. The secular squabbling (there are two contentious camps among those humans favoring reintroduction) belies major consequences that may determine the fate of the last big wilderness south of Canada, one big enough to contain self-regulating populations of all the Rocky Mountain megafauna, including the besieged grizzlies. Those animals will necessarily live beyond our control, which we modern humans so fear to relinquish. This is far less esoteric than it appears.

The grizzly can tolerate us, but we have chosen not to return that tolerance. As a practical matter, grizzlies are not much of a threat to humans or their livestock. But they are not exactly safe either—no guarantees, the grizzly is a risky proposition. It is an animal that lives beyond the dictates of our agronomy and management plans. The danger of grizzlies to people can be minimized through education if only we would take the time to know and learn about the bear. Above all, we humans are a species who fears the unknown, the bear we no longer know. We fear the bear in the tame, fragmented, developed landscapes we produce. The overriding habitat need for bears is security from humans. We shoot grizzlies on sight, so the bear needs wilderness. But *security* is a relative term; empty country is as safe as a dense thicket. And a region with a few people who don't fear and kill grizzlies is almost as good as empty country. The Yaak could figure prominently in this equation.

The Yaak is a microcosm for much of what's left of wild America: a small human population (good), much public land (97 percent Kootenai National Forest), little roadless area because of a massive network of logging roads (bad), all the northern Rocky Mountain megafauna living since the Pleistocene south of Canada, lowland forests influenced by Pacific maritime weather, not particularly spectacular in terms of towering mountains and glaciated peaks, but great wildlife habitat, and absolutely no protected wilderness.

Grizzly experts generally think the C-Y, at twenty-six hundred square miles, is too small in terms of bear survival (areas smaller than four thousand square miles have historically tended to go extinct, wink out in terms of grizzly populations). The population is officially listed at thirty-five to forty grizzlies, though it could be far less. The Cabinet Mountains and the Yaak Valley together comprise one of the more heavily logged ecosystems in the West. Yet this tiny reservoir of wild animals in the Yaak is critical to long-term survival of all grizzlies south of Canada—the genetic and geographic connection to bear populations in Canada.

Why not start by giving grizzlies and their habitat some protection in the Yaak, and then working backward toward Wyoming? It is the cheapest and easiest thing to do. Maintaining grizzlies in the C-Y would buy us time to work out reintroduction back into the Bitterroot and would hold out hope for the isolated Yellowstone bears.

Can some kinds of logging proceed along with protecting grizzlies? Possibly. Selective cutting aimed at a graded mill market has long been advocated by ecological foresters. It's the big timber companies that need to clear-cut in the national forests. Logging roads are another problem.

Two cheap, democratic ideas that come to mind that could be undertaken right away to help Yaak grizzlies would be to close a bunch of logging roads and to legislate some cores of wilderness habitat. The thing grizzly bears need most is territory with damn few (and preferably unarmed) people. Keeping hunters from killing grizzlies—mistaken for black bears, intentionally poached, or in misperceived cases of bear danger—is the major challenge to bear managers everywhere. Closing logging roads is the easiest way. They need to be obliterated to reopen secure habitat for bears. The U.S. Forest Service could effortlessly close many of these seldom-used roads, but it doesn't. The real lobby for keeping logging roads open comes not from the timber industry, which has no more use for them, but from the powerful off-road vehicle lobby, well funded by the timber and mining industries and corporations like Mitsubishi.

It will take real courage to restore the grizzly anywhere. As my friend David Quammen, one of the most fiercely independent, informed voices living in the northern Rockies, wrote: "The political obstacles are breathtaking, [implying] nothing less than reinventing the status of large areas of public and private land. It implies rethinking the relationship between grizzlies and human society." The great bear is wilderness incarnate—both risky propositions to people, as they should be.

Now I am back home, sitting quietly at the Grizfork, cleaning my pistol, thinking about world peace, restless, angry about this seemingly impossible task—the staggering, ubiquitous threats to wild habitats everywhere—one more reason we could use a little victory in the Yaak. I put on a tape of a late quartet by Beethoven (old courage-giver) and go to the fridge, pop open a Corona, and squeeze in a wedge of lime. The cat is sitting on my lap, so I reach for a nearby magazine, a journal about wilderness activism and conservation biology. The text is dry and precious—no words really burning off the page—without the immediacy of bear shit steaming in the trail.

No matter. I pull heavily on the beer and read on, looking for useful clues and fortitude for our fight to win back wilderness in the Yaak. We have entered the most precarious time in the 3.5 billion years of life on earth, the article states, the highest rate of extinction ever, greater than the mass extinctions of the Cretaceous era 65 million years ago. There is wholesale devastation of tropical rain forests, the loss of temperate-zone old-growth forests, accelerating desertification, and the beginning of the death of the seas by rapacious drift-netting and other commercial fishing. It goes on.

Bummer, I say to myself, reaching for another Corona. The esoteric lineal argument escapes me. I look out at the dark sky, alive with stars seldom seen, the shadow of a mule deer running across the pasture, wanting only missing bear. My pal old Ed Abbey once wrote: "I believe in nothing I cannot touch, kiss, embrace . . . .The rest is only hearsay."

I need to take a break from all this, so I head up into the Bitterroot Divide, west of the Centennial Valley, finally bushwhacking up a steep creek that reminds me of my father, who died three years ago. The uninhabited grizzly country runs more than two hundred miles up north, to the sparsely inhabited Cabinets, then into the Yaak. Sixty miles to the east lie the hazy summits of the Centennial Range, occasionally visited by Yellowstone's grizzly bears. In between is a lot of private land, open ranch country, and a freeway. Quammen, again, said this about those grizzlies: "Yellowstone's population of 'Ursus arctos horribilis' is probably as important as any endangered species, any sub-species, any population of animals on earth, insofar as it helps the planet's most arrogant people to recall the acrid taste of an ancient ecological fear." He was talking about the small chance of being killed and eaten by a larger, more terrible being. "We need that knowledge," he wrote; "we need that dimension of humility."

This day I was only picking mushrooms, knowing there might be a few yellow chanterelles on the gentler north-facing slopes under spruce. I came up a small draw with a trickle of water running down it. A dense cluster of fir and spruce occupied the creek bottom just beyond a small wallow. In the mud lay the track of a large bear, with more tracks leading into the thicket. I looked around, feeling a paralyzing rush of déjà vu. Then I remembered—grizzlies have a cognitive complexity and are aware of their own track making. One of the more disconcerting experiences in nature is to have a bear set up an ambush for you. One April I watched a big grizzly trace my snowshoe tracks out of a clearing into the lodgepole forest; the bear was walking on top of the tracks I had made coming in. After waiting ten minutes, I started to follow the huge tracks, but it was almost dark and something made me stop short. A chill of premonition ran up my spine. I turned and quickly got out of the woods.

The next morning I followed the prints out onto the crusted snow. The grizzly had followed my snowshoe trail for nearly a hundred yards, then veered off to the right in a tight circle to an icy depression behind a large deadfall ten feet off my trail. More tracks led away.

The sign told me that the night before this grizzly had backtracked me, then circled around next to the trail and bedded behind a log that would conceal him, waiting for me, ten feet away from the track of my snowshoes. The icy bed spoke of a long wait. This had been the second time I had known a grizzly to set up what looked like a deliberate ambush for me. What it means, what the bear intends, I don't know; maybe it is only curiosity. Still, I had known a distinct if momentary perception of a malicious intelligence lurking behind that log.

But here, in the Bitterroot, there were no grizzlies, not yet at least. I struggled to hold in that immense distinction inside of me.

CHAPTER 27

DEAR RICK

By   David   James   Duncan

LOLO, MONTANA

Dear Rick,

Excuse this ludicrous stationery, they were samples, only two more pieces to get rid of! Hey, goddammit! I read your latest letter asking for help as I was walking down the driveway a few minutes ago, felt my heart slither down into my fucking socks, don't know what to say, really, just want you all to know that my heart goes out to you, stands by you, which is worth a grand total of no saved acre, saved life, saved tree. I don't have a "but at least" sort of turnaround that can salvage these sentences either, and never will. I just stand by you all in sickness, in the sickness of a humanity that chooses to be a planetary cancer. When people mention Mark Hatfield's name to me to this day I go insane, rage or cry, see fawn slicks (stillborns), the way they curl up against death like a dog in front of a woodstove but shine like something all wrong, obsidian in the ferns, you never forget that, and my friends sprayed with 245T and jailed and hurt by cops like the northern kids who a decade earlier tried to slow the juggernaut of niggerhaters, but with none of the respect—this country *believes* in killing its wilds—and my neighbors K and G, whose water supply was up in the stand of Sitkas so huge and magic that when I made tiny twig chairs and tables and set them on a queen-sized bed of moss-covered bent spruce trunk ten feet up one giant tree in the air with silverware smaller than splinters and plates smaller than buttons and a day later their girls, Megan and Johanna, two and four, saw the set table, they felt God had come for them, had filled their lives with Bible words like *beatitude* and *plenteousness*, and they believed it so hard they named the whole place Fairyland and worshiped it and no one who walked up there thought it was silly, you heard their awe even in a whored-out word like *Fairy*, then came process time, EIS time, doom time, but my crazy friend Harry went walking up the hill to the first green forest service truck he spotted on the new spur road anyway and begged some confused forest service grunt, didn't know how to pursue the fucking process, just stood in front of those five-hundred-year-old trees and that green truck like anyone who ever loved would have to do and told him, "This is wrong. Save Fairyland. Be a human being and save this place. Little children grew up here, little children worship it," best goddamn protest I ever heard of, though of course, what happened, Fairyland became stumps and five-pound Sunday *L.A. Times,* and the stumps got sprayed, leaving us obsidian in the ferns, and all those poor fuckers at that meeting you were at who don't even know they're fuckers, and God's sons all ordering us to love them even more than they hate those of us who try to love the world, Jesus Buddha Krishna the whole lot ordering us to stay nailed to the ground and spiritually save the very earth fuckers who never save anything so we're luckless fucks sometimes, for all our good fortune, is what I'm feeling about you and me, man, and our good monk, Thomas Merton, who could not drive past the Indian professional beggar kids in Bombay without giving them money even though it's known, Merton knew, that giving money supports an industry of child maiming and child slavery, I tell you, this same Merton could *not* live where you live or I once lived and screen our chain saws to find his fucking "root of inner wisdom" every day. Man, he may have said something to help us stay away from too many conferences, too many cause meetings, too many scattered thoughts, scattered writings, scattered naturelovercirclejerks, but you were dead right to pull yourself up short: Merton did not say anything to keep us from bleeding inside when those trees go down. To bleed *is* to be in touch with inner wisdom, to bleed *is* to love.

When I drove in February through your country, coming back from Bonners Ferry, what I saw was my old country, the Oregon Coast Range, Fairyland and all, still standing: It rose from the dead; and it was doomed to death all over again: And I hurt all over again just knowing you all are in the thick of that. I know words of consolation, some of the best ever spoken, know heart-healing secrets and a thousand things still worth loving, but today, my friend, I'm just sick and sorry and standing by you in that.

CHAPTER 28

AN ALASKAN VISITS THE YAAK

By Carolyn Kremers

IT'S TOUGH TO LIVE IN THE LOWER FORTY-EIGHT. EVEN IN THE West—where I was born and mostly lived until I was thirty-four—it feels like the wildness is gone or about to be. Highly at risk. Endangered. And somehow, each time I come down here from Alaska, that feeling transfers from the wildness (or lack of it) to my inner spirit—and I start feeling endangered, too.

Currently, I'm living in Spokane, Washington, teaching creative writing and literature at Eastern Washington University and returning to Alaska in summers. One of our graduate students lives in the Yaak Valley of western Montana, and last February he invited one of my classes and me to "come out to the Yaak" for a weekend. The class was a form and theory literature course in contemporary creative nonfiction, and one of the books I'd assigned was *The Book of Yaak*, by Rick Bass. We planned to discuss it in class the following week.

The drive from Spokane to the Yaak is green—even in winter, which it was. El Niño had brought Spokane little snow (mostly ice), but as soon as my silver Subaru and I left I-90 for Highway 95—at Couer d'Alene in the Idaho panhandle—the colors beyond the windows became white and green. Spruce green.

I glanced right and left at the forests, feeling thirsty, drinking them in. Like I said, it's tough to live in the lower forty-eight. The ceaseless activity of 190,000 people in Spokane (and, worse, their cars) makes me feel like a moose calf that has skittered onto a four-lane highway.

As I drove north on 95 and then east on 2, the ranches and farm country between Sandpoint and Bonners Ferry gave way to a steep, winding road into the Cabinet

Mountains, past clear-cut whole hillsides: huge tree stumps poking up from the forest floor, stumps ten or twenty times bigger around than anything that grows in the heart of Alaska. Near the eastern edge of Idaho, the road began to curve more gently, stretching out with the wide meanders of the Kootenai River that flows down from Canada. I stopped a few times, getting out of the car to listen—for the river and birds, the chatter of squirrels—and to smell the needled trees and winter air.

I grew up in Colorado, and it's always good to return to the Rockies and smell them. They are altitude and freedom and great granite outcroppings wind-scoured clean—opposites of the scraggly trees, thick brush, and wet, squishy tundra of Alaska's interior. I love the Rockies—I will always love them—even though now, in truth, I know that my heart lies elsewhere.

Soon after entering Montana, I glanced at the map Jeff had drawn for our class, and his note:

> *Take Highway 2 to the Yaak Highway—*
> *turn left and go to the 9-mile mark—*
> *mine is the first house on the right after the guardrail.*
> *If you get to the 17-Mile Bridge, you've gone too far!*

Just past the guardrail, I glanced at the odometer: 132 miles. It was hard to believe, but the drive from Spokane to the fabled Yaak had taken less than three hours, including my stops to breathe free.

I pulled into the first driveway on the right and followed the snowy road to a space behind two parked cars. Was this it? Knocking on the door of the building that looked most like a house, I expected to see Jeff.

The door swung open to a young woman from our class and the sudden heat of a woodstove. "Come on in," Laura said in her gentle southern accent (she's from Kentucky), flashing a pixie smile. "I'm glad you're here."

I saw a jumble of backpacks and cross-country ski boots on the floor, and two big dogs, and soon Laura was stirring something garlicky on the propane stove. "For the potluck tonight," she said. A tall young man with glasses put down a book and shook my hand: quiet, punkish Eric, with Barry Lopez's *Crossing Open Ground*.

"Some of the students are taking a nap," Laura explained, "and Tracy's in the shower. Oh, and Jeff and Kai and Gailyn are out making a video. Of the Yaak. They're gonna use it for their class presentation. It should be pretty funny. You know them."

I laughed, setting down the pot of spicy Santa Fe beans I had made that morning in Spokane, and dropped my green backpack and trusty sleeping bag into the pile. Then I sat on a bench by the door to put on hiking boots. I knew what I wanted to do first.

That night there was hot food—Laura's spaghetti, a neighbor's cheese enchiladas, and Jeff's barbecued emu, which I (usually vegetarian) had never tasted before. I wanted to see a picture of an emu, so Jeff got out his dictionary.

A large, nonflying Australian bird, similar to the ostrich but smaller.

Drinking our beer, Erica, Lisa, and I inspected the crude ink drawing and caption: EMU (5 ft. high). We laughed. For an instant, I felt like we were all—the three women, the man, the book, the emu meat—inside a cartoon. Such joy.

There was wine, too, and a campfire with s'mores, and taking turns pushing two little girls in the swing above the snowdrifts, with orange flickers in the dark, and wood-smoke, and the Milky Way hung with a quarter moon. Later, there was Jill singing to guitar inside the warm living room, everyone sprawled on the red-and-blue futon couch and the floor, with candles and the woodstove and, later still, bodies everywhere, on beds and in sleeping bags on all the floors: writers asleep and youthfulness, and the hope that accompanies both . . . *dreaming*.

The next morning I woke before seven. I felt my way down the dark stairs and left a note on the kitchen counter for Jeff and the others. Then I snuck away, carrying my backpack and stuffed sleeping bag out the heavy wooden door and down the path to a muddy car. The overcast sky was just beginning to offer light. I wanted to drive around the Yaak and take a ski, before heading back to Spokane. And more, I wanted to get a better sense of this "wild."

Sitting in the front seat of my car (who is called Trickster, for his delight in honking the horn whenever either of my hands slips off the rim of the steering wheel and lightly touches one of the two oval buttons located way too close by), I spread out my road map of Montana. I could see that the area known as "the Yaak" is a section of the Kootenai National Forest, outlined by Highway 508—and, later, by 68—in a sort of lumpy rectangle. This road is a two-lane asphalt ribbon that rolls off the main highway just four miles past the Idaho-Montana border. The road follows the curves of the Yaak River gently northeast to an intersection and a place called Yaak—just a few buildings, I would discover, including the Dirty Shame Saloon, a Laundromat, and the Yaak Tavern and Mercantile. Then the route cuts south through thick forest and steep mountains—the Purcell Range of the Rockies—and rejoins Highway 2 at the lumber town of Libby.

According to Jeff, within this lumpy rectangle are scattered private landholdings, some the result of subdivisions sold by Champion International, the timber corporation responsible for many of the Yaak's large clear-cuts. Other private holdings include old mountain ranches and homestead properties. Here and there throughout the Yaak, wealthy and not-wealthy people have built log or frame houses and other outbuildings. I've read that only 3 percent of the 471,000 acres of land in the upper part of the valley is privately owned. Like Alaska, the rest is owned and managed by the government. Unlike much of Alaska, though, most private property in the Yaak is accessible by automobile, for only about one-third of this forested valley has escaped roads.

In the mid-1960s there was only one main road through the valley: the not-yet-paved Highway 508. Now, although much of the area still has no phone service or electricity, twelve hundred miles of roads mark the hills, most the result of logging.

The human population in the Yaak is not large—perhaps 150 people who stay through winter. I am amazed. Twelve hundred miles of road for 150 people is inconceivable in Alaska. Most Alaskans who live in "remote," sparsely populated areas must rely on boats or planes for transportation in and out. They make their own trails—by snowmachine, four-wheeler, dogsled, or on foot or skis. If the area is crisscrossed by logging roads—as some parts of Southeast Alaska are—it is not considered remote.

The people who live in the Yaak do all sorts of things. Some are retired, some work for timber companies or the Forest Service, some commute to jobs in Libby or Troy. Some work at the Dirty Shame or the Merc, help operate the ski area, or run snowplows in winter. They do road repairs and trail maintenance, make jewelry, write stories, design clothing, raise children, work as seasonal hunting or fishing guides.

Besides people, though, the Yaak is home or resting place for hundreds of species of plants, animals, fish, and birds. They're like a whisper of what surrounds me now and of what I cannot see—and likely won't without living here.

Mushroom, huckleberry, raspberry, orchid, lichen, violet, fungus, fern. Gray wolf, grizzly, black bear, beaver, moose, coyote, elk, deer, mountain lion, bobcat, woodland caribou. Wolverine, marten, lynx, fisher, weasel, porcupine, lemming, bat. White sturgeon, bull trout. Great gray owl, boreal owl, golden eagle, bald eagle, grouse, woodthrush, chickadee, raven, loon.

The list goes on.

This breathtaking variety, I've learned, is partly due to the fact that, in the Yaak, two major ecoregions overlap: the Pacific Northwest and the northern Rockies. One of the Yaak Valley's essential roles in this part of the American West, then, is as a *corridor of wildness*—a place that helps lace the ecosystem together.

Turning Trickster around in Jeff's driveway and heading north on 508, I tried to remember what I had learned about such corridors. According to conservation biologists, populations must not become fragmented or cut off from one another. If they do—if they become "islands"—those populations become unable to mix with fresh genes, and they go extinct. To allow for mixing, there must be paths that individuals can take to get to each other.

Before moving to Spokane, I'd not been aware of this concept of corridors of wildness. As a little girl and, later, an adult, I had visited many national parks in the lower forty-eight—Yellowstone, Rocky Mountain, Zion, Arches, Glacier, the Grand Canyon, the Everglades, the Great Smokies. I'd loved them all: the variety of their ecosystems—the geysers, alligators, red rocks, delicate alpine flowers—and the fact that the land could not be bought or sold but would be held in trust, by the U.S. government, for the enjoyment and appreciation of generations to come. And that these lands would be protected "in perpetuity" from private ownership and business development.

But I had been naive.

In contrast to Alaska, the American West is becoming increasingly fragmented, particularly by roads, clear-cuts, housing and business developments, and dams. And the current situation in the Yaak Valley, a comparatively remote area of the West, is something to sit up and pay attention to. The Yaak exhibits the combined diversity of all the ecosystems of the West, because it *links* north to south and west to east: British Columbia to Idaho and Oregon, Montana to Idaho and Washington. I have been stunned to learn that, without this link and others like it, the four largest national parks in the Rockies—Yellowstone, Rocky Mountain National Park, Glacier-Waterton, and Banff—cannot survive. They, too, will become endangered and may eventually become "extinct," if cut off from the genetic diversity that is crucial for physical and spiritual survival.

After learning this, I've thought many times of the controversies in Alaska over management of national forests and wildlife refuges, including use of those lands for mining, logging, sport hunting, sport fishing, and oil and gas exploration. Since moving from Colorado to Alaska twelve years ago, I've read numerous articles about the challenges that face Alaskan fish and game and forest managers as they seek to strike a balance between the human population's needs and desires, and the migrations and traditional habitat requirements of thousands of other life forms. Alaska is a state that encompasses more land than Montana, California, and Texas combined and that has a human population of only 500,000.

In Alaska the moose and bears, otters and whales, salmon and sandhill cranes eat and move as they please—as they have for centuries—and the people are reminded of the power of nature every day. Alders take over cleared land, rivers erode banks and change course. Ice jams cause floods. Trees fall on power lines. Permafrost cracks roads. Salt air rusts vehicles. Darkness brings depression. When the tip of the fireweed blooms atop the rest of the purple-red stalk of flowers, the lovely wand quickly turns to white, fluffed seed, and everyone knows: *Summer is over.*

The imposing, ever-changing environment is central to what goes on in Alaska, among humans and not, and the Alaskan ecosystem is largely healthy and intact—if also, as everywhere on earth, at risk. In Alaska, one is not inclined to consider "corridors of wildness," perhaps, because the whole state and its surrounding waters create such a corridor. In fact, wildness predominates, and the tiny road system, short railroad lines, and bobbling public ferries provide corridors for *humans* to move among all the other living things.

I drove the entire lumpy rectangle of Highways 508 and 68, from Jeff's house near Yaak Falls, northeast to the Dirty Shame at Yaak, then south, past Turner Mountain Ski Area. I was startled at the number of logging roads, off-road vehicle (ORV) trails, and marked forest service trails branching to my left and right. Near a place Jeff had recommended, I parked the car and changed into my backcountry ski boots. Lifting my blue-and-white Fischer Country skis off the roof, I snapped them on.

As in Spokane, winter in the Yaak had been unusually warm with El Niño, and I discovered that the snow on this trail—or road of some sort—had melted and then frozen into layers of ice. I trudged up the wide route, wishing for climbing skins. I'd take one stride and slide partly back, then stride again. I inched uphill, feeling like one of Lewis and Clark's overloaded canoes. Huge snowflakes fell on my nose and eyelashes, though, making me smile. Here was a memory of warm winter in Colorado. I shed thick mittens and unzipped my fuchsia fleece anorak, skiing hatless with thin Capilene gloves.

The snow kept falling and falling. I would get wet, but I knew that Trickster waited faithfully below. I needed this ski, this Sunday morning in the Yaak. I needed this *silence*.

Back in the car, I drove on. The land flattened, and the road joined Highway 2 at the center of Libby. The beehive stack of a sawmill loomed into view, then many gas stations (I stopped to fill up), and, after about twenty more minutes of driving, I reached Troy and the school building where Jeff teaches.

Trickster and I had circumnavigated the Yaak. It felt like an island. It was smaller than I had imagined—and more populated, crisscrossed by roads—but it was also magical. And real. And just as I had imagined, as all wild places are, the Yaak was blessed with mystery. The river and mountains felt like Yup'ik Eskimo elders, like they held the wisdom of the past and perhaps could see the future, and they were waiting patiently to see if we young ones would see it, too.

I realized, more than ever, how much I miss (living in the city of Spokane) the *wild* and my relationships with it, and why people in the Yaak must love their valley so much. It's not the place so much as the *feeling*—the sense that you can hear things like the riffles of the river and the rustle of a few forgotten, dry leaves on a branch. The assurance that ice in the river will move and change, and that water will run over and under it, around and through—that a bear might pass in the evening by the porch, a black bear in summer seeking food—or an eagle is circling on the updraft as you walk up the road to meet Jeff's friends, Shamus and Laura. People build their own houses in the Yaak, as do people in Alaska, and each season they discover where the best berries are. They know how to plant gardens, where their drinking water comes from, the meaning of snow. What the stars look like at night, whether a storm is coming, how to fix a roof leak or an engine, the *wack!* of an ax on wood, who's sick in the valley, what needs to be done before nightfall or the first frost or the mud at breakup.

And it's not that these things can only be done or known in wild places—in the heart of Alaska or in a magical valley like the Yaak. It's not that only the privileged few—those with money and those without—can do or know these things. It's that it's so dang hard to get back to this harmony—this *stillness* away from people, automobiles, and malls, away from jet planes, paperwork, and plastic. And not to just touch it (which is hard enough) but to rest inside it, live within it, be part of it, and know and understand we're part of it every day and every season, for years. For ever. And we're *only* part of it. And this harmony—this stillness and change, beyond technology and human artifice—will continue, whether our species chooses to rest inside it and honor it or not. It will continue in the face of destruction.

That's what's tough about living down here.

Corridor, from the French and Italian *corridore,* derived from *correre* and its Latin root *currere.* "To run." The English word *current*—originally "running" or "flowing"—derives also from this root.

I don't want the Yaak to be an island. I don't want to be one, either. I want us both to be corridors. And I want there to be many corridors in the lower forty-eight, many opportunities for the exchange and flow of life—and spirit—in all its diversity.

That's partly why I wanted my class to read *The Book of Yaak.* And why I'm glad Jeff invited us to his home. There are things we can do—each one of us can do—to understand and honor the corridors. But something is whispering . . . *We're all into this pretty deep.*

I think it is saying we've got to do these things now. And we've got to do them every day, each in our own way—not just for our own beloved places but for the whole of it, for the sake of all the land and all the people, all the spirit—if we want to continue to get out of our cars and breathe free.

CHAPTER 29

GROUSE, GROUSE, GROUSE

By Bob Shacochis

IN 1989, AT THE END OF THE SUMMER, MISS F. AND I FLOUTED common sense by moving from Florida to Italy by way of Montana.

Our beloved Tyrone had died, and we were delivering our new Irish setter pup, Issabel, to our friends' ranch, deep in the federal wilderness of the Northwest, where she would presumably prosper in dog paradise until we returned in a year from overseas. North of Libby, Montana, we turned off the state road—the power lines and the phone lines ended—and drove thirty-five rugged miles on a one-lane loggers' track toward the valley where Rick and Miss E. resided. Every mile or so, white-tailed deer pranced across the road. Miss F., having too much imagination for her own good, refused my suggestion to peer over the steep edge of the shoulderless byway to where, far below, a moose sucked on marsh weeds. Two weeks earlier, Rick had called Florida to report he had seen a grizzly bear, and now, as the wild and daunting vista unfolded, I had one bad thought on my mind: Once we dropped Issabel at the ranch, we would never see her again, because some fierce beast was bound to devour her. Maybe Rick's bear, maybe a wolf or a mountain lion. Hell, I thought, maybe the untamed folks up here in the high country themselves, since they were known for exercising their right to bear arms and for eating anything they surprised roaming the forest. Life consumed life. Period. That's where we were taking Issabel, back into an almost lost world, where truths were bald and instincts—man's included—were ancient. We crept around a blind curve, trying to avoid being obliterated by renegade logging trucks, when Miss F. squawked and threw up her hands. Two flying butterballs, sluggish and heavy as water balloons, catapulted out of the underbrush into the side of our pickup.

"Were those chickens??!" wondered Miss F., a little disbelieving.

They were grouse, and we were both reminded of the time we lived in Iowa, with kamikaze pheasants careening out of the corn stubble dead-on into our car. If you're not thinking "Lordy, free food!" you come to resent this birdbrain behavior rather quickly, this crossing of paths that were never meant to cross.

At the ranch, Rick and Miss E. displayed the laconic passion of seasoned naturalists; they wanted to know what sort of critters we'd spotted on our way in. I told them about the grouse, and Rick, his eyes brightening, glanced expectantly toward the truck.

"You stopped and got them, didn't you?"

"Naw," I said, shrugging. I had no experience thinking that way. None. In fact, once, in the islands, on the way to a party with a West Indian friend, we ran over a manicou— an opossum. My friend pulled over, put the roadkill in the trunk, and, at our destination, built a fire in the driveway, tossed the opossum in the flames, drank a beer while the hide carbonized to a black crust, raked it from the coals, peeled off the char, and ate the fucker, licking the bones. "Have some," he encouraged me. "It's good meat, mahn."

"You're a savage," I said. "You'd eat your own mother. You'd eat a dog."

"Dog ain't so bad, ya know," he teased, laughing at my squeamishness.

Back in Montana, Rick shook his head and looked at me as if I were a bit queer. "Man," he said, "that grouse, that's good meat."

Rick and Miss E. are not shy about serendipitous windfalls of good meat. That's the way they are, no apologies. Rick's pa, a Texan oilman, made sure his son received an education in self-reliance as it is understood in the roadless out-of-doors. Miss E. was similarly well equipped for the wild side, preferring as a companion a .357 magnum handgun, a gift from her mom in Mississippi.

I, on the other hand, was born into a wussy family, nary a hunter among our tribe. Except for pond fish and Annapolis blue crabs, what didn't come from the supermarket didn't exist. Like most ten-year-old boys, I had a BB gun, which I employed in the persecution of songbirds. When one of my older brothers joined the NRA, I enlisted too, but after earning about five inches' worth of marksman's bars, nothing in the world bored me more than firing a .22 at a circle on a piece of paper. Not until my first year in college, on my roommate's family's farm in Missouri, did I seize the opportunity to assassinate something with a bullet. I picked off a squirrel in an oak tree, tore away half of a cardinal's head, then contemplated the limp dead things at my feet and said, simply, *I'm not doing this anymore.* I was more relieved than remorseful, having finally fractured the mystique of death, which, after self-defense, is the true attraction of guns.

I regarded this as a fairly normal rite of passage for a teenage boy, sort of like condemning yourself to hell for all eternity by telling lies in the confessional. I didn't quite feel I had learned a lesson: No mentor was at my side, teaching me to respect the animal kingdom by propelling lead into a select few of its subjects. What happened was more or less juvenile delinquency: I had felt the mindless compulsion, I acted on it, that was that, and I imagined I was finished with it because I had also slain whatever pathetic small blood lust was there, trying to define itself within my character. Or so I imagined. So we all imagine.

We were still in Montana when grouse season opened, as did deer season for bowhunters. Rick and I took Issabel for a romp on the mountainside; he stowed his shotgun and bow in the truck, and we set out for an area that had been logged maybe twenty years back. Issabel ran far ahead of us, carefree, rising in and out of sight like a dolphin in the waves. Then she would brake, riveted by a seriousness, a spell of concentration that was as magnificent as it was amusing. Birds! her body whispered, this most exquisite tension of muscle and nerve. The closer we came, the more her restraint faltered, and at last she would lose control, rocketing into the scrub to be dazzled by the elusive muffled rhythm of wing beats.

Rick was almost impressed. He and Miss E. owned two Mississippi hounds, as obedient and hard-nosed as marines. Issabel was sweet, stubborn, and a bit goofy. How much and how often she and Rick would contradict each other in the months ahead was anybody's guess.

"Look at that," Rick marveled, watching the pup turn to stone. "You train her for the field?"

"I didn't," I said. I trained her only to be kissy-face, to bring joy to our lives, to come or stop or sit without endless shouting.

"She's a natural-born hunter."

"Seems to be," I agreed. Issabel sprang into a clump of huckleberry bushes and launched another covey of grouse. Rick fired twice, missing. The thought that I could do better never crossed my mind—there was no way in creation I could have—but I asked if I could hold the gun for a while, and that was okay with him.

Having the shotgun in hand, hefting its weight, made me magically more alert; otherwise, I felt no different, experienced no power thrill, no transformation into the great white hunter because, frankly, I had already decided I wanted to eat a grouse. After walking the forest with Issabel for two weeks, I was ready, my spirit was ready. Understand that if I could have clubbed a grouse with a stick or conked one with Rick's slingshot or strangled one (or hit one with a car), that would have been fine, too. The gun wasn't the point—the point was the decision to kill and eat. My days of moronic adolescence were long past. I had awakened into a role more threatening to the animal world: I was a cook with a lethal curiosity, intent on expanding my culinary universe, willing to sidestep the middlemen and venture to the source.

Well, why not? Eighty million buffalo had been slaughtered not for their food value but so that the American continent could be converted into wheat fields and pastureland. If there is no more authentic wilderness or wildlife left in America, it is because we've domesticated the land to grow tomatoes, corn, beans, rice; to graze cattle and sheep; to build chicken coops. Every salad we stab our fork into carries an enormous environmental price tag—the vast herds of antelope, the wolf packs, tens of thousands of bears, not to mention the Native Americans, the forests, the aquifers, the rivers, all the lost species. What happened to the wilderness, to nature? Easy answer. We cleared it, plowed it, planted it, packaged it. And then we ate it. All of us.

Having industrialized the production of food, having regulated and sanitized the fundamentals of survival, we the people of the twentieth century have made hunting an anachronism, a nostalgic fantasy, an ultra-macho indulgence, and, worse—for its hypocrisy—a cruelty. When Miss F. and I finally found our way to Rome, I was reminded, perusing Italian menus, that both high and low cuisines also welcome the gastronomic expression of wildness. Venerate it, in fact, as a luxury, one regarded identically from two opposed points of view. The aristocrat's roebuck, the peasant's hare—symbols of extravagance and crudity, yes, but also vital points of contact with nature's ever-more-circumscribed bounty. Without these points, the natural world's remaining essence becomes that-which-is-forgotten. Our most damning crime against nature is not progress but disassociation.

Over and over, the polemic looped through my mind on my walks in the Montana mountains with Issabel. I was neither royalty nor rustic, but I had resolved to eat wild game, and therefore I had soberly resolved to kill what was precious and free, as long as it was legal to do so and the animals were plentiful—a meaningless term, I know, except to fish and game authorities. I would not kill a moose any more than I would shoot a bald eagle, and I would never hunt what is most like us: that is, anything that kills. The killers—mountain lions, bobcats, bears, wolves, coyotes, et cetera—are taboo. They wanted what we wanted: meat, good meat. Birds I wanted: grouse, ducks, pheasants. Maybe an elk or a deer. Maybe.

We walked down the slope of the mountain, Rick and I and the dog, a perfect sky above us, as if we were descending from the sun, an appropriately hubristic conceit for hunters. Soon enough, Issabel flushed another pair of grouse. I raised the gun, held my breath, aimed, and led one of the birds in its low glide through the pines, my index finger taut against the trigger. These were the barbaric thoughts that boiled in my mind: Split the breasts, grill with apple wood, smother in a Calvados sauce, garnish with Rainier cherries.

Issabel flushed three birds, four birds, five, each flight described by the barrel of my shotgun. They were such bottom-heavy fliers, I could have hit them with a rock. I could sense Rick standing a respectful distance behind me, anticipating the report. But I never pulled the trigger, never took a shot. After half an hour, I handed the shotgun back to Rick, unable to explain myself. Maybe I didn't want to miss. Maybe I didn't want to do the dirty work.

Rick's luck was better. We took two birds home to Miss E., who added two more from the refrigerator and baked them stuffed with apple slices, basted with white wine. It's impossible to tell you how delicious they were, the meat tangy from the grouse diet of larch needles, just as it's impossible to tell you why I never squeezed the trigger. Only this: I am going to try again this fall, out in the woods with Rick, because I have feasted on grouse and deer and elk at his table, and they did not come wrapped from the supermarket.

Miss F. sends me off with rules of her own. Don't shoot the dog, and don't shoot Rick. In that order.

There's a culinary paradox we budding neo-primitives like to sharpen our teeth on around the campfire, and it is this: To serve wild meat properly requires a cook's most elegant and refined skills. Try, for instance, the following recipe for Pheasant Nelson, which I cooked last spring in Washington, the place once billed as the Evergreen State but that is now promoting itself as, get this, the Gourmet State, since the logging industry has more or less toppled the old image. You'd think Seattle was Siena these days, as measured by espresso bars. And superlative cooking.

PHEASANT NELSON

2 carrots, finely chopped
2 stalks celery, finely chopped
1 large onion, finely chopped
½ cup asparagus tips, finely chopped
2 cloves garlic, minced
¼ cup prosciutto, cut into short, thin
  strips
1 bay leaf, crushed
Sprig of thyme
½ cup butter

4 breasts of pheasant
Salt and pepper to taste
¼ cup flour
6 tablespoons chicken stock
1¼ cups white wine
Bouquet garni
1 cup each chanterelles and artichoke
  hearts
1 cup cream
¼ cup Calvados

To enhance the flavor of the game, prepare a *mirepoix* by sautéing the carrots, celery, onion, asparagus tips, garlic, prosciutto, bay leaf, and thyme together in ¼ cup of the butter for 20 minutes or until tender. Dust each pheasant breast with salt, pepper, and 1 tablespoon of the flour. Over moderate heat, fry the breasts in the *mirepoix* until golden. Allow the *mirepoix* to brown and even burn. Add the breasts, chicken stock, white wine, and bouquet garni to a second saucepan. Cover and cook for 20 minutes over low heat. Remove the pheasant and drain the liquid by half. In a skillet, sauté the chanterelles and artichoke hearts. In the first saucepan, remove all but ¼ cup of the *mirepoix,* then deglaze the pan with the cream. Add the remaining ¼ cup of butter and allow to boil for 1 minute. Add the liquid from the second saucepan and the Calvados. Add the pheasant breasts, chanterelles, and artichokes, then allow the sauce to bubble for a few seconds and serve.

Serves 4

CHAPTER 30

WHIRLWIND IN THE YAAK

By Terry Tempest Williams

Narrow, winding roads above the river
A moose mirrored in water
Fog
Rain
Moss, ferns, flowering dogwood, trilliums, huckleberries,
*   thimbleberries, an understory so rich, a canopy so high—*
Pines
Spruce
Firs
More pines
More spruce
More firs
Little light in the forest
Too much light in the forest
A clearing
A clearing of stumps
A clear-cut
More clear-cuts
Chain saws
Bulldozers
Stretchers
Trucks, flatbed trucks, trucks ready and waiting to haul the
felled bodies of trees

Down the roads
Up the roads
The roads, dirt roads, dusty roads, winding roads
Roads carving up the mountains
Fog
Rain
Erosion
Soil bleeding into the rivers
Muddy rivers
Rivulets streaming down the hillsides
More clear-cuts
More slash and burn
Smoke
Fire
We cannot see the forest for the trees
Slashpiles, piles of paper, this sheet of paper
Must we cut these trees?
A reprieve of uncut forests
Pines
Spruce
Firs
Hemlocks
Cedar
Larch
Deer eyes
Flicker cries
Homestead
Rock wall
Home made of wood in a clearing
Two small girls dressed in chintz are waiting on the porch
A door opens
I see a cultured life in the wilderness

Breakfast with friends on the porch
Screened porch
A man sits comfortably in a rocking chair
A woman tends to her garden
Great Blue Heron stands in the meadow watching, waiting
The sound of chain saws rise from the forest
Smoke
Fire
By the hands of man, trees are felled
One by one
Clear-cuts
More clear-cuts
Logging trucks storm down the road transporting the bodies of
  trees
To the mill
To the lumber yard
To be sold
One by one, two by fours
Hauled to Home Depots on
Narrow, winding roads
Roadkills
R a coooooooon   rab b i ts q u i r r e l
m aggggggg pie,   d eer
doefawnunborndead
Deer eyes on the edge of the forest
We are all complicit living in our homes made of wood
My home is made of wood
Here in the Yaak, the sky turns green
A green sky is followed by stillness
A circle wind arrives
Tall pines bend and sway, bend and sway
Tall pines bend and sway more furiously

Tall pines snap
The circle wind
is recognized
for what
it is a
tor
na
do
We run for cover
Everywhere trees fall,
   slam to the ground,
   trunks break,   branches
shatter,
a random uprootedness threatens our safety.
In seconds, the woods have changed—
The wind is gone
We emerge out of hiding, humbled, witnesses to a whirlwind
   we didn't know was coming.
Windfalls
Clear-cuts
What is natural and what is not when it comes to the evolution of
   destruction?
Deer eyes glare from deep inside the forest
       —Silence—
If I am a hunter, it is for this eyeshine in the dark
       not to kill,
but to see.

CHAPTER 31

LATITUDE/LONGITUDE

By Sandra Alcosser

47.460 DEGREES NORTH
114.882 DEGREES WEST

We braid Bitterroot to Clark Fork to Jocko to Flathead

Clark Fork to Bull to Yaak

North over Wild Horse Plains through Paradise Valley.

*A white stage floats highwater between outcrops of soft pink silts
that with the slightest persuasion might collapse.*

*A glacial lake exploded through here thousands of years ago, but today
only a man on stage nervously points toward the sky.*

*The larch broaden and begin to droop as we race—deciduous, soft green needle
leaves on spur shoots. Solitary naked flowers. Papery cones. They take us in, slow
and hush us.*

*Larch will outlast oak. If we stepped outside our vehicle we might bend
to drink water from the lupine's cupped palm. We might trill.*

*Under small twinflower, violet, heathers, huckleberry shrub—frail branchings—
we might sink into forest floor, sink into duff, sink into vanish.*

*Larch timbers built into oldest of castles outlasted stone. A tree might live eight
hundred years after a century of rapid growth.*

48.833 DEGREES NORTH
115.708 DEGREES WEST

*A bird barely escapes our windshield, its body a tiny projectile that reaches the
crotch of a V, and at the moment of impact, pivots, feathers away. Too fast to be
identifiable, a bird escapes us in one piece.*

Travel, by definition, ecstatic.

*Raphael painted his great work on canvases of larch. Gilded madonnas
rising from crimson air.*

*We come around another curve below the speed limit (too fast) to see a lone boy,
clothes the color of asphalt , chasing a gray kite down the center-line of pavement.*

He is lost in that dream of wind current, the way it makes the dark triangular object
dip, yes up, and spin.
Speed a function of distance over time.

We speed north early summer evening—
to enter a longhouse in the Yaak Valley used for basketball, theater, and church,
to read poetry from behind a pulpit to neighbors who have come from the forest
to listen on hard wooden benches, on homemade rockers.

We are not driving recklessly, we are below the speed limit. As we pass through
this forest strung with Old Man's Beard, we hear nothing, smell nothing.

A vacuum between danger and dream.

There is nothing fast about the growth of trees.

Nothing fast about poetry—the line itself a furrow,
an act of attention, a unit of sense.

The god of speed is the god of commerce, travel, thievery.
On his planet the atmosphere is thin.
The stars move three times faster across his sky.

46.632 DEGREES NORTH
114.078 DEGREES WEST

We map to hold ourselves in place.

Before latitude / longitude, a navigator might sail no more than a day or two
from sight of land. Even then he had to carry elaborate
star maps in his mind: parrot fish, falling gourds.

For eighteen months I have been traveling

I live on Como Stony in the Bitterroots.
Carlton Creek Drainage
south of Lantern Ridge.

While I was gone a corporation took away the forest
behind my house, highgrading,
leaving only defects behind.

This forest was a gift. Two percent of the United States presented
in the nineteenth century to Northern Pacific
to finance the building of a transcontinental telegraph and railway.

True? The greatest forest fires of American history hit forests with a high percent-

age of spruce/ pine/ fir in areas exposed to dry winds on mountain sides where relative humidity drops below 30% due to logging and road building.

In the valley where I live, planners sometimes wear bulletproof vests.

48.833 DEGREES NORTH
115.708 DEGREES WEST

The road is hypnotic no matter what speed.
No one and no one and no one forever as the wool-like bolt of gray
unwraps before us over dense green.

Threatened / Sensitive / Disappearing

woodland caribou   wolverine   goshawk   falcon   moonworts
big-eared bats   small lady's slipper   short-head and torrent sculpin
water howellia   kidney-leaved violet
black-backed woodpecker   round-leaved orchid   green-keeled cottongrass
bog birch   crested shield-fern   Spalding's catchfly
northern bog lemming   gray wolf   fisher   grizzly bear   lynx
harlequin duck   golden and bald eagle   salamander   trout
flammulated, boreal, great gray owl

Twenty-five thousand miles of logging roads in Montana.

2/3 of Montana citizens say no to more roads on nationally protected lands.

Push and pull between our speed and the landscape
on the other side of the windshield.

42.460 DEGREES NORTH
71.349 DEGREES WEST

In the last eighteen months wherever I traveled people talked to me about their
forest. In Massachusetts I ask a visiting scholar from Japan if he knows who wrote:
Green leaves, young leaves
Speaking of what took place
600 years ago

He says it sounds like Issa, the poet whose name means
a single bubble in steeping tea.
The scholar draws Issa's shrine. Made of cedar, replaced ritually every twenty years,
the wood is no longer available. The shrine for Japan's great eighteenth-century poet
has to be imported.

We walk Estabrook Woods where the American Revolutionary War began, where the
Minutemen marched, and Paul Revere rode, where Thoreau wrote in his journal. A boys' prep
school wants to turn acres of these woods into playing fields.
After all, Walden Pond almost became
a condominium development.

What if we each had an allotment for our lifetime and could decide: this for the
furniture of my family, the grain running longitudinally;
this for my house and the house of my grandchildren.
This for the pine marten.

Our most intimate response in life is to resources—air water food clothes shelter—
braided into the chemistry of our body and brain.

A family of five uses seventy-five trees each year for paper products.

95% of the forest in America logged, 4% left in dispute, and 1% protected.

Must we speak a language of usefulness when we speak of forests.
Usefulness = quantifiable mass.

48.851 Degrees North
115.657 Degrees West

Larch wood is durable, heavy and hard. Straight and free from large knots. Rich in resin
though not easily ignited. It does not splinter.

Traced in the air by radiations of light, three dimensional and symmetrical.

Rotting larch home for woodpeckers, owls, songbirds, osprey, bald eagles, Canada geese. Soft needles food for blue and spruce grouse Light seeds, 143,000/per pound with large wings, can fly 400 feet from parent tree.

A felled tree leaves a stain
(that's how forensic scientists follow Jefferson's designs at Monticello—they turn car lights on the
field at night to study the stains of Jefferson's trees).

There is a value to objects that is neither monetary nor utilitarian.

A history of the heart.

You could make your own forest. If you were good with your hands.

Holes, apertures, hairy surfaces. Rough hessian smeared with wax.

After all, the whole world is made of fiber. And if you could somehow weave it back together.

It would be necessary of course this forest.

The tribal history and religion of most cultures rooted in the tree.

Inexhaustible life with delicate expendable leaves, roots underground and branches rising to the sky moving between hell and heaven, linking different worlds.

Tree = true.

The Egyptians left the heart in the mummy because they knew it was the center.

All centers—symbols of eternity. Time the periphery wheeling around the unmoved.

47.594 DEGREES NORTH
115.346 DEGREES WEST

We court speed to escape time. We become less intimate, better able to objectify.

As I see the man on the white stage, he sees me as a speeding white automobile on the road above. I am noise.

His stage a pontoon boat from which he casts a line. Over the sound of wind in the canyon, the shussing of river, he cradles a cell phone and points at the sky.

When I enter a car and drive as fast as I can, I become a weapon.

The forest
ovate pinnacled bobbing light
the forest shapes our brain
our history (the wheel)
our eye

If you gave us a way to choose would we choose wisely.

From granite and volcanics stirred, dissolved. From tide pools.
from mosses and liverworts.

Would we choose beauty, would we choose history, rootedness, dwelling place.

An isolated cell never turns into wood; it must be stimulated by the pressure of
others.

Is there another way.

Seventy million years ago came summer green leaf-dropping trees.

CHAPTER 32

THE YAAK

FOR RICK BASS

By Alison Hawthorne Deming

1

At the party in Missoula everyone
was excited about the poetry slam
in Troy. I said I'm going north
to take a walk in the woods with
Rick Bass, and all they could talk
about was how last year Denis Johnson
lit his book on fire after reading
from it. I said I'm going north
to take a walk with Rick Bass,
then someone heard me and asked,
You're going to the Yaak? (like it's
a god not a place which it is) that's not
the middle of nowhere, it's beyond it,
the edge.

I drove along
the Clark Fork, road that follows
water's lead, up out of the plains
and hills to the thick place
where mountains and rivers
and forests work together without

interference until those scabs
of harvesting come. Still
ravines of blue-green darkness
called me, larches and hemlock,
and the hand-drawn map
that took me into them.
Grizzly country, where I stopped
to admire ice layered blue
on Hell Roaring Creek.

When I arrived
Lowry barefoot on the porch—She's
driving a silver limo!—the celebrity of
any visitor coming to the far away.
Mary Katherine—was she reading,
painting, something inward? Rick
planting bulbs in the near-frozen
ground. Elizabeth heating soup.

The first walk—I'm not afraid of
the bears, she said, but the lions
will stalk you. One walked
right by the window. Last winter
right here—near the cabin made
of the homestead's salvaged beams—
I saw two little black bear cubs.
Here a pack of wolves—
usually only one. Here,
he said,

(what they've witnessed
of the untamed world marking
their landscape like
animal scent) under a tree
like this (big larch with
yellow rain of needles
spilled like sawdust—
I thought at first
it was the work of
woodpeckers drilling and
leaving a mess behind—
but, no, then the fallen
needles looked like light
the tree had spilled
in a halo on the ground),

in a place like this, he said,
sheltered and dry, in winter
you might see five or six deer
lined up, stores, left by
a lion—and then more larches,
a few giant elders, others
reaching the age when
the bark is thick enough
to withstand a fire, and then
the spot where wildfire bloomed
and they came with buckets, the
girls with watering cans, for days,
and long after they thought
the fire was out, night after night,
the ground glowed red.

Walking home,
we crossed the brown hummocky grass,
circle of marsh round as
the iris of an eye, opening,
across which the ravens
          call and call.

2

In the dark before sunrise
we eat cheese toast and dress
so thick we walk like moonmen
across the crusted marsh
and into the sleeping woods. Yesterday
tracks in snow—a very big animal,
they'd said, bending down to see,
urine spattered, buck sign on
three trees that mark the trail
where the does keep passing,
the buck's arousal
scraped into wood,
saplings bark-bare and raw
where he rubbed and rubbed his scent.

Rick's set up out of sight, my job
to lie beneath a giant larch,
await the light, rattle antlers
and grunt the buck's call,
riling the old stud to defend
his dominance.

On ground
hallowed by scat and spit
and pillage of wolf, bear, and lion,
stories now are prey—one hunter
found two skeletons, antlers
deadlocked, bucks fixed in
combat's embrace then
the shared quiet end, though
each must have cried out
against its helplessness;
another hunter—tone of voice
the mark of his aroused
admiration—watched a buck
work a circle of five does,
moving from one to the other,
mounting and jerking
until he'd had them all.

3

I love to think
my animal presence
is equal to being
predator or prey, no agent
of dominion, rather
subject to the rule
of violent need—all I might
inflict might be inflicted
on me. But truth is harder
than desire. The human mind

makes seeds that spew and drift
and carry us far from our will
or wish to be benign. Most of what
we generate floats only
through neurological space,
making us confuse what
we dream with how we live.
It's time to leave the forest,
go home for pancakes and coffee,
and let the ravens and squirrels
move on to smaller complaints.
We creak up out of hiding,
our footsteps loud, stopping
the snowshoe rabbit that freezes
on the haunch of a snowy deadfall.
Pure white, except the godly
brown eyes, it watches us, thinking
nothing that my human mind
can comprehend—not, Should I
escape, or, Am I hiding well enough,
or Great-Force-of-Mystery
protect me. It just thinks
the stillness its body demands.

CHAPTER 33

LOOKING OUT/LOOKING IN

By Laura Sedler

I HAVE NEVER DREAMED ON MOUNT HENRY LOOKOUT. LYING there, crowded up against my husband on the narrow bed, my sleep is light and shallow. Occasionally the forest radio crackles and hums, a midnight transmission from some far-off fire. Meanwhile, the moon and stars illuminate the mountaintop through the multipaned windows that encircle the cabin, and the wind whistles constantly around the rails of the catwalk, changing pitch with each shift of direction. I peer out from the blankets often, checking the progress of the night by the positions of the heavens, until finally a slight suggestion of dawn appears to the east. By five A.M. the westernmost peaks of Glacier National Park are outlined by the growing dawn, and I am thinking ahead to the smell of coffee and a chilled foray down the tower stairs. By six, the Yaak River Valley is full of yellow light and mist rises steaming from the water. Smoke drifts from scattered chimneys, marking the places where people live.

My first trip up the mountain was in August 1986. My husband, Shamus, was putting in two days of relief duty for the regular lookout. Our oldest son, Jesse, and I hiked up to join him, bringing dinner, extra supplies, and a bottle of wine to savor with the sunset. It was a warm, sultry day at the trailhead at the end of Solo Joe Road; scattered cumulus drifted in from the west. I was unprepared for the two-mile hike in. The trail rose steadily, at times quite steeply, winding through open flats of lodgepole and larch, past gray talus slopes, and finally into a scattered forest of white-bark pine, bear grass, and alpine fir; blue gentian, whortleberry, and saxifrage carpeting the ground. A red-tailed hawk screamed across a rocky opening as I paused, sucking in the thinning air. At each switchback I stopped, looking back over my shoulder as more and more of the valley spread out below, the far mountain ridges coming into view as we climbed. Negotiating the final pitch, I swore I would never again carry so heavy a pack up that mountain. It was a vow I have repeated often; somehow a bottle of clear, red Bardolino always makes it to the top.

There was magic for me in that first visit: a recognition of an unfulfilled, unknown desire to be in high places; a need to view this valley I have called home from a larger perspective.

In the spring of 1987, Shamus was offered the lookout's job for the season. He accepted; he would spend the next three summers looking out from Mount Henry. Living up there, in solitude and splendor, the lookout wrote:

> *A 14 X 14 Fire Lookout Tower*
> *on top of a 7,000 ft. mountain*
> *is a private place.*
> *The glass walls don't change that.*

Every place has a history, a record of natural events and influences. The original look-out on Mount Henry was constructed in the 1930s. It sat at the apex of the mountain, just above the last of the twisted pines that mark the timberline. Set on a foundation of rock, it was built with timbers hauled up by horses and mules from the lower slopes. At that time, before the advent of spotter planes and sophisticated radios, there were nine towers in the Yaak Valley. From Mount Henry, you could see towers on four of the surrounding peaks. Squatting in the lee of the west wind, backed up against the old foundation wall and glassing Lost Horse Peak for the remnants of one of those old structures, I imagined the lookout watching for the smoke from his neighbor's cooking fires, wondering what the others were up to; each of them living on their own private summit. Packing up the trail with a couple of mules in early summer, the lookout would settle in for the fire season; supplementing his bare supplies with fresh game, berries, and sweet trout caught at dusk in the clear, green lake that sits at the foot of the northeast col. Spotting a fire, he would pack up his mules—shovel, ax, buckets, and grub—and head out to fight it. The lookout would slide into the rhythms of the mountain; moving to the dance of the wind and the hum of sun-warmed granite through the fleeting summer of the northern Rockies.

The original lookout cabin is gone now; the remaining foundation walls make a good place to sit and write, doze or daydream. Beside them stands an elevated wooden tower that was built in the 1950s. These days, a helicopter flies in each June bringing tanks of propane to fuel a cooking stove and small refrigerator. Exploring down on the south side, nearby the spiny quarter-mile trail that leads to the closest spring, I found on one of my visits a few weathered posts marking the corrals where the mules were kept. At the spring, an old tin dipper still hangs by the deeply shaded spring where my husband comes each evening to fill his water jugs. The dipper speaks to me of a long history of lookouts and visitors drawn to this water, sweating and thirsty; grateful for the sweet coolness, grateful to be down out of the wind. Tall-ribbed veratrum, a scattering of purple asters, and creeping yellow mimulus mark the seep, even in the driest of summers.

I went up the mountain many times those three seasons in the late 1980s that Shamus was lookout. Our son Edward—the youngest at seven—sometimes stayed the week, taming golden-mantled ground squirrels and building elaborate card houses as the tower shifted in the winds. The experience marked his drawings and stories for years to come. Often another of our four sons would join me; making the dusty drive to the trailhead, I would gather my spirits and make the climb, carrying fresh supplies. Reaching the top, drenched in sweat, the lookout would welcome me warmly with a towel and a cup of tea. Lying on the narrow bed in the late afternoon, having nothing to do—nothing to do—I would nap in the greenhouse heat of the westering sun. Eating dinner while hawks circled the tower, I felt intensely happy, at home. Seeing my home valley from this high place, and somehow able to place myself more precisely in the pattern of a larger world, I felt change in my heart, and a lifting of my spirit.

There have been many words written from the tops of mountains: novels, essays, books of poetry. On Mount Henry an open journal waits on the small gray desk to receive the comments and wisdoms of all who make the climb; most accept the invitation. Generations of earnest young students and seasoned loners have signed up to spend their summers in small glass-lined cabins, watching the forest and seeking solace, earning a living and living alone. Each person brings to the job their own particular set of expectations and aspirations. What they find is the mountain and the surrounding forests, just as they are. Awakening to the life of the place—the smell of juniper and shrill company of the rock picas and marmots, the subtle shadings of lichens and mosses outlining the steep rock slopes—a soul may begin to settle in; surrendering to the inescapable forces of wind, weather, and time. With an open heart, you might become the mountain. Toward the end of his last full season on Henry my lookout wrote:

> *All of my time has become*
> *now.*
> *My pacing is not to leave this mountain,*
> *I know I never can.*

I have at home a volume of poems by Robinson Jeffers that have been beautifully paired with black-and-white photographs of the Big Sur coast. Jeffers spent a lot of time alone on those high ridges overlooking the Pacific, and the volume is titled *Not Man Apart.* Approaching nature, we don't always know what to say. We have come to feel awkward and out of place, like intruders at a gathering of beings to whom we are only distantly related. Going onto the mountain—building towers, suppressing wild-fires, measuring its rhythms—the mountain is altered. We may be altered too.

Today I am back on the mountain for a visit, pondering the completion of this essay and what I want to say. It is a cool, cloudy day, and strong gusts of wind shudder the tower. Above the windows children's drawings, sketches, and photographs have been tacked up by people to whom this place has become home, some of my own among them. An entry in the tower journal by a woman from Canada reads: "The Geese were migrating the day I was here, September 18th 1991. Large flocks have been passing to the west of the tower, honking and carrying on. From up here you can look down on them and see the wing bars quite clearly. There is a dusting of snow from yesterday and I heard elk bugling on the way up the trail. I hope to return again, it has been lovely. Thank you, Mount Henry, for sharing this day with me." Looking once more out over the valley where the people live, I feel part of the whole. Looking out and looking in.

CHAPTER 34

HERE'S TO YOU, MR. ROBINSON

By John Wickersham

MOUNT ROBINSON MARKS THE EXTREME NORTHEAST BOUNDARY
of the Yaak. And although it is one of the few truly high points in an otherwise
rounded feminine landscape, it does not occupy a central place in the Yaak consciousness. Unlike Mount Henry, its neighbor to the south—a mountain that rises from the
valley floor in striking, solitary fashion and looms on the horizon from almost any van-
tage point—Mount Robinson straddles the Canadian border, lurking in the northern
shadows like a bandit. It is a hard mountain to see from most places in the valley, yet
everyone knows where it is. For most people, the mere mention of the name elicits a
wry smile and a knowing nod. "Interesting country," they say, while also admitting that
they've never been there. Mount Robinson seems to violate the law of mountain
locales; it is higher than almost every other mountain in the area, yet it does not draw
people to it. In this case, higher is not necessarily more attractive, an anomaly among
mountains.

It is outlaw country and, as such, Mount Robinson gathers more legends and stories
than it does visitors. Down in the valley, people talk about a plane that crashed up
there in the 1950s. By itself, this is not much of an oddity; planes crash in the mountains with alarming regularity. However, this particular plane was carrying, so the people say, a cargo of gold bullion. Nobody has ever found anything up there and, very
likely, the stories are just colorful exaggerations, bandit tales. The mountain has apparently cached the gold in one of the many secret nooks flanking its craggy ridges. Or it
swallowed it up. Or it just sat there, passively stoic, indifferent, while the people in the
valley made up their stories. Not even the mythical prospect of hidden treasure,
though, seems to be inviting enough to bring people to this remote corner of the Yaak.

Mount Robinson is on the shrouded fringe of a forgotten valley. Gold or no gold, the mountain's a treasure; it is the centerpiece for seven thousand acres of roadless, tangled wildness.

Like Pancho Villa or Geronimo, Mount Robinson protects his border stronghold carefully, always seemingly ready to slide off into Canada at the slightest provocation. Access to Robinson country is, therefore, a problem. From the west, it is guarded by a maze of old logging roads. On the map, these roads look like bacteria on a microscope slide, squirming this way and that, but never leading anywhere except old harvest units, now overgrown with alder and lodgepole pine thickets. If you make it past the clear-cuts, you still have to find your way through a swampy, mosquito-infested forest of spruce and subalpine fir. And most of the time you can't even see the mountain. You trust your compass but invariably wind up lost, bleeding, and bug-swollen.

So after repeated failures from the west, I decided finally to cross out of the Yaak watershed, following the road down from Porcupine Creek, through ponderosa pines splashed with yellow balsam root, to Koocanusa Reservoir. Skirting the west flank of the reservoir, I follow Young Creek to the Lake Geneva Trailhead. From there, the trail winds through a beautiful forest of spruce and fir to Lake Geneva, a clear mountain tarn surrounded, as Thoreau noticed at Walden, by "eyelashes" of old-growth spruce. The lake rests in a glacial cirque; boulder-strewn ridges and cliffs rise from its shores. Mount Robinson's summit, though, is not yet visible above the ridgeline.

The lake's surface is broken repeatedly by rising trout; slow-motion ripples float toward the shore. Strange, I think to myself, for fish to be so active in the middle of the day. As I slip off my backpack and rest on a moss-covered log, I soon realize why the fish are jumping. Thick clouds of mosquitoes appear as if from thin air, conjured by the same demented backcountry spirit. Continually swatting my arms, legs, face, and sweat-drenched shoulders, I decide that motion is probably the best antidote. After quickly filling a small day pack, I half jog to the steep hillside on the north shore of the lake. Sweat drips down my face, mingling with spruce needles and dirt, as I scramble through the last thirty feet of rocky ledges in the ridgetop. Pausing to wipe my face on my T-shirt, I convince myself that sweat-stung eyes and brush-raked legs are vastly preferable to the hordes of voracious mosquitoes at the lakeshore below. Wispy, low-level clouds swirl among the trees; the top of Mount Robinson appears for an instant, then fades away like a dream.

On top of the ridge, I follow a well-established elk trail, meandering through car-sized boulders and stunted spruce, fir, and white-bark pine. Gray jays and Clark's nutcrackers scold me from perches only a few feet from my head; their inimitable squawks sound jarringly foreign yet utterly native, rooted. Beautiful violet penstemon and scarlet rock cress cling to the thin soil and sprout from impossible angles in the cliff crevices. Juncos and white-crowned sparrows dart among the lower branches while a raven glides from somewhere beyond the ridge, its wings noisily slicing the thick, diaphanous afternoon light. The lake shimmers below.

The elk trail takes me around the ridge where I see remnant, patchy forests laced with logging roads stretching out to the west. Koocanusa Reservoir, the Tobacco Valley, and the pale blue outline of the Whitefish Range are visible on the eastern horizon. A pine-scented breeze brushes my face. Elk trails always remind me of mountain streams; they seem to flow between trees, around rocks. With elk, the shortest distance between two points is anything but a straight line. In fact, straightness is a human construct. While we bridge rivers and blast roads through mountainsides, elk seem to be content just to wander up, down, around, in and out. I feel like an elk today as I scramble over boulders and duck beneath tree limbs.

Lake Geneva is no longer visible as I pass behind a rocky shoulder on Mount Robinson's north flank. On this particular ridge there is a ghost forest of huge old white-bark pine—killed by blister rust fungus, most likely. While most white-barks are gnarled and wind-stunted, these are thick—some are three feet in diameter—and their bare branches, ghastly pallid, scratch the sky fifty or sixty feet above me. Like the people of the Yaak Valley, these trees were renegades, recluses. They were holed up on this remote ridge for three or four hundred years—a quirky, odd bunch with their multiple tops, twisted boles and broad, spreading branches. And while most of the old hermit trees are dead or dying, some are still hanging on, defiant. There are deer and elk pellets scattered among the old trees like dark hailstones—the ghost forest apparently still proving adequate summer shelter even while it no longer contains many living trees. A Cooper's hawk flashes through the oddly filtered light, banks, and heads downvalley.

The stark outline of Mount Robinson's summit ridge now appears to the south, a dilapidated wind-worn fire lookout marking the top. Though the weather has cleared in the surrounding valleys, Mount Robinson still holds a sheet of vaporous, phantom-like clouds around it like an outlaw's mask. They scuttle by, dissipate, and reemerge. The ridgeline to the summit is dotted with delicate-looking subalpine larch, small in comparison to their lower-elevation cousins, but hardy and resilient. This is an often harsh place of wind and snow, and these trees are survivors. The ridge grows steeper, and sheer cliffs mark its boundaries on either side, sliding abruptly to the valley bottoms below. After some frightening missteps and fatigued stumbles, I emerge on the summit.

The valley unfolds before me in pelagic waves. The uneven afternoon light, coupled with the intermittent clouds, gives the surrounding sea of mountains the illusion of motion. Gary Snyder's image of "blue mountains constantly walking" comes to mind as I take in the panoramic view. A Townsend's solitaire sings from the top of a dead larch while a hermit thrush's flutelike warble drifts up on the afternoon thermals from the valley floor below. Spotted saxifrage, western spring beauty, and sulfur buckwheat add color to the lichen-covered rocks that are strewn about the summit.

As my eyes adjust to the oddly diffuse light, I notice the extent of the clear-cuts. Mount Henry, Grubstake Mountain, and Caribou Mountain rise from the valley floor through a literal maze of barren harvest units, like pieces of a jigsaw puzzle spilled across a green tablecloth. It is a sight as severe as it seems anomalous, unnatural. The clear-cuts just look so out of place in the gentlish forested landscape of the Yaak Valley. The words of the English poet Gerard Manley Hopkins echo in my mind as if dropped down an empty cistern: "O if we but knew what we do when we delve or hew, hack and rack the growing green!" Written more than a hundred years ago, the words are hauntingly powerful today. Has the past century given us any profound insight into the inner workings of forests? Do we realize any more today "what we do"? The clouds reconvene and the view is suddenly lost. I leave the top feeling displaced, disheartened.

As I am walking down the summit ridge, though, I think about my home state of Colorado. I live in the San Juan Mountains where there are more than seven hundred thousand acres of federally protected wilderness areas. However, there are only a few grizzlies left, perhaps none at all. There are rumors of lynx and wolverine, but there haven't been any reliable sightings in years. There are no wolves. Colorado's is a paper wilderness, conspicuously empty, even hollow. It strikes me that there are many more components to wilderness than easily delineated roadless areas. Federal protection is no substitute for thousands of years of evolution. Congress cannot create wildness; it can only hope to preserve what is left. It may be another hundred years or more before the San Juans echo with the howls of wolves, before the sight of a grizzly track on a melting snowfield prompts atavistic shudders in Colorado. The Yaak, despite the proliferation of "management" on its forests, despite the glaring absence of designated wilderness and its omnipresent roads, is still wild. True wilderness has a foothold in the Yaak; in Colorado it must wait patiently, dormant, to reemerge. The Yaak's is a wilderness not on paper but on the ground and beneath the skin. Wildness is a feeling, palpable, yet not very easily quantified. And it still exists in the Yaak, in places like Mount Robinson—remnant and isolated cores of what once was. Mount Robinson is like a time capsule, preserving, if tenuously, that feeling. But for how long?

I continue walking north along the ridge over a jumbled topography of quartzite talus and huge frozen-bubble formations of dusky Purcell lava—evidence of volcanic activity millions of years ago. I wonder what this place will look like millions of years from now. The dynamic nature of landscapes is overwhelming. If nature abhors a vacuum, she is certainly irritated by long-term balances, by equilibria. It is somewhat of a comfort to know that our puny human actions—our dams, roads, and clear-cuts—though ugly, disruptive, and harmful in the short term, will be nothing but a faint scar in the fossil record millions of years from now. The laws of thermodynamics confirm what Yeats wrote at the beginning of this century: "Things fall apart, the center cannot hold." And while things do indeed "fall apart," they also re-form, a continuity we can't possibly understand, a pattern we dare not predict. Although Yeats concluded his poem with the bleak specter—"What rough beast, its hour come round at last, slouches toward Bethlehem to be born"—we can only hope that our minimal understanding and our frighteningly myopic decisions today will not create

CHAPTER 35

SOLSTICE

By Roy Parvin

THEY WARNED US ABOUT THE DOGS. TOLD US, IF WE KNEW
what was good for ourselves, not to bring them. That dogs and grizzlies don't mix and
to hike with a dog in such country, in grizzly country, well, it's plain bad news, an accident waiting to happen.

We brought the dogs anyway. Two Border collies, sheepdogs, a strain of canine
expressly bred not to bark else they'll scare the herd, scattering them to kingdom come.
Besides, they—our dogs, Maggie and Kody—are family, the closest Janet and I will
ever get to children, and we take them everywhere including this green place in the top
shelf of Montana, a place with a name that looks like it's from some long-dead language: Yaak.

Today is the summer solstice. We've driven a thousand miles and change to get here.
It was a rough winter in the part of the world where we live, so bad that spring never
really took root at all, the rains continuing unabated clear into June. The idea came on
the whip-and-spur, to visit the Yaak, a sunny whim to spend the longest day of the year
in a place where a day might last almost forever.

We drove so fast, it was Idaho before we knew it. Now it's the next morning and the
rest of the day yawns before us like a promise, enough time for anything. For starters,
we hike up Northwest Peak, a moderate tramp in deep timber. Every ten steps or so I
rattle a pop can filled with change to keep the grizzlies off our backs. Other than that,
we hike in silence. It is enough to just be here and though we've never been here before
before, this tilt of land feels oddly familiar: We know cousins of the spruce and red
cedar we walk under.

We've come from somewhere that is not altogether different than Yaak. A wild place with many trees and not many roads, populated by a hardy few who've taken root under the old growth. In truth, each wild area is unique, as individual as people, and it's wrong to lump them in a single category.

However, I do detect a similar type of earth-blood coursing through such places. Places that are big and muscular in their rawness and yet are, paradoxically, fragile as a china cup. Places that have given and given—in terms of timber and ore—and should be allowed to simply rest. Pulling in the valley this morning, we saw the clear-cuts that stud these sheer hillsides, standing out like a shaved head. The Yaak looks tired of being dug out and cut down.

The place from where we've come—I protect it with a fierceness that extends down its name, the not altogether unreasonable fear that whenever I utter it to someone from the outside world something gets subtracted, lost forever. That we shouldn't be here in the Yaak does not escape me. We try to walk as quietly as possible, despite the clatter of the soda pop can. I try to convince myself we're exchange students, from one wild place to another.

Like all good guests we come bearing gifts from our particular neck of the woods. When we visited the North Slope of the Brooks Range on a dogsled expedition, I tucked in my parka slivers of puzzle bark sloughed off a ponderosa pine that grows outside our cabin home. I left them, like an offering, along a frozen oxbow of the Sagavanirktok River. On a mesa above the San Juan River in Utah it was a snowball— the last remnants of the terrible blizzards of 1993—stored in the icebox since then for just such an opportunity, transported into the desert inside a cooler with dry ice. Now a few speckled granite river rocks plucked from our creek ride low in my day pack.

A couple of miles through the haunting green filter of spruce and fir and we reach tree line, the remainder of the trail traversing open talus. There's an ancient lookout cabin at the top, we've been told, that's filled with cookware and other artifacts from a bygone time. Wind whips across the open face of rock. There's still snow in places.

At the crest we nibble fruit but the view itself is what fills us up, the humped shoulders of the Cabinet Mountains. According to our maps, Canada is so close, we can almost reach out and touch it. A ghosted moon keeps its steady vigil, waiting on an evening that perhaps will never come. You can dream on days like today—you can dream on any day, of course—but today, the longest day of the year, in a place such as this, it feels like your dreams somehow have a better shot at coming true. I think about living forever, Janet and me and the dogs. I think about the rugged forested place we've come from, and about the Yaak, too, the sweet long shot that perhaps the wilderness just might outlive us all.

The sun and clouds are playing a slow-motion game of hide-and-seek. From up here, this high rocky aerie, the land looks unbroken.

Behind us, on the ridgeline, the lookout's walls are stoved in like a crumpled hat. The door opens with rusty complaint. What we find inside are not the quaint cookery and enamelware that were promised but liquor bottles of all description, enough to stock a hotel bar, and walls covered in a riot of graffiti. Though we're not the ones guilty of leaving this trash heap, somehow it feels that way, the granite river rocks I've carried all these miles pressing heavier against the shallow of my back.

Outside in the open air I notice a lone stump of alpine larch. There's writing on this, too, but not the scrawl of meaningless names and dates. It reads 180 YEARS OLD: A WASTE. What's left of the tree is about as big around as a salad plate, wouldn't be any more than a teenager in our woods, but the rings are as tight as the whorls of a fingerprint. For the moment, the threat of grizzlies feels awfully remote.

It's afternoon, the same endless day, the sun still high up the ladder of sky. We've spent the fat middle of day lazing along a stretch of the Yaak River, behind the mercantile store, reading, napping, tossing sticks for the dogs, the slow drift of the river as it passes us by.

It is sunshine and magic and right now I have no complaints. High above, a hawk glides in the blue. I feel like I've dropped thirty years, am eleven again, the newly minted summer as bright and shiny as a penny.

Someone in the mercantile has told us about a property he caretakes, a spread of seventy acres, somewhere we might want to see. His directions are more whimsy than precision—navigation by wind-leaning lodgepole pines, distances described in stone throws—and we overshoot the correct turnoff our first tries but that's okay. Today we have all the time in the world.

The sign for Yaak is no bigger than the cover of a book. It simply says YAAK—no elevation or population data. Yaak: like a typo, like a name the land might have given itself if it could talk. There are only two signs, coming and going. As we wheel down the road now, we encounter signs of a different nature, advertising parcels for sale, a picket fence of signs, one every couple hundred yards, like the "before" picture to something, or a warning.

It's a ranch, the property, or was once that. The grass stands if not as tall as an elephant's eye at least as high as Janet's. In the middle distance a high-gabled barn is coming undone one board at a time; it looks like the prow of a great ship gradually sinking into the earth. If there's a story to this spread's demise—and there must be; everything has a story—the land isn't giving up its secret. That's fine with us. You can't trust a place that gives up its secrets too easily.

Everything is golden: the sky, the grass, the wide valley. We walk toward the fringe of trees in the far distance, where we know the river must be. The dogs play a canine version of tag, disappearing entirely in the giant spokes of grass, only a constant rustling, the occasional arch of a back bounding above the surface, like porpoises breaching the sea.

The going turns boggy and we double back. Over by the farmhouse we flatten out a square of grass and lie back and stare up at a patchwork sky. After putting so many miles on the car—and ourselves yesterday—we're going nowhere fast and I'm delighted to be along for the ride.

It's well past the dinner hour but still light by the time we return to town, to the Dirty Shame Saloon. We could do with food and drinks of certain descriptions and it's a good place for such things, better at least than it sounds, a low-hulking ceiling inside, the entire wall behind the bar papered in folding money, bills pasted up by travelers with inscriptions of where they came from, the promises of their return and the ready funds to buy drinks with when they do.

We can still smell the sun on our skin, the sun's still holding outside for that matter, shows no sign of tiring, and we're practically drunk on it by now, happy enough to sit up at the bar amid the gabble of conversation. A couple of fellows are getting pleasantly stinko a few stools down, arm-wrestling for drinks and cigars. The bartender—a woman whose name is Willie—smokes cigarettes as long as a wand, talks to us in a howl of a voice, dishes the lowdown on what's been happening lately.

Everybody knows everybody. They ask us where we're from and we tell them, even the name of the place; it's okay: We're among friends. We discuss this and that and nothing in particular, trading horror stories about the respective winters we endured.

And so it goes. It's a good deal later when another couple enters the bar. Everything stops for a beat, the chemistry of the room changing if only for a flicker, and it's clear that these folks aren't locals either. They sit at a table behind us and the questions go out, about where they're from. Massachusetts, they say, Boston. A call carries down the bar, to a fellow we'd talked to earlier. He looks like the very definition of mountain man, a waterfall of a beard, a build stout enough that he could have been hewn from the red cedar we hiked through this morning.

It turns out he's from Beantown, too, and he goes over to talk with them, brings his drink, and we can hear them discussing the Bruins and Fenway and other matters we could never hope to understand, each sentence his voice refashioning into the drawn-out vowels of a New England accent.

It's beautiful here, one of the couple tells him, and they all agree that it is. What do you do here? the other one wants to know and Mountain Man tells them the how and why he came to be here. It's a good story and I don't feel so bad for eavesdropping. And then it seems the conversation has reached the end of its string, nothing else to say. But one of the couple pipes up, We love it here, could imagine living here. What does real estate cost in the area? Do you know of any that's available?

I lean back to better hear how Mountain Man would answer. How does anyone answer such a question? I've been asked the selfsame often, regarding our little wedge of paradise, and I never know what to say.

After the longest silence he tells them gently, Yes land's available. Anything's available for a price. But if you come here, there'll be less of the valley for me. You seem perfectly nice, but do you see what I'm saying?

Janet glances over, her time-to-go look. We've eaten and drunk our fill, but it's not that. We've spent the longest day of the year in this lovely place and it has worked its spell, our long, dark winter seeming far behind us now. But the tight circle of hours we've been here—maybe even that small amount is too much for this tired valley. We didn't leave trash or graffiti in our wake. We covered our tracks pretty well.

But something's lost, there always is. That's how it works, little by little, until one day there's nothing left for the place to give, until it's the same place in name only, the magic going out like a guttering candle that's finally extinguished for good. And the truth of that, quite literally, hits home and I suddenly miss the trees of our forest more than I can say.

We settle up the tab, leave a tip but not a dollar bill to tack up over the bar. It's dark outside, finally dark. Inside the car, the dogs eagerly admit us back into the fold. It occurs to me that everybody had it wrong, warning us about bringing the dogs up here. It's we who shouldn't be in this country. The Yaak might need many things but more people aren't one of those.

We point the car toward the wild place that we call home, follow the picket fence of FOR SALE signs out. We stop briefly at the curve near Hellroaring Road. I take in hand the granite river rocks that I plucked from our creek, deposit them at the base of a tree. If we're lucky, nobody will ever know we were here.

ABOUT THE AUTHORS

Sandra Alcosser lives in the Bitterroot Mountains of western Montana. Before moving to Montana, she directed Poets in the Park, Central Park, and has been a poet-in-residence for Glacier National Park. Her latest book of poems, *Except by Nature,* received four national awards, including the Academy of American Poets' James Laughlin Award for the best second book of poetry in America. James Tate selected Alcosser's first book, *A Fish to Feed All Hunger,* to be the Associated Writing Programs Award Series winner in poetry. Alcosser directs the MFA Program in Creative Writing at San Diego State University each fall and has been a recent visiting writer at the University of Michigan and the University of Montana.

Rick Bass is the author of seventeen books of fiction and nonfiction, including, most recently, *The Hermit's Story,* a fiction collection published by Houghton Mifflin, and *The Book of Yaak.* He lives with his family in the Yaak and is a member of the Yaak Valley Forest Council, the Montana Wilderness Association, Cabinet Resource Group, and Round River Conservation Studies.

Before turning to freelance writing full time, **Bob Butz** was the managing editor for *The Pointing Dog Journal* and *The Retriever Journal.* He was a contributing editor for *Sports Afield,* and is currently contributing editor of *Traverse: Northern Michigan's Magazine.* Butz also writes lifestyle, interview, environmental, and sporting articles for numerous publications including the *New York Times, Book Magazine, Outside,* and *Land Rover Journal.*

Douglas H. Chadwick is a resident of northwestern Montana, a wildlife biologist, and the author of half a dozen books on natural history and conservation. He has also written a couple of hundred magazine articles. A frequent contributor to *National Geographic,* he has reported on subjects from Australia's coral reef ecosystem to primates in the Congo, Norwegian whales, and back home to Montana's grizzlies.

Scott Daily lives in the Yaak Valley with his wife and daughter. He has worked with the Yaak Valley Forest Council for five years on projects involving habitat conservation, preservation, and restoration. Scott's work has appeared in several publications, including *Orion, Earthworks, Ohio Afield,* and *Pennsylvania Outdoor Times.*

Alison Hawthorne Deming is Associate Professor in Creative Writing at the University of Arizona, and Director of the Arizona Poetry Center in Tucson. She is the author of numerous collections of nonfiction and poetry, including *Temporary Homelands, Science and Other Poems, The Edges of the Civilized World,* and *Writing the Sacred into the Real.*

Mike Dombeck served as the acting Director of the Bureau of Land Management and chief of the U.S. Forest Service. He is Pioneer Professor of Global Environmental Management at the University of Wisconsin–Stevens Point and UW System Fellow of Global Conservation.

David James Duncan is a father, fly fisher, river activist, clear-cut survivor, and author of *The River Why, The Brothers K, River Teeth,* and *My Story as Told by Water,* which was nominated for the 2001 National Book Award in nonfiction. He also believes in civility and apologizes for the language in this letter. He never imagined anyone would want to publish it.

Amy Edmonds is a wildlife sciences technician working and writing from a riverside log cabin in northwest Montana that she shares with artist Lee Secrest and two dogs. She's seen but one wild lynx, and is grateful for the encounter.

Jeff Ferderer has a great life. He is a native Montanan, which he considers a blessing. He and his companion and partner, Kris Whipple, share their lives in a place along the Yaak River. Jeff has a wonderful family, including two beautiful daughters, Jennifer and Tiffany, who are grown and living their own adventuresome lives, currently in Oregon. Jeff has the best job, teaching English and coaching track at Troy high school. And he has a big white dog named Kootenai, who also has a happy life living in the Yaak Valley.

Jim Fergus was a field editor and monthly columnist for *Sports Afield* magazine, and writes a monthly column on the AllOutdoors.com Web site. His work has appeared in numerous national magazines and newspapers; he is also the author of the nonfiction *A Hunter's Road* and the novel *One Thousand White Women: The Journals of May Dodd.* He lives with his dogs in northern Colorado.

Tom Franklin is from Dickinson, Alabama. The recipient of a Guggenheim Fellowship, he was the John and Renee Grisham Writer-in-Residence at Ole Miss in 2000–2001. Currently he is the Tennessee Williams Fellow at Sewanee College in Sewanee, Tennessee. His first collection, *Poachers,* was published by William Morrow in 1999. The title novella appeared in *New Stories from the South* and *Best American Mystery Stories of the Century.* He is writing a novel, *Hell at the Breech,* due out next year from Morrow.

Debra Gwartney lives in Oregon and is a freelance writer, teacher, and the mother of four daughters.

Sue Halpern lives in the Adirondack Mountains of New York with her husband, Bill McKibben, and their daughter.

William Kittredge recently retired from teaching at the University of Montana. He has books forthcoming from the University of California Press, University of Kansas Press, and Milkweed Editions.

Carolyn Kremers writes literary nonfiction and poetry, and currently teaches at the University of Alaska Fairbanks. She has also served on the faculty of the MFA/Creative

Writing Program at Eastern Washington University in Spokane. She is the author of *Place of the Pretend People: Gifts from a Yip'ik Eskimo Village.* Her essays and poems have appeared in numerous anthologies and magazines, including *American Nature Writing 1999, Brevity, Creative Nonfiction, Manoa, Newsday, North American Review,* and *Runner's World.* Currently she is completing a second book of nonfiction, *Then Came the Mustang,* and seeking a publisher for her book of poems, *Upriver.*

Laurie John Lane-Zucker is cofounder and managing director of The Orion Society. He is an editor and contributing writer for its two magazines, *Orion* and *Orion Afield.* This piece originally appeared in the premier issue of *Orion Afield.*

Tim Linehan is an award-winning hunting and fishing guide for Linehan Outfitting with his wife, Joanne, in Yaak, Montana, and a board member of the Yaak Valley Forest Council, as well as a member of Trout Unlimited; he hosts *Trout Unlimited Television.*

Bob Love lives with his family near the confluence of the Middle and North Forks of the Flathead River, and is grateful for the blessings associated with that.

Bill McKibben is an author and environmentalist whose writings have appeared in periodicals ranging from *The New York Times* and *Natural History* to the *Atlantic* and *Rolling Stone.* A former staff writer and author of hundreds of articles for *The New Yorker,* his first book was *The End of Nature.* McKibben lives with his wife, Sue Halpern, and their daughter Sophie in the Adirondack Mountains of upstate New York.

A writer, journalist, and editor, **Gregory McNamee** is the author or editor of twenty-one published books and more than two thousand articles, essays, reviews, interviews, and other periodical pieces. He lives in Tucson, Arizona.

Ellen Meloy's books of nonfiction include *The Anthropology of Turquoise* and *The Last Cheater's Waltz: Beauty and Violence in the Desert Southwest.* She is the recipient of a Whiting Writer's Award. *Raven's Exile,* her account of living in a remote canyon on Utah's Green River, won the admiration of readers and river lovers everywhere. A one-time resident of Montana, Meloy now lives in southern Utah.

Roy Parvin lives in the woods in the far north of California. His collection of short stories, *The Loneliest Road in America,* was published by Chronicle Books in 1997. A second collection, *In the Snow Forest,* was recently published to critical acclaim.

Doug Peacock, a fierce advocate for grizzly bears and wild country, is the author of the classic *Grizzly Years.* A board member of Round River Conservation Studies, he and another board member, Terry Tempest Williams, serve as that group's ethical benchmark for all their decisions. He lives outside Livingston, Montana.

Robert Michael Pyle is the author of numerous books of natural history, including *Chasing Monarchs, Where Bigfoot Walks,* and *Walking the High Ridge.* He lives in Washington, where he is active on behalf of the Dark Divide roadless area.

Writer and naturalist **Janisse Ray** is the author of *Ecology of a Cracker Childhood,* which won the Southeastern Booksellers Awards for Nonfiction in 1999, the Southern Environmental Center 2000 Award for Outstanding Writing on the Southern Environment, and the Southern Book Critics Circle Award for Nonfiction in 2000. She is a founding board member of Altamaha (Georgia) Riverkeeper, and divides her time between south Georgia and north Florida, where she lives with her partner, Raven Burchard.

Pattiann Rogers has published nine books of poetry—most recently, *Song of the World Becoming: Poems New and Collected, 1981–2001.* She has received two NEA fellowships, a Guggenheim Fellowship, a Poetry Fellowship from the Lannan Foundation, five Pushcart Prizes, three prizes from *Poetry,* two from *Prairie Schooner,* and two from *Poetry Northwest.* New poems will be appearing in *Field, The Paris Review, Georgia Review, Orion, Poetry,* and *The Antioch Review.*

Lynn Sainsbury works as a seasonal biologist/forester for the Forest Service. Over twelve years she has worked in nine states, most recently Alaska. She winters in western Montana, in a small off-the-grid house that sits on a ridge overlooking the Potomac Valley. Two cats share her house with her. Her time is spent taking classes at the University of Montana; gathering firewood and venison; volunteering for Women's Voices for the Earth (an environmental justice organization); fixing old trucks; doing carpentry work; and sometimes sitting in front of a computer and writing.

Laura Sedler was born and raised in Southern California in the 1950s and 1960s; she first came to northwest Montana in the summer of 1968. An instant love affair with the trees, rivers, and mountains culminated in a permanent move to the area in 1971. She has lived and breathed at her home in the 17 Mile Creek Valley with her partner, Shamus, since 1975. A late life career blossomed after raising four sons and stepsons: She now works and writes as a community-based social worker in hospice and home health. A longtime practitioner and student, she also teaches yoga.

Bob Shacochis, the author of five books, is a novelist, journalist, and educator. "Grouse, Grouse, Grouse" is excerpted from *Domesticity*, his collection of essays about food and love. He lives in Florida and New Mexico.

Annick Smith is a writer of essays and short fiction whose film-producer credits include *A River Runs Through It* and *Heartland*. She writes for *The New York Times*, *Los Angeles Times*, *Audubon*, *Travel & Leisure*, *Modern Maturity*, and *Outside*; is the author of *Homestead* and *In This We Are Native*; and was coeditor with William Kittredge of *The Last Best Place: A Montana Anthology*. Born in Paris and raised in Chicago, Smith has lived for thirty years on her homestead ranch outside of Missoula, Montana.

Todd Tanner and his wife, Molly, are residents of the Yaak Valley. Todd is an outdoor writer as well as a retired fishing and hunting guide. His stories have appeared in a number of sporting magazines, including *Field & Stream*, *Sports Afield*, *Fly Fisherman*, and *Sporting Classics*.

Steve Thompson has worked on and written about wildlife, wilderness, parks, and sustainable forestry issues in Montana for the past eleven years. Since March 2001 Steve has been employed as the Glacier field representative for the National Parks Conservation Association. He and his wife, Kerrie, live in Whitefish, Montana.

John Wickersham has worked as an English professor, a ski instructor, and a conservation biology instructor. He was last seen somewhere in the backcountry of the mountains of southern Colorado.

Terry Tempest WIlliams is a ceaseless defender of the unprotected wilderness areas of Utah—particularly the redrock desert—and is the author of *Refuge, Leap,* and, most recently, *Red: Passion and Patience in the Desert.* She lives in Utah with her husband, the writer Brooke Williams.

Chris Wood is the conservation director of the watershed programs of Trout Unlimited. He helped develop the roadless rule as the senior policy and communications adviser to the chief of the Forest Service. He thanks the members of the Forest Service Roadless Area Conservation Team.

WHO TO WRITE, HOW TO HELP:

Please send a letter to the following addresses asking that the Yaak's last roadless areas be protected:

Forest Supervisor
Kootenai National Forest
1102 U.S. Highway 2 West
Libby, MT 59923

YVFC
155 Riverview
Troy, MT 59935

Dale Bosworth
U.S. Forest Service
Box 96090
Washington, D.C. 20090

Senator Max Baucus
U.S. Senate
Washington, D.C. 20510

And feel free, please, to send a copy of your letter to your own elected officials.

INDEX